SPIN CONTROL

THE WHITE HOUSE OFFICE OF

COMMUNICATIONS AND THE

MANAGEMENT OF PRESIDENTIAL NEWS

JOHN ANTHONY MALTESE

THE UNIVERSITY OF NORTH CAROLINA PRESS   CHAPEL HILL & LONDON

© 1992 The University of North Carolina Press

All rights reserved

Manufactured in the United States of America

The paper in this book meets the guidelines for permanence and durability of the Committee on Production Guidelines for Book Longevity of the Council on Library Resources.

96 95 94 93 92

5 4 3 2 1

Library of Congress Cataloging-in-Publication Data

Maltese, John Anthony.

Spin control: the White House Office of Communications and the management of presidential news / John Anthony Maltese.

p. cm.

Includes bibliographical references and index.

ISBN 0-8078-2034-2 (cloth : alk. paper)

1. Presidents—United States—Press conferences. 2. Government and the press—United States. I. Title.

JK518.M35 1992

353.03'5—dc20   91-50788

CIP

SPIN CONTROL

TO MY PARENTS, MAY AND JOHN

CONTENTS

ACKNOWLEDGMENTS

I am grateful to many people for their help in the preparation of this book. I am especially indebted to Francis E. Rourke, who spent countless hours reading my work and offering thoughtful criticisms and advice. He shared his wisdom at virtually every stage of this project's development—from its inception as a seminar paper, through its growth into a doctoral dissertation, and finally to this. Through it all, he proved to be a trusted mentor and a faithful friend. Robert L. Peabody also guided me through much of this research, and I am grateful for his kindness, wisdom, and support as well.

Many others have also helped along the way. I would like to offer a special word of thanks to the many individuals who worked in or with the Office of Communications and who granted interviews and shared their valuable time with me. I am also grateful for the Gerald R. Ford Foundation's generous grant, which supported my travel to the Ford Library in Ann Arbor, Michigan. The staff there—as well as the staff at the Nixon Presidential Materials Project in Alexandria, Virginia, and at the Jimmy Carter Library in Atlanta, Georgia—proved to be absolutely invaluable. I would especially like to thank Paul Guitté, James Hastings, Joan Howard, Byron A. Parham, and Sue Ellen Stanley from the Nixon Project; David Horrocks, Leesa Tobin, and Paul Conway from the Ford Library; and David Alsobrook, Martin Elzy, Bert Nason, and David Stanhope from the Carter Library. In addition, Samuel Kernell kindly shared transcripts of a symposium at the University of California at San Diego called "The Presidency, the Press and the People," and Benjamin Bradlee, Charles Colson, and Herbert Klein responded to my written queries.

I also owe an enormous debt to Scott M. Cutlip, dean emeritus of the School of Journalism at the University of Georgia. He is a man who has studied the Office of Communications since its inception and who generously gave me his files concerning the office. The files included notes from many interviews that he had conducted with journalists and members of the Office of Communications in the early 1970s. They also included many unpublished documents, as well as an extensive clipping file. He shared his time as well as his research with me, and he offered thoughtful comments on an earlier draft of this manuscript.

Many others read parts of my manuscript and offered their suggestions. They include Kristin Bumiller, Alvin Cohan, Del Dunn, Charlie Euchner, Arnie Fleischmann, Louis Galambos, Robin Kolodny, Norma Kriger, Brian Mirsky, Norman Ornstein, Donald Rumsfeld, Margita White, and three anonymous referees for the University of North Carolina Press. I presented portions of this manuscript at the Midwest Political Science Association Meeting and at presidential conferences dealing with Gerald Ford and Jimmy Carter at Hofstra University in Hempstead, New York. I appreciate the comments of fellow panelists, including Michael Grossman, Jerry Jones, Bruce Miroff, Jody Powell, and Sarah McClendon. I also appreciate the feedback from colleagues at the Johns Hopkins University and the University of Georgia who listened to my various research presentations on this topic.

Among the many others to whom I owe thanks are the late Bertha W. Beekman, for her love and indomitable spirit; Beekman W. Cottrell, for following in her footsteps; David L. Paletz, for sparking my interest in politics and the media; J. Woodford Howard, for patiently encouraging me to continue this research even as my field of specialization turned to public law; Peter and Beth Digeser and Janine Holc, for always being around to listen and give support; Tim Conner and the Strines, for their companionship and good-natured pummeling; Chris Allen, Larry Biskowski, Steve Engelmann, Paul Faustini, Paul Gurian, Dick and Judy Katz, Thom Kuehls, Karen Maschke, Nancy Maveety, and Steve Stribling, for many hours of bridge; Kim Hellier and Phil Kronebusch, for their Minnesota charm; Evelyn Scheulen and Evelyn Stoller, for countless favors and good advice; Scott Ainsworth, Lief Carter, Tom Lauth, Susan Nees, and Susette Talarico, for easing my transition to Athens; Ron and Ann Surace, for being part of my family; and the staff of the University of North Carolina Press—especially Paul Betz, for his friendship and editorial guidance.

Many others have supported me in countless ways throughout the writing of this manuscript. I must, however, especially thank two graduate school roommates, Tim Smith and Mike Tolley. They not only put up with my foibles but also were—and are—inspiring colleagues and the best of friends.

Most of all, I am indebted to my parents, John and Eva May Maltese, for their constant support, unerring faith, and abundant love.

J.A.M.

May 1991
Athens, Georgia

SPIN CONTROL

CHAPTER ONE

INTRODUCTION

Congressman Dick Cheney leaned back in his chair and swung his feet up onto his desk. He was in a good mood. In a few hours he would leave for the White House where President George Bush would introduce him to reporters as the president's nominee for secretary of defense. President Bush wanted the announcement to be a surprise, so Cheney was going about his morning schedule as usual. I happened to be part of it—one of the occasional string of academics who passed through Cheney's office to ask questions about his experiences in government. That morning we were talking about Cheney's tenure as White House chief of staff for President Gerald R. Ford.

My allotted time was running out, and our conversation drifted from specifics about the Ford administration to more general issues of presidential-press relations. To have an effective presidency, Cheney reminded me, the White House must control the agenda. An essential element of that control, he explained, is the ability to maintain discipline within the administration itself. Any appearance of disunity among the president's ranks will be seized upon by the media as an opportunity for a story—one that will undermine the president's agenda.[1]

Communications experts often note that the media are preoccupied with conflict. By the media's own definition, news is drama, and drama thrives on conflict.[2] As an example, Cheney pointed out that conflict between policymakers over the implementation of the federal budget makes for a much more interesting story than one that concentrates on the dry details of the budget itself—even though the dry details of the budget are ultimately more important. Besides, he added, conflict is easier for reporters to cover: "It's much easier for them, for example, to get into covering and focusing upon an alleged personnel clash between the secretary of defense and the secretary of state over what the arms control policy is going to be than it is to talk about the policy itself, which most of them don't understand."[3]

As a result of the media's preoccupation with conflict, good-faith debate within the administration is sometimes depicted as serious dissension among the ranks. Furthermore, stories about real conflicts increase the tension between those at odds and make the president look like a poor manager.[4] To maintain control of the public agenda, then, the White House must not only minimize exposure of internal conflict but also aggressively promote the messages that it wants conveyed to the American people. Bluntly put, the White House must attempt to manipulate media coverage of the administration. "That means that about half the time the White House press corp is going to be pissed off," Cheney continued, "and that's all right. You're not there to please them. You're there to run an effective presidency. And to do that, you have to be disciplined in what you convey to the country. The most powerful tool you have is the ability to use the symbolic aspects of the presidency to promote your goals and objectives. You're never going to get anywhere if you let someone step on your lead, or if you step on your lead yourself." That means you've got to control what information you put out, he emphasized. "You don't let the press set the agenda. The press is going to object to that. They like to set the agenda. They like to decide what's important and what isn't important. But if you let them do that, they're going to trash your presidency."[5]

The responsibility for doing just what Cheney was talking about rests with the White House Office of Communications. That office is charged with long-term public relations planning, the dissemination of the "line-of-the-day" to officials throughout the executive branch, and the circumvention of the White House press corps through the orchestration of direct appeals to the people (appeals that are often carefully targeted to particular constituencies in specific media markets). The goal is to set the public agenda, to make sure that all parts of the presidential team (the White House staff, cabinet officers, and other executive branch officials) are adhering to that public agenda, and to aggressively promote that agenda through a form of mass marketing. Focus groups and polling data are used to fashion presidential messages; sound-bites are written into the public pronouncements of the president and his underlings to articulate those messages; public appearances are choreographed so that the messages are reinforced by visual images; and the daily line is enforced to prevent the articulation of conflicting messages. "Surrogate speakers" take the messages to local constituencies through speaking tours while local media markets are penetrated by means of direct satellite interviews with administration officials and are co-opted by the distribution of editorial memos explaining administration policy and by camera-ready graphs and articles, "radio actualities" (or audio press releases), and briefings for local reporters and editorial writers.

The ultimate goal is to influence—to the extent possible—what news will appear in the media about the administration and its policies. Originally associated with political campaigns, such tactics were perfected by Richard Nixon in his 1968 bid for the presidency. In a scathing account of the campaign, Joe McGinniss called Nixon's tactics "the selling of the president."[6] But Nixon brought the tactics with him to the White House. As Nixon aide Charles Colson said, "Nixon had a fetish about [trying to] dominate the news from the government." The president was especially successful in 1972—the year of his triumphant visits to China and the Soviet Union and his landslide re-election. Colson added that in 1972, the White House came "as close to managing the news as you can do." Daily public-opinion polls helped to determine "what issues were sensitive with the public" so that "you could tell one night how people were reacting to things, and the next morning back off or intensify what you wanted to say with almost simultaneous polling."[7]

It was Nixon who created the White House Office of Communications, and every president after him has ultimately felt compelled to embrace it. Quite simply, what seemed so shocking to McGinniss and others in the 1968 campaign is now common practice—not only in campaigns but also in day-to-day governance. Nixon's techniques were followed most successfully by the administration of Ronald Reagan, which copied the Nixon practice of a tightly regimented line-of-the-day coupled with limited press access and direct appeals to the people. Again, polling data helped to formulate the line, and efforts were made to see that certain stories dominated the news. Television was paramount to Reagan (as it was to Nixon), and the White House set up a tracking system of network newscasts to see how many minutes were devoted to each of the stories that the White House was promoting. Based on that tracking system, the White House modified its efforts to communicate its stories more effectively.[8]

The White House embrace of public relations techniques has corresponded with an increasing dependence on public support for the implementation of presidential policy. No longer does public support merely elect presidents.

Now public support is a president's most visible source of ongoing political power. More than ever before, presidents and their surrogates take messages directly to the people in an attempt to mold mandates for policy initiatives. A strategy of presidential power based on such appeals is known as "going public."[9] As defined by Samuel Kernell, this understanding of presidential power assumes that the elite bargaining community that implements policy is neither as isolated from public pressure nor as tightly bound together by established norms of elite behavior as it used to be.[10] As a result, policymakers are increasingly susceptible to the influence of public opinion.[11] A key to presidential power, then, is the ability to harness (or manufacture) that opinion. The result is a sort of unending political campaign.[12]

All of this is a far cry from what this country's founders expected. Scholars of the presidency, such as Jeffrey Tulis, remind us that before this century, popular presidential rhetoric was largely proscribed because it was thought to "manifest demagoguery, impede deliberation, and subvert the routines of republican government."[13] That approach reflected the founders' fear of "pure" or "direct" democracy. Although the founders felt that public consent was a requirement of republican government, they nonetheless felt that the processes of government should be insulated from the whims of public opinion. Thus, they attempted to instill deliberation in government through such things as indirect elections, separation of powers, and an independent executive. In short, the now commonplace practice of direct public appeals was shunned during the nineteenth century because it went against the existing interpretation of the constitutional order.

Over time, however, the source of presidential power shifted from narrowly defined constitutional underpinnings to a broader plebiscitary base.[14] This shift placed a new set of institutional demands on presidents. Initially, presidents responded to the new demands by forging a professional relationship with reporters as a means of reaching the people. Theodore Roosevelt began the practice of meeting regularly with reporters (often during his late-afternoon shave). He even provided a room for them in the newly built executive office wing of the White House.[15] Later, Woodrow Wilson established regularly scheduled presidential press conferences. The new system of presidential-press relations was perfected by Franklin D. Roosevelt, who formally created the White House Press Office. FDR coupled the institutionalization of the Press Office with his own repartee with reporters, a skill that he used with magnificent effect at his informal biweekly press conferences. There was strict control over how reporters could use material from press conferences (as there had been from the start of the new presidential-press relationship), but the system—as Kernell points out—was one of "hard news, openly conveyed."[16]

The growth of the broadcast media altered that relationship. Most noticeably, it eroded the intimacy. Presidents were no longer as dependent on reporters to convey their views to the public. Radio and television became a direct means of reaching the masses. Even presidential press conferences came to be used more to meet the people than to meet the press when the practice of televising them "live" began in 1961.

As presidents became more adept at taking their message directly to the people—thereby performing an end run around intermediary interpreters—reporters became less willing to accept the strict "ground rules" that presidents had once proffered for access. In the process, the adversarial aspects of the presidential-press relationship were emphasized. The reliance on unfiltered public appeals that reflected the new strategy of going public raised new institutional demands. Those demands were filled by the White House Office of Communications.

It is important to note that the functions of the Office of Communications are very different from those of the White House Press Office. Rather than targeting local media outlets, the Press Office caters almost exclusively to the needs of Washington-based reporters who frequent its domain on a regular basis. Rather than coordinating the news flow from the entire executive branch, the Press Office is primarily concerned with providing information from the White House itself. And rather than engaging in long-term public relations management, the Press Office seldom moves beyond the short-term goal of disseminating the news of the day and responding to reporters' queries. Thus, whereas the Press Office is primarily reactive, the Office of Communications is primarily proactive.

This study of the Office of Communications is largely about how the White House attempts to control the public agenda by making presidential news. It also serves as an example of how modern presidents have attempted to increase their control over the executive branch and the policies of government by placing more power in the hands of the White House staff.[17] Just as presidents in the earlier part of this century came to use the Bureau of the Budget as a central clearinghouse of legislation—a means of asserting presidential (rather than departmental) judgments, choices, and priorities in molding a legislative package under executive auspices—presidents today have come to use the

Office of Communications as a means of asserting control over the communications agenda of the executive branch.[18]

From the White House perspective, control of the agenda is an essential component of successful policy-making. But such manipulation can raise serious problems from the point of view of democratic theory. For instance, it has eviscerated our presidential campaigns of much of their content. Now it is threatening to do the same to day-to-day government. Style is substituted for substance. Complicated issues are transformed into simple slogans and slick sound-bites. The very real threat is that our ideal of a bold and deliberative government will be dashed by timid, self-interested policymakers who shy away from responsibility for their actions and delude themselves and their constituents with their own symbolic spectacle.

Although the Office of Communications was not established until 1969, some of its functions had been carried out informally in earlier administrations. For instance, Dwight D. Eisenhower's press secretary, James Hagerty, made a point of coordinating the federal government's public relations operations through informal meetings between himself and departmental public information officers.[19] Some felt that this sort of liaison was not enough. In 1954, Robert Humphreys suggested to President Eisenhower the creation of a structure much like the Office of Communications.[20] Humphreys, who was then publicity director of the Republican National Committee, had been active in Eisenhower's public relations efforts during the 1952 campaign.[21] But Eisenhower did not act on Humphreys's proposal, nor did John F. Kennedy when a similar plan was presented to him for the creation of a "super-press secretary" to coordinate all executive branch communications to the media. Nonetheless, Kennedy's press secretary, Pierre Salinger, continued the practice of meeting once or twice a week with officials and information officers from various departments. The personnel included in the meetings varied but usually consisted of eight to ten people. Under Salinger, a primary purpose of the meetings was to gather information for Kennedy's televised press conferences. No doubt the meetings also served to keep the participants abreast of what was happening in other departments, thus providing some element of coordination.[22]

By the end of Lyndon B. Johnson's administration, the White House Press Office maintained close contact with departmental public information officers (or "PIOs"). Johnson's last press secretary, George Christian, had a man on his staff by the name of Lloyd Hackler who was responsible for talking with departmental PIOs every morning to determine where various issues would be handled and to make sure that different parts of the administration would not convey conflicting messages. In fact, Christian noted that he felt the Johnson Press Office had a better system for dealing with PIOs than did any previous administration.[23]

Aside from these *ad hoc* efforts, a few formal structures for coordinating the flow of news from the executive branch had existed before the creation of the Office of Communications. However, those structures were short-lived and were almost always a response to national emergencies. The most notable was the Committee on Public Information, which President Woodrow Wilson instituted on 14 April 1917—just eight days after America entered World War I. Chaired by George Creel, a liberal crusader and former journalist, the committee was set up to coordinate the flow of government news about the war and to rally public support for American intervention in the European conflict.[24]

Apart from serving as a mechanism for coordinating the flow of information from government, the so-called Creel Committee was an unparalleled instrument for going public. It flooded news bureaus with official information about the war. Indeed, its torrent of handouts helped to make the press release a Washington institution.[25] The committee also introduced the visual equivalent of a handout by providing a weekly quota of five hundred feet of motion picture film to each of the four makers of weekly newsreels.[26] In addition, the Creel Committee produced its own films, published its own daily newspaper, distributed syndicated articles by some of the nation's leading writers, and encouraged the creation and distribution of artwork to promote the war effort.[27] It also published pamphlets that were used to justify American intervention in the war, highlight the "German menace," and extol the virtues of American democracy.[28] All told, the Creel Committee independently distributed more than seventy-five million pieces of literature.[29]

Still, the Creel Committee's most innovative way of directly reaching Americans was through the use of what were called Four-Minute Men, who spread the administration's gospel to movie theater audiences throughout the country in carefully tailored, four-minute speeches given between the silent motion picture features. The Creel Committee existed before the age of radio, and Four-Minute Men were used as an alternative method of providing a "nationwide hookup" for the distribution of a single spoken message.[30] Eventually, there were some seventy-five thousand four-minute speakers around the country who worked under the supervision of local chairmen and in cooperation with theater owners. The topic of the speeches was determined by guidelines from the *Four-Minute Men Bulletin*, which was regularly distributed to local chairmen by the Creel Committee. Thus, speakers all across the country were talking about the same message at the same time. The operation was so successful that it was expanded to include divisions for women, school-age children, and college students. The most important feature of the program was that the messages were being transmitted by peers—sometimes in languages other than English. In New York City alone, sixteen hundred speakers reached a half million people each week.[31]

Quite apart from propagandizing the war, the Creel Committee helped to depict the president as the preeminent national leader and the prime mover of the war effort.[32] Thus, the committee turned out to be "a kind of embryonic 'propaganda ministry' for the national Executive, which in turn meshed with Wilson's desire to reach the populace directly."[33] As such, it did much to solidify the change from congressional to presidential government.

Nonetheless, the Committee on Public Information ceased to exist after the war. Within twenty-four hours of the signing of the armistice, Creel issued orders to stop all domestic activities of the committee. As he later put it, "I had the deep conviction that the Committee was a *war organization* only, and that it was without proper place in the national life in time of peace."[34] In addition, the administration seems to have feared that Congress, which had been wary of the Creel Committee during the war, would turn openly hostile toward it in peacetime.[35] As a result, the Creel Committee took no active part in publicizing President Wilson's effort to join the League of Nations. Instead, Wilson set out on his own to rally public support through a grueling whistle-stop train tour, which ultimately led to his physical collapse.

Many of the activities of the Office of Communications have resembled those of the Creel Committee. Both organizations were meant to coordinate information flow from the entire executive branch, engage in a wide array of tactics for going public, and focus attention on the president as the prime mover and shaker in American politics.

Short-lived efforts to coordinate government publicity were later introduced during the 1930s. The most notable of these was the creation of the Office of Government Reports (OGR) by executive order in 1939. The office was designed as a centralized public information office that would serve as a clearinghouse for the distribution of information about the activities of government agencies and as a tool for keeping the Roosevelt administration abreast of public opinion on governmental activities.[36] The director of the office was Lowell Mellet, a former Scripps-Howard editor, who was described during his tenure as "quiet, studious, and an almost 'evangelical' liberal."[37] After America's entry into World War II, the functions of the Office of Government Reports were consolidated into the newly created Office of War Information (OWI). Making the Office of Government Reports (a presumably permanent organization) a part of the Office of War Information (an obviously temporary organization) was a mistake from the point of view of those who wanted to establish a full-time government publicity operation, since the move all but guaranteed that the OGR's functions would die with the end of the war.

The Office of War Information was similar to the Creel Committee, but it was less aggressive in its approach.[38] The director of OWI was Elmer Davis, a journalist and popular radio commentator. It was quickly evident that the office did not have the same sort of power that the Creel Committee had enjoyed. Americans were already united behind America's entry into the war as a result of the fall of France and the bombing of Pearl Harbor. Thus, a propaganda campaign such as that undertaken by the Creel Committee was unnecessary. President Harry S. Truman abolished the Office of War Information in 1945 by executive order. A suggestion that a similar office be reestablished during the Korean conflict was not acted on.[39] From the abolition of the Office of War Information until the establishment of the Office of Communications, the coordination of news flow from the executive branch was carried out on an *ad hoc* basis, usually by the White House press secretary and usually for the benefit of the president.

It was under the administration of President Kennedy that many of the new tactics of going public were introduced and made commonplace. Kennedy was the first president to allow his press conferences to be broadcast "live" on nationwide television. As one Kennedy aide, Theodore Sorenson, later said, the use of live coverage was meant "to inform and impress the public more than the press" and to provide "a direct communication with the voters which no newspaper could alter by interpretation or omission."[40] Kennedy also began to cultivate ties with the media outside of Washington as a means of bypassing the scrutiny of the White House press corps.[41]

Kennedy's new tactics of going public, as well as the older practice of informally trying to coordinate government news flow, were continued during the presidency of Lyndon Johnson. For instance, in a memorandum to the president dated 25 January 1966, Press Secretary Bill Moyers suggested that

Johnson utilize local media markets as a means of going public: "When the President chooses a locale outside of Washington to talk about world affairs or domestic issues, the regional newspapers give it extra play. The President has favored them by making his pronouncements in their area, and whatever he says is bound to be accepted much more favorably."[42]

Still, George Christian said that the Johnson administration really did "very little outreach to media outside Washington." That was largely an innovation of the Office of Communications.[43] The traditional bias of the Press Office toward major East Coast media was understandable, since those media were more accessible. For instance, Christian explained that even major newspapers from distant locales were not read in a timely way by the White House. They simply could not be, since they were not received as quickly as East Coast newspapers. At best, other newspapers were received a day late. As a result, the White House was more sensitive to what East Coast newspapers were saying and therefore gave them more attention.

Johnson himself was obsessed with the news and the flow of information from his administration. "President Johnson lived and breathed the news," Christian once said. "Not many people get up at five or five-thirty and start reading half a dozen newspapers, then tune in all three morning news shows on TV, and watch all of the Sunday interview programs and the news documentaries, and monitor the AP and UPI tickers in [their] office all day, and tune in the CBS radio news every hour on the hour."[44] Johnson was also obsessed with what people in his administration were saying to the media. He even tried to institute a system whereby every media contact had to be cleared by the Press Office. For instance, after Joseph Califano met with the reporter Joseph Kraft without official permission, Johnson wrote: "Joe—may I *again—again* ask you and *all* your *associates* to please meet with press members during your association with my administration upon request of [the press secretary] only. This request has been made before and will not be made again."[45] Of course, no such system can really work. "You can't make somebody report [their press contacts]," Christian noted, "you can just ask them to. So from my standpoint it was a flawed system, but I went through the motions to try to find out what everybody else was saying."[46]

In 1966, Johnson asked Robert Kintner, who had been a Washington journalist and president of both ABC and NBC, to perform some of the activities that later came to be associated with the Office of Communications.[47] Kintner was known as a hard-driving, tough executive during his days in broadcasting—"not," according to one colleague, "[someone] you'd call charming or personable."[48] But he was a friend of Johnson's, and he joined the administration as cabinet secretary and special assistant to the president in March 1966. In that capacity, he served as a liaison with the cabinet and agency heads. He also chaired White House staff meetings, cultivated media contacts, and gave advice on how to improve the president's image.[49]

Shortly after Kintner's arrival, Bill Moyers wrote him a letter in which the press secretary outlined Kintner's duties. As cabinet secretary, he would receive weekly reports from the departments and agencies. Moyers suggested that he use those "to keep the President informed and, more importantly, to keep the departments and agencies prodded on matters of interest to the President and the White House." The president had been impressed with Kintner's contacts in the world of journalism, and Moyers noted that "quiet and discreet cultivation of those contacts can be most useful." He went on to write: "The President is going to want your creative and sustained thinking about the overall problem of communicating with the American people. Some call it the problem of 'the President's image'; it goes much beyond that to the ultimate question of how does the President shape the issues and interpret them to people—how, in fact, does he lead?" Finally, Moyers added that Johnson wanted Kintner's advice on formulating a strategy for electing as many Democrats as possible in the 1966 midterm elections. Such a strategy would include how best to use "the Democratic National Committee, radio and television, and the President himself."[50]

Nonetheless, Kintner never achieved much power in the White House. According to George Christian, Kintner ended up doing only about 50 percent of what he was originally mandated to do. In part, Kintner was thwarted by the way the president operated. As Christian put it: "There was no chief of staff, all the senior staff were more or less independent of each other, and they all dealt directly with [the president]. As a result, it was difficult for anybody to ride herd on anybody else at the senior level. There wasn't any way that Joe Califano or Harry McPherson or Bill Moyers or Walt Rostow was going to be coordinated by someone else. They didn't have to. They had access." Indeed, they had access that Kintner did not have. "So no," Christian concluded, "he did not fill the role of a communications czar."[51]

In short, despite several previous attempts, no administration had succeeded in institutionalizing a lasting mechanism like the Office of Communications. Before Nixon, most coordination and public relations activities were carried out in an *ad hoc* manner or were simply left to chance. Since then, the Office of Communications has become an indispensable part of planning and implementing the strategies of the modern public presidency.

The chapters that follow trace the development and evolution of the White House Office of Communications.[52] Its size and precise structure have changed from administration to administration to meet the needs of the incumbent president. For a brief time the name was changed, and more recently the Office of Communications has become an umbrella term for a number of offices working within its jurisdiction. (See the organization charts in the Appendix.) This fluidity is not surprising, since the Office of Communications is part of the president's personal staff in the White House Office. No president, however, has felt able to do away with the basic functions of the office. Indeed, the very continuity of those functions over a span of twenty years and through the administrations of five presidents of both political parties is indicative of the office's importance.

My approach to the study of the Office of Communications combines political science with political history. Over the last five years, the Nixon Presidential Materials Project, the Gerald R. Ford Library, and the Jimmy Carter Library have opened a huge body of papers relating to the office. I have been among the first scholars to tap these papers and have supplemented them with over fifty personal interviews, most of which are on the record and are listed in the Bibliography. Some of those whom I interviewed shared additional documents with me from their own files. These included internal memoranda from the administration of Ronald Reagan.

To the extent that I have performed the task of a historian, I have been mindful of a remark that former White House Chief of Staff H. R. Haldeman made to me. As our interview drew to a close, he said that his experiences had led him to read history from an entirely different viewpoint. "I read it with the assumption that virtually all of it is wrong," he said. "It's only a matter of *how* wrong it is, because it's virtually impossible to re-create accurately an ongoing entity—what happened and why it happened, even with access to all the memos and all the tapes."[53] As I have sifted through thousands of pages of documents and listened to different people give vastly different accounts of the same event, I have realized more than ever before how differently each of us perceives the reality around us and how relative our vision of history is. In presenting my vision of this office, I have tried to be as little wrong as possible.

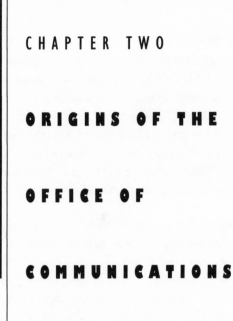

CHAPTER TWO

ORIGINS OF THE

OFFICE OF

COMMUNICATIONS

Controlling the public agenda was especially difficult for the White House in 1968. It was a year of bitter turmoil. Robert F. Kennedy and Martin Luther King, Jr., were assassinated. Protest against American involvement in the Vietnam War was at its height. Race riots, student uprisings, and bitter clashes between demonstrators and police were commonplace. In Chicago, the Democratic National Convention nominated Vice President Hubert H. Humphrey as its presidential nominee in the midst of violent protests outside that included the hurling of rocks and feces by demonstrators and clubbings and gassings by police. In living rooms across America, families saw the images on television: American boys dying in Vietnam, urban ghettos in flames, rancor and discord in the streets, and college campuses awash in protest. In Washington, President Lyndon Baines Johnson was even forced to call out federal troops to protect the White House. Conflict was everywhere.

Most alarming to those in power was the fact that opposition was spreading to middle America—and it was doing so, many of them felt, with the help of the media. In the wake of the Tet offensive that was launched against South Vietnam in January 1968 (producing massive American casualties), the CBS television news anchorman Walter Cronkite went to Vietnam to view the situation for himself. He was appalled by what he saw. On 27 February 1968, Cronkite—one of the most trusted men in America—went public against further escalation of American involvement in the war. In a CBS special television report, Cronkite concluded, "It seems now more than ever that the bloody experience of Vietnam is to end in a stalemate."[1] After the broadcast, President Johnson told his press secretary, George Christian, that "losing" Cronkite was the equivalent of losing "Mr. Average Citizen."[2] Christian later recalled that Cronkite's report caused "shock waves" to roll through the government.[3]

Two weeks later, on 12 March, Minnesota Senator Eugene McCarthy, who campaigned against U.S. involvement in the war, all but beat Johnson in the New Hampshire primary. Although Johnson won the Democratic vote by 49.5 to 42.4 percent, the addition of Republican write-in votes to the total gave Johnson a lead of only 230 votes—and this, as Theodore White has written, "in what was supposedly one of the most patriotic and warlike states of the Union."[4] To the media, McCarthy was the clear winner.* Four days later, Robert Kennedy entered the race against the president for the Democratic nomination, and on 31 March, Johnson withdrew his candidacy. Johnson's fall was partly blamed on what was at the time called a "credibility gap."[5] Despite his long-running obsession with the media and his attempts to cultivate news organizations as president, Johnson ultimately failed to communicate effectively with the public.

In a speech before the National Association of Broadcasters the day after he withdrew his candidacy, Johnson spoke about his failure to communicate. "I understand, far better than some of my severe and perhaps intolerant critics would admit, my own shortcomings as a communicator," he said. But he clearly placed some of the blame on the media for his failure to communicate. "You of the broadcast industry have enormous power in your hands," he told

---

*Ironically, McCarthy's "victory" was almost totally illusory. Not only did McCarthy in fact lose, but many people in New Hampshire voted for him because they felt that Johnson was not pursuing the war *aggressively* enough. Thus, many of the votes were not really votes for McCarthy and his antiwar stance, but were votes against Johnson. It should also be noted that Johnson (who had not yet declared his candidacy) was not officially on the ballot. Therefore, those who wanted to vote for him had to write in his name (Turner, *Lyndon Johnson's Dual War*, 235–36).

them. "You have the power to clarify and you have the power to confuse. Men in public life cannot remotely rival your opportunity—day after day, night after night, hour after hour you shape the Nation's dialogue."[6] Johnson elaborated on that theme in an article he published the next year. "The President and his Cabinet officers have a number of instruments for conveying their policies to the people," he wrote. "Yet what happens to their explanations of policy in print, or on the television screen, may be something far different from what they intended. Policy may be distorted. Rumors of dark motives or of unspecified dissent, may be given equal prominence with the expressed purposes of the administration. Failure and conflict will certainly be emphasized wherever they can be found or presumed."[7]

Former Vice President Richard Nixon agreed with that assessment. He had long been wary of the press, and his impression that members of the press were siding with liberal opponents of the war only reinforced his feeling that they were part of his political opposition. Nixon was waging a comeback campaign for the presidency in 1968, and he was determined that his campaign apparatus would maintain control of his public agenda. To ensure that his messages would not be distorted by the filter of "hostile" media reporters, Nixon circumvented reporters and took his messages directly to the electorate. He did so with the help of sophisticated advertising techniques and carefully orchestrated uses of the media.[8] Nixon had shunned such tactics in his 1960 race for the presidency against John F. Kennedy. His failure to embrace such tactics in 1960 is somewhat ironic, since Nixon is commonly thought to have had a keen sense of the importance of going public from the beginning of his career in politics. After all, his 1952 "Checkers" speech had shown what an enormous impact a direct televised appeal could have on public opinion. Yet Nixon's method of going public in 1960 reflected an understanding of public appeals that was not yet fully attuned to the modern media age.

Nixon did, of course, participate in the famous televised debates with Kennedy in 1960, but even there Nixon displayed a rather naive understanding of the requirements of television. He "lost" the crucial first debate largely because of his failure to take care of his own appearance. He refused to wear makeup and finally relented only to the application of some mostly ineffective "beard stick" to hide his five o'clock shadow. His appearance was further undercut by the fact that he had been hospitalized just the week before the debate to combat a severe infection. The bout had left him ten pounds underweight, and he sported a shirt collar that was a full size too large. During the first debate he wore a light-gray suit that only accentuated his haggard appearance and made him look anemic against the light-colored backdrop of the television studio. The image that millions saw was that of a nervous, haggard, sweating Nixon versus a relaxed, robust, confident Kennedy. What the two candidates said no longer mattered.*

Aside from the debates, Nixon employed a campaign strategy in 1960 that stressed personal campaigning over television appeals. Thus, he undertook an exhausting schedule of personal appearances that revolved around a promise to visit all fifty states during the general election campaign. The strategy not only was grueling for the candidate but also wasted valuable time and resources. Nowhere was this more apparent than in the final hours before election day. While Nixon was flying off to Alaska to fulfill his campaign promise, Kennedy was visiting key northeastern states with large electoral votes and major media outlets.

Kennedy displayed a remarkable understanding of the media throughout the 1960 campaign. Indeed, it was Kennedy who perfected many of the modern tactics of going public. Nixon learned his lesson and was determined not to repeat his mistakes in 1968. In June 1967, H. R. "Bob" Haldeman wrote Nixon a memo outlining the flaws of the 1960 campaign and offering advice for 1968. With a background in advertising, where he had served as an executive for the prestigious firm J. Walter Thompson, Haldeman had served as Nixon's chief advance man in 1960. It was Haldeman who suggested that Nixon rely on television to circumvent hostile reporters and take his messages directly to the people. Reminding Nixon of his exhausting schedule in 1960, Haldeman wrote, "The reach of the individual campaigner doesn't add up to diddly-squat in votes."[9] Television was the answer, he concluded. "The time has come for political campaigning—its techniques and strategies—to move out of the dark ages and into the brave new world of the omnipresent eye."[10]

The approach that Nixon adopted shielded him from reporters. He relied instead on staged television events to communicate with the people. For instance, Nixon made frequent use of televised question-and-answer sessions that followed the "man in the arena" concept. As Nixon described it, "I stood

---

*There is a story—almost certainly apocryphal—that John Kennedy's brother, Robert, visited Nixon in the dressing room before the first debate. Searching for conversation, Nixon reportedly said, "How do I look?" to which Kennedy quickly replied, "You never looked better!" (in Baus and Ross, *Politics Battle Plan*, 325).

alone, with no podium, in the center of a stage surrounded by an audience in bleacherlike tiers."[11] Members of the press corps were excluded from the sessions, with the exception of local media representatives who occasionally supplemented the questions of private citizens. The tactic of shunning the press suited Nixon just fine. As he later wrote in his memoirs, "I was bored by the charade of trying to romance the media."[12] Among those in charge of Nixon's image was Roger Ailes, who later tailored the image of George Bush in the 1988 presidential campaign. The slick images transmitted to the American people showed a relaxed and confident Nixon. Meanwhile, Nixon's new ring of advisors kept a tight rein on his schedule and cordoned him off from unnecessary contacts. In the media, there was talk of a "new" Nixon.

The antagonistic political climate of 1968, President Johnson's credibility gap, Nixon's new approach to using the media in his race for the White House, and a split between Nixon's old and new guard all influenced the establishment and initial evolution of the White House Office of Communications. It is probable that the creation of the office also reflected Nixon's fear and distrust of the federal bureaucracy. From his perspective, the bureaucracy had been captured by liberals. Thus, Nixon may have seen the office as a means of keeping tabs on the entrenched bureaucracy and preventing that bureaucracy from disseminating information unfavorable to the White House and its policies. Still, most important among the short-term reasons for establishing the office was the need to create a post for Nixon's longtime press aide and friend, Herbert George Klein.

Klein, a former reporter and editor with the *San Diego Union*, had been a friend and confidant to Nixon since 1946. Most notably, he had served as Nixon's assistant press secretary in the 1956 vice-presidential campaign and as press secretary in the presidential campaign of 1960 and the California gubernatorial campaign of 1962. It was, in fact, Klein's election-night press conference in 1962 (announcing Nixon's concession to Edmund "Pat" Brown) that an exhausted Nixon interrupted to berate the press and announce: "Just think how much you're going to be missing. You won't have Nixon to kick around anymore because, gentlemen, this is my last press conference."[13]

But Nixon was back in 1968, and so was Klein. Along with the "new" Nixon came a new title for Klein—"Manager of Communications." For all practical purposes, he was still press secretary (indeed, he was often referred to as such by the media), but his role was rather different from what it had been when he was press secretary during Nixon's 1960 presidential campaign. For one thing, he presided over a larger press operation than he had before. The new operation also had a somewhat different thrust. More attention was now paid to establishing links with the media outside Washington and New York, as well as coordinating the flow of news from all parts of the campaign apparatus—from state organizations to national committees such as "Farmers for Nixon." Klein's operation also scheduled speeches by "surrogates" (party leaders and others who campaigned on behalf of Nixon).[14] Much like the Four-Minute Men used by the Creel Committee, surrogates took messages directly to the people through community speeches across the country. In many ways, Klein's operation served as a transition to the White House Office of Communications.

One of the greatest differences in Klein's new post was that he no longer constantly traveled with Nixon, as he had in 1960. Klein still met frequently with the press, conducted briefings, and answered questions, but his real role was that of a principal coordinator for the overall press operation. Ronald Ziegler—a member of Klein's staff who had been hired at Haldeman's suggestion[15]—was assigned the task of traveling with Nixon and shepherding the press on a day-to-day basis.[16] Ziegler had previously been an aide to Haldeman at J. Walter Thompson.

Of course, another difference was that in 1960, the print medium had been the center of focus for the Nixon campaign. By 1968, the center of focus was television.[17] Aside from Klein's operation, there were other communications advisors in 1968—notably Harry Treleaven (who, like Haldeman, came from the J. Walter Thompson advertising agency) and Len Garment (Nixon's law partner), who were in charge of the overall "packaging" of Nixon. Likewise, Frank Shakespeare (previously a division president of the CBS network) served as Nixon's television advisor.[18]

Ostensibly, Klein's new title gave him more power than he had had in 1960. However, there is some indication that Klein's new position was part of an effort to "kick him upstairs." Nixon's inner circle in 1968 was different from the one he had had in 1960, and Klein was no longer part of it.[19] Chief among Nixon's "new guard" was Haldeman. Although both Klein and Haldeman profess to have been friendly on a personal basis, they differed over how best to serve Nixon.[20] Actually, Haldeman had been around Nixon campaigns for some time. He had worked on Nixon's advance team during the vice president's reelection campaign in 1956, and Robert Finch (Nixon's campaign

manager in 1960 and clearly one of Nixon's "old guard") had made him the chief advance man for the 1960 campaign. However, Haldeman came to see what he thought were weaknesses in the old guard—weaknesses that he later tried to do something about.

Haldeman reportedly felt that Finch and Klein had been largely responsible for Nixon's loss in 1960. He felt that Finch had not kept a tight enough rein on Nixon's schedule and had allowed the candidate to succumb to sheer exhaustion through the strategy of visiting all fifty states. John Ehrlichman, who worked under Haldeman as Nixon's "tour manager" in 1968 and had worked as an advance man in 1960, shared that belief. He later wrote that Finch "had no talent whatever for running a campaign . . . or running anything else requiring much consistency and firmness."[21] To these men, the names of Finch and Klein (who were longtime personal friends as well as campaign associates) were practically synonymous. The new guard apparently felt that Klein had contributed to Nixon's problems by making the candidate too accessible to the press, thus allowing too much room for error and wasting valuable time that could have been spent elsewhere.[22] Klein—known for his cluttered desk and his tendency to be late for meetings—may also have been too disorganized for their tastes. Some (or most) of that dissatisfaction may have reflected Nixon's private feelings. The columnists Rowland Evans and Robert Novak have written that even in 1960, Nixon "complained privately about Klein's 'crybaby' recommendations for easier press access."[23] In 1989, Ehrlichman noted that the period between 1960 and 1968 had brought about "a qualitative difference in Klein's relationship to Richard Nixon," although he claimed not to know specifically what had caused that difference.[24]

The fact that Ziegler—the press spokesman traveling with Nixon—had previously worked for Haldeman at J. Walter Thompson was no coincidence. Although Ziegler was Klein's representative with the traveling group, Haldeman directed that group, and Ziegler was someone he could control. Haldeman also helped to distance Klein from Nixon—probably at Nixon's instigation. As Klein later wrote: "It seemed to me that too many of the decisions we [advisors] were debating were being made by Haldeman. I said so. I did not have the ready access to the former Vice President I needed or had been accustomed to. He was too isolated."[25] Finch, who was lieutenant governor of California and had only an honorary role in the 1968 campaign, also noted the difference: "Herb was not meeting daily and hourly with Nixon as he had when we were running the 1960 campaign. It was just a totally different construct."[26] Margita

White, an aide to Klein in the 1968 campaign, said that Klein's lack of direct access to Nixon was compounded by the fact that he no longer traveled with the presidential candidate.[27] Klein himself worked in a labyrinthine building that Nixon seldom frequented at 450 Park Avenue in New York City—across the street from the headquarters of the campaign manager, John Mitchell.[28] According to Klein, Haldeman was zealous in distancing him from Nixon: "I sometimes found Haldeman checking telephone calls to the candidate and questioning me as to why I had tried to phone Nixon directly, not through him. He felt that was how the system should work—through him."[29]

Nixon, stressing the theme "law and order," narrowly defeated Democrat Hubert Humphrey and the third-party candidate George Wallace in the November election. Having done so, Nixon was keenly aware that he would be entering office under severe handicaps. The nation was divided—more so, he later claimed, than at any other point since the Civil War.[30] As a conservative Republican, he faced a bureaucracy that he felt was controlled by liberal Democrats. Congress too was a problem. Indeed, Nixon was the first newly elected president in 120 years to take office with both houses of Congress controlled by the opposition.[31] And then there was the news media, which Nixon felt was compounding the nation's divisiveness and undermining governmental authority. He had seen how the media had reacted to Johnson, and he was particularly concerned about how these opinion makers (whom he viewed as disproportionately liberal in their outlook) would treat him. Nixon's distrust of the media was long-standing, and it was only compounded by the political landscape of 1968. He openly admitted in his memoirs that he then considered "the influential majority of the news media to be part of [his] political opposition."[32] He was determined not to let them trash his presidency.

At the outset, Nixon made an apparently genuine effort to stress national unity and allow for the airing of divergent views within his administration. He initially wanted some Democrats in his cabinet. Hubert Humphrey and then Sargent Shriver were offered the ambassadorship of the United Nations, and Senator Henry Jackson of Washington was offered the position of secretary of defense. All three declined. He also made an effort to recruit blacks. Senator Edward Brooke of Massachusetts joined Humphrey and Shriver in turning down the U.N. position, and Whitney Young (executive director of the Urban League) turned down an offer to head the Department of Housing and Urban Development. In the end, Nixon's cabinet was totally white, male, and Republican.[33]

Nonetheless, Nixon seemed eager to allow for divergence of opinion among his advisors—especially in the area of domestic policy. As Carl Brauer has pointed out, Nixon deliberately set up an internal debate on domestic policy by giving an active voice to both Daniel Patrick Moynihan (a Harvard professor and Democrat who had served in both the Kennedy and Johnson administrations) and Arthur Burns (a conservative Republican who had served as director of the Council of Economic Advisors under President Dwight D. Eisenhower). The fact that Nixon was ultimately unwilling to mediate that debate led to the eventual rise of Domestic Affairs Advisor John Ehrlichman as a broker between the two.[34]

In the end, few of Nixon's initial intentions came to fruition. During the transition, he said that he wanted a strong cabinet that would do the work of government through the departments. He promised an "open" administration. And he initially let it be known that he did not want a strong chief of staff in the mold of Eisenhower's Sherman Adams. These intentions, like the attempt to spur healthy internal debate over domestic policy, eventually atrophied.

Nixon chose H. R. Haldeman to be his White House chief of staff. From the outset, Haldeman exerted a great deal of power as chief of staff, but it was the power of a gatekeeper and broker rather than a policy advocate.[35] As Haldeman later wrote: "I envisioned my job at the White House as that of a manager, and was determined to be the best manager a President ever had. That meant I had to be tough. I was tough."[36]

Haldeman is often accused of having isolated Nixon—of building a "Berlin Wall" around him with the help of two other advisors of German extraction, John Ehrlichman and Henry Kissinger. Haldeman vigorously denies this. Nixon was well aware of what was going on around him—a fact that is obvious to anyone who has made use of Nixon's presidential papers. Once in the White House, Nixon sometimes wrote memos signed "Haldeman" so that they would not be traced back to him. For the same reason, some close aides—such as Charles Colson—marked memos to "Haldeman" when they were really for Nixon.[37] As Haldeman put it, his staffing system was not meant to keep Nixon in or others out but rather to give Nixon "the opportunity to control his time and his access to the advisors he knew would be most useful."[38] Nixon himself wrote that Haldeman was "a funnel rather than a filter" who would "examine the paperwork to ensure that opposing views were included and then bring them" to the president for a decision.[39]

To the extent that Nixon appeared isolated, it was because he preferred to make decisions based on written memos rather than face-to-face exchanges. He disliked confrontations, hated to say "no" in person, was uncomfortable with small talk, and was unable personally to fire anyone. Thus, the man who said "no" (and said "no" straightforwardly—even zealously) was Haldeman. The man who denied access was Haldeman. The man who demanded "zero defects" and expected every job to get done was Haldeman. As Haldeman has written: "My style at work was exactly the opposite to Nixon's. I was brusque, direct, I 'chewed people out.' I would come straight on at a problem or person, hammering culprits over the head, verbally. Nixon would attack the same problem or person by coming in at the side, often through subordinates, when the victim wasn't looking, and trying to strike his blow unseen."[40]

Haldeman's direct style and his zeal to get things done intimidated many and gave rise to his being depicted as Nixon's "Prussian guard." Haldeman himself said at the time that he was "Nixon's son-of-a-bitch."[41] He has since admitted that he took his job too seriously and pushed people too hard.

> My wife, getting glimpses of my operation and relationships with the staff, especially the junior men, very perceptively has since observed that it wasn't *Nixon's* character or moods that allowed Watergate to happen. She points out that *my* character and demands pushed people to become "little generals," which was out of character for them. . . . My demands were always expectant of results. . . . It was push, push, push for concrete action. In that setting the action got more and more out-of-hand as wilder schemes were proposed to get more answers and satisfy what they thought were my expectations.[42]

During the transition period after the 1968 election, tensions between Nixon's old and new guards continued. Nixon's old friends and advisors were distanced from the president and relegated to less influential positions. Robert Finch was a prime case in point. John Ehrlichman has written that the changes were made "to make room for more able and efficient newcomers."[43] But some—including, it seems, Herb Klein—felt that it was a power play by Haldeman. Finch echoes that feeling: "Even though [Haldeman] had been hired by *us*, in effect, in the 1960 campaign . . . [he had] very strong feelings about how the White House ought to be run. . . . I think it's clear that Haldeman wanted his own crew."[44]

Quite obviously, Haldeman's approach to Nixon loyalists did nothing to win their affection. He made it clear that everyone who wanted a position in the

White House—no matter how close the person was to the president-elect or how much service had been rendered in the past—was applying for a job. Nothing would be handed to anyone on a silver platter. Thus, the announcement of who would serve on the White House staff was purposely delayed for weeks.[45]

When announcements were finally made, Haldeman made some enemies. For instance, Haldeman was adamant that Nixon's personal secretary, Rose Mary Woods—who had served Nixon since 1951—could not occupy space next to the Oval Office, the desk area of every other personal secretary to the president since the West Wing of the White House had been built during Theodore Roosevelt's administration. He insisted that if he was to be Nixon's gatekeeper, there could be no one else close at hand who could grant access. He knew that Eisenhower's secretary, Ann Whitman, had sometimes been used to circumvent Sherman Adams, and he would not allow this to happen under him. When Woods was informed of the decision, she was furious. She hated Haldeman from that day on. As Nixon's close associate and speechwriter William Safire later wrote:

Nixon had to break this Haldeman-first news to Rose personally, a task he hated, and she reacted with the grief-stricken fury one might have expected of a loyal woman scorned. Rose and Nixon rode down in the Pierre Hotel elevator [in New York] afterward, and the President-elect spoke to her twice; she would not speak to him; Bryce Harlow, the only other person in that confined space, refers to it as "the longest elevator ride ever taken by a man who had recently been elected President of the United States." . . . There was a purpose in Haldeman's choice of Rose Woods as the first person with whom to do battle. If he could interpose himself between the President and Rose, he could do damn near anything.[46]

It was in this context that the planning of Nixon's White House press operation took place. Very early in the transition period, Nixon decided against a strong press secretary in the mold of Eisenhower's Jim Hagerty. As Haldeman recently stated: "Nixon wanted someone as press secretary who would transmit to the press what the president wanted transmitted to the press. He did not want someone who would function in the Hagerty mold of being an alterego to the president in terms of spokesmanship. And Klein—by his nature and by his relationship with Nixon—really fit the Hagerty-type role in Nixon's view."[47] John Ehrlichman echoes that assessment: "It was pretty well determined that the press operation would be run out of the President's office. The President wanted a [press secretary] who was not a Jim Hagerty. He didn't want his media representatives making policy, or even being involved in policy, except to the extent that they announced policy. So, this whole thing was very specifically planned and calculated as a downgrading of the press secretary's role to a ministerial role."[48]

Nixon and Haldeman decided that this downgraded press operation would be headed by Ron Ziegler. Ziegler would not hold the title "Press Secretary" but would simply be a press spokesman. The purpose of this seems to have been twofold. First, Nixon and Haldeman wanted to send a message to the press that they held the press in "a certain contempt."[49] Second, they wanted a press aide that they could control. Ziegler was subservient and young (twenty-nine years old) and came from a background in advertising (where he had worked for Haldeman) rather than journalism. As Charles Colson noted: "Nixon was able to program Ziegler. He was absolutely programmable. I mean, Ziegler was like Charlie McCarthy. He would go out and say *exactly* what Nixon said, with *exactly* the tone Nixon wanted. Klein would not. So Ron was the perfect press guy for Nixon—for his tastes."[50]

The fact that Klein would not simply parrot what his superiors told him to say appears to have been an important factor in his not becoming press secretary—a post that many observers had felt was his for the asking. "Haldeman recognized that he couldn't control Herb," says Robert Finch. "He was not about to be dictated to."[51] Jeb Stuart Magruder (who later became deputy director of the Office of Communications and was in frequent contact with Ziegler) wrote that Ziegler never uttered "a syllable that had not first been approved by Nixon or Haldeman. That got him the job over Herb Klein and others who had been known now and then to express a personal opinion or an independent thought."[52]

Klein's problems may have been compounded by the fact that he was a journalist, having served as an editor of the *San Diego Union* and on the board of directors of the American Society of Newspaper Editors. He enjoyed the company of reporters and was widely viewed by them as a professional. Some felt that this made Klein all the more suspect to Haldeman. Haldeman, however, has described the decision in less sinister terms. He says that it was actually Nixon's decision to distance himself from longtime personal friends. According to Haldeman, "Nixon viewed Klein and Finch in human terms, as people, which meant that he would have trouble dealing with them on an official basis."[53] In fact, Haldeman claims that Klein's experience as a working journalist with close ties to that constituency made him "uniquely able to deal on a peer level" with editors and other media representatives in a post separate from the White House Press Office.[54]

It was Finch who initially gave Klein the informal news that he would not be named press secretary. Haldeman furnished the details later. Whatever the motivation for the decision, Klein was disappointed. He had expected to be press secretary and he had expected to be a strong one.[55] As Haldeman noted: "Having worked with Nixon when he was vice president and known Jim Hagerty well and all, I think Herb saw himself as potentially becoming another Jim Hagerty." Hagerty, it should be noted, is often viewed as the greatest White House press secretary not only for his immense skill in running the Press Office but also for having defined the role of the modern press secretary. "And so," Haldeman continued, "there was disappointment on his part that he never became that."[56] As for Ziegler, he was apparently surprised to be chosen over Klein. "I was approached about it in Florida," he said. "It was not a position that I sought or visualized that I would even be offered." And although Klein was disappointed about the choice, he apparently exhibited no bitterness toward Ziegler. "There was no tension at all," Ziegler said. "As a matter of fact, Herb was my mentor. We were together in the Wyndham Hotel in New York, and during the transition I would go discuss with him the [press] briefings [I would give]. At least from my standpoint, there was never really any tension that existed, and I don't think there was from Herb's."[57]

Aside from whatever personal regret he may have felt, Klein was appalled that Ziegler's post would be downgraded. He said so to Haldeman. Klein eventually helped to convince Haldeman and Nixon that Ziegler's title should be upgraded to press secretary, which it was—just one week before Nixon's inauguration.[58] In the meantime, Klein set out to fashion a different sort of role for himself in the administration. He was aware of the new demands imposed on presidents by the rise of the modern presidency. Conversations that he had had with former presidential press secretaries confirmed the need to coordinate the press activities of the entire executive branch. But—partly because of his experience as a newspaper editor—Klein also wanted to serve as a liaison with newspapers and broadcasters throughout the country.

The idea for a post separate from the Press Office had begun percolating early in the transition. "We started talking about it in the Hotel Pierre [Nixon's transition headquarters in New York] after the election when we were first putting together the Cabinet," says Finch. "At least that's when I first talked about it." Initially, the post was thought of as a mechanism for controlling the flow of news throughout the administration. What they wanted, Finch continues, was "an orchestration for the administration's multiple voices."[59] According to Haldeman, Bryce Harlow, who had served as the director of Eisenhower's congressional liaison office—a role that he reprised in the early part of the Nixon administration—was one of the originators of the idea. "Harlow strongly advised the President and me and others that we should give careful consideration to coordinating the spokesmen and press secretaries from the various Cabinet departments because of the constant problem of the non-unified 'line.' In other words, one department may have a different view of a given issue than another department. As a result, the administration appears to be speaking with multiple voices. And so there was a feeling that a White House Director of Communications could be a unifying force in all that."[60]

Although it is widely thought that the Office of Communications was created for the benefit of Herb Klein, most of the principals deny that. John Ehrlichman has categorically stated, "The Office of Communications was not created for Herb Klein's benefit." He believes that the office would have been created whether or not Klein was on the scene.[61] Ziegler concurs: "The judgment was made that Herb should not be press secretary, but I do not think that was directly tied to the creation of the director of communications post. The creation of the Office of Communications was based on need, and I think that proposition is supported by the fact that the office has continued as a vital function."[62] Still, such a post became a convenient place to put Klein so as to smooth over whatever ill feelings may have been created by the choice of Ziegler as press secretary, and Haldeman admits that the desire to bring Klein into the administration in some capacity was a "moving force" for acting on the suggestions for such a post.[63] After all, Klein was one of Nixon's oldest friends.

Toward the end of November 1968, the finalized plan for the new office was presented to Nixon at a meeting that included Klein, Ziegler, Haldeman, and Ehrlichman, among others.[64] Nixon seemed enthusiastic about the new post, and the group decided that Klein should be called "Director of Communications," a title that Lyn Nofziger had used to describe his job for California Governor Ronald Reagan (who had beaten Pat Brown—Nixon's old nemesis—in 1966).[65] Of particular interest to the president-elect was the television aspect of the new Office of Communications.[66] He was eager to use various means to take his message directly to the people so that the elite media would not "distort" it. Likewise, Nixon was pleased with Klein's intention to accommodate local media because he felt that they were more likely to be supportive of his policies than were the Washington-based ("eastern establishment") media, which he viewed as adversarial and disproportionately liberal. In other words, Nixon felt that local broadcasters and editors could be used as yet another means of circumventing the "establishment" media and taking his message directly to the people. Although Nixon may not have thought of it in exactly those terms, Klein's management of television and his links with local media would serve to institutionalize a means of going public.

Klein's appointment was announced on 25 November 1968. The *New York Times* noted that Klein had been appointed with what appeared "to be unusual supervisory powers over all Government information services."[67] Unlike Ziegler's rank, Klein's formal position was at the highest level of Nixon's personal staff. The appointment was announced by Ziegler, who said in his statement:

President-elect Nixon intends to emphasize in his administration the need for free access to information in all departments of government, to the extent that it does not endanger national security. The execution of this responsibility will be one of Mr. Klein's primary responsibilities. In this position, Mr. Klein will serve as a spokesman for the executive branch as a whole. He will coordinate the activities of public information officers in every branch [sic] of government.[68]

The *New York Times* noted, with perhaps some overstatement, that no government information officer had "ever been given such a broad mandate."[69] There was immediate concern that Klein would act as an "information czar" and restrict the flow of information from the government. Klein sought to allay these fears. In a question-and-answer session following Ziegler's opening remarks, Klein told the assembled reporters: "Truth will become the hallmark of the Nixon administration. I'm charged directly by the president to emphasize [to] every department of government that more facts should be made available. With this kind of emphasis, we feel that we will be able to eliminate any possibility of a credibility gap in this administration."[70] He seems to have believed what he said.

CHAPTER THREE

THE NIXON YEARS

BEGINNINGS AND EVOLUTION

At the outset of the Nixon administration, the position of director of communications was perceived by outside observers to be more powerful than the downgraded press secretary post.[1] The Office of Communications and the Press Office were two entirely separate operations. Press Secretary Ziegler was responsible for day-to-day briefings and contacts with Washington-based reporters. Communications Director Klein was responsible for the larger coordination of news flow from the executive branch, for maintaining links with local editors, publishers, and broadcasters, and for scheduling interviews and television appearances by administration officials and other proadministration spokespeople (such as members of Congress and party officials). Whereas the Press Office was responsible for dealing with reporters' daily concerns, the Office of Communications was charged with mapping a long-range media strategy. As Klein put it at the time: "Ziegler is the spokesman for the president; I am [spokesman] for the administration."[2]

Klein was also the early favorite with the media. He was, after all, one of them. He had started out as a reporter—working in the 1940s for the *Post-Advocate* in Alhambra, California. In 1959, he was named editor of the *San Diego Union*, a conservative Republican newspaper that was part of the Copley chain. Later he served as a director of the American Society of Newspaper Editors. But beyond all that, Klein had a certain aura that the press found attractive. Perhaps it was the softening influence that he seemed to have on Nixon. R. W. Apple wrote about that quality in the *New York Times* when

Klein was appointed director of communications. Recalling a hectic whistle-stop tour of Ohio and Michigan during the 1960 campaign, Apple wrote how hecklers had thrown eggs and tomatoes at Nixon while other demonstrators had been caught putting dynamite on the railroad tracks that Nixon was to ride over. Nixon was already exhausted from a long campaign, and this was the last straw. It was Klein who calmed the distraught candidate. As Apple recalled, "After an hour or so of conversation with [Klein]—a man with a voice so soft that he seemed to swallow his words, a man as relaxed as Mr. Nixon was tense—the then vice president gradually unwound."[3]

Klein—who Robert B. Semple, Jr., described as "a short, stooped, habitually sad-faced man"—possessed a soothing quality that was conducive to openness and trust.[4] Dom Bonafede echoed the image of Klein as Nixon's "soft voice" in an article in the *Nation*:

A sandy-haired man of medium height, with an executive bulge and a passive mien, Klein at the age of 52 evokes an aura of sincerity. . . . For more than two decades, he has been accepted by the national press as one of the "good guys." To malign Richard Nixon was permissible, but for some reason it was unsportsmanlike to indict his mouthpiece as an accessory. . . . With monotonous predictability, the same hyphenated adjectives have been applied to him: soft-spoken, even-tempered, crinkly-eyed, mild-mannered.[5]

Ziegler, on the other hand, was initially treated by reporters with suspicion. They complained that he was too young, had too little experience, and had no background in journalism. He was often compared—unfavorably—with such predecessors as Jim Hagerty, Pierre Salinger, George Reedy, Bill Moyers, and George Christian. He openly admitted his subservience to superiors such as Haldeman. As he told an interviewer at the time: "I would never say anything unless I've been authorized to. I'm out there to give what the President thinks, not what Ziegler thinks."[6] Not only did he have no independence, but it also appeared that he would not participate in what *Time* magazine called "the high counsels of government."[7] Indeed, it seemed that Ziegler was not always informed of all the facts concerning particular events.[8]

Ziegler was also kidded—and criticized—for sprinkling his answers to reporters with advertising clichés. Soon his roundabout, jargon-laden replies at press briefings came to be known as "ziegles," "zigzags," or "ziggies."[9] Much of the jargon that reporters found so glaring in 1969 is now commonplace. For instance, the term "photo opportunity" has found its way into the vernacular—thanks, in part, to Ziegler—and it is hard to think of someone snickering at a press secretary today for talking about a particular policy being "implemented" within a particular "time frame."[10] Arguably, Ziegler's choice of vocabulary was disconcerting to reporters because it underscored the changing style of presidential-press relations. The FDR system of "hard news openly conveyed"—part of an elite bargaining relationship between reporters and officials—was giving way to direct forms of communications that circumvented this relationship. To have an adman as press secretary was to turn a cold shoulder toward the old system. The new system seemed more preoccupied with image and hype—one reason, perhaps, that so much was made of Ziegler's old summer job at Disneyland as a tour guide ("Welcome to the world of make-believe, folks. My name's Ron and I'll be your guide down the river of adventure.").[11] Reporters were quick to point out that Ziegler had also handled the Disneyland account (actually a prestigious one) when he had worked for Haldeman at J. Walter Thompson. Even when Ziegler tried to be self-deprecating—calling a cocktail party for the White House press corps a "press relaxation opportunity"[12]—the words seemed to grate. While Klein evoked feelings of trust and openness, Ziegler evoked feelings of suspicion and evasiveness.

This dichotomy in the way the two were depicted by the media led to some strains in the relationship between Klein and Ziegler. As Haldeman put it, the relationship between the two had "its ups and downs." "Herb tried to be helpful," he said, "and Ron tried to work with Herb, but there was an inevitable conflict."[13] Klein himself has noted that in the awkward first months of Ziegler's tenure at the Press Office, Ziegler somewhat resented the respect and attention that Klein was receiving.[14] The initial fear among the media that Klein might be transformed into a propaganda czar had been quickly put to rest, and Klein and the Office of Communications enjoyed a rather blissful honeymoon with the media.

That honeymoon was aided by the fact that Klein immediately set to work to fulfill his promise of making the administration open to the press. Klein appears to have honestly believed that his job was to bridge the "credibility gap" that had developed during the Johnson administration. He tried to do that by providing the media with access to government officials. During his first two months on the job, Klein was reported to have arranged one hundred interviews with cabinet-level officials.[15] Margita White (Klein's administrative assistant) later said that those first months were used to open up access

President Nixon conversing in the Oval Office with Communications Director Herbert Klein (left) and Press Secretary Ronald Ziegler. (Courtesy Nixon Presidential Materials Project)

wherever possible. "Openness," she continued, "was the hallmark of Herb Klein's office."[16] The press seemed to agree. A report to the National Press Club later reported that the Office of Communications had won "the thanks of many Washington news people for the help [it] gave in opening up the bureaucracy and arranging interviews with policymakers."[17] Even Joseph Spear (an assistant to the syndicated columnist Jack Anderson)—not one to tout the openness of the Nixon administration—has written:

> Whenever a reporter had difficulty obtaining information, a call to Klein usually opened the door. Newsmen were surprised with his performance, and his reputation reached the point that a mere threat to "call Herb" proved sufficient, in many cases, to convince a stubborn information officer to cooperate. Washington journalists also gave Klein high marks for making officials available for interviews. He constantly urged administration functionaries to cooperate with the press.[18]

As we shall see, this openness soon led to renewed tensions between Klein and his superiors.

INITIAL FUNCTIONS OF THE OFFICE OF COMMUNICATIONS

Initially, the Office of Communications consisted of Herb Klein and four senior staff members: Paul Costello, who served as Klein's assistant in dealings with the written press; Virginia Savell, who headed up the Speakers' Bureau, which was used to arrange speeches around the country for administration officials; Alvin Snyder, who was responsible for liaison with the broadcast media and for arranging television and radio interviews with administration spokespeople; and Margita White, who was the administrative assistant (a sort of "staff secretary" who coordinated work assignments throughout the office).[19]

One of the first things that Klein did was to take formal steps toward coordinating the flow of news from the various departments. Under the direction of Costello (a former political reporter for the *Boston Herald*), each of Klein's four chief aides had jurisdiction over particular departments and kept in daily contact with their public affairs assistants. For instance, the Defense and State departments were monitored by Costello, and the Justice and Treasury departments were monitored by White.[20] In addition, each department submitted two reports a week to the Office of Communications. These contacts, in turn, became the basis of daily reports that were given to Klein.[21] The aim of the office was to coordinate information from the various departments, not to dictate how their individual press offices were to be run.[22] Nonetheless, the Office of Communications sometimes drafted press releases for use by the departments, at least for particularly delicate issues.[23] By the time Nixon left for a European summit—just over a month after his inauguration—the system was in place, and Nixon was requesting that Klein supply him with a daily rundown of the major releases that were expected to come from the departments while he was gone. He also had Haldeman instruct Klein to coordinate the timing of the releases so that there would be "at least one major announcement each day from one of the departments."[24] Nixon was eager to keep the administration in the news on a daily basis.

Information transmitted by the public affairs assistants also provided the basis for "fact sheets" outlining particular administration programs. The office distributed these fact sheets directly to some seventeen hundred daily newspapers and thousands of radio and television stations around the country. These activities were part of an effort to create an open administration and to bridge the credibility gap that had developed under President Johnson. Klein, from his firsthand experience as an editor, realized that most newspapers were dependent on wire service reports, which were often sketchy and inadequate. Therefore, he felt that fact sheets could be of great informational value to editors and broadcasters. At the same time, he felt that they could lead to a better understanding—and perhaps acceptance—of administration policies. Nonetheless, he was keenly aware that such mailings could smack of propaganda, and he made every effort to see that they consisted of "cold facts."[25] Two of the earliest mailings dealt with postal reform and the antiballistic missile system.[26] Another, a biography of Warren Burger, was sent out to some thirty thousand publications when Nixon nominated Burger as chief justice of the Supreme Court in the spring of 1969. The strategy seemed to be successful. Hundreds of editors wrote letters to the office expressing thanks, and many of the mailings apparently spurred small newspapers to give more coverage to those topics than they ordinarily would have.[27]

Klein was also concerned that the departments were "creaky and antiquated" in their dealings with the media. He tried to get departmental officers to make more use of the broadcast media, and he briefed each member of the cabinet on how best to use television. When necessary, cabinet members were rehearsed for television appearances.[28] Klein found the domestic departments to be particularly weak in terms of public relations. Thus, he made an effort to hire new people in departmental public affairs offices, and he set up regularly scheduled meetings that included himself and the public affairs officers from all the departments (much like the meetings that Jim Hagerty had initiated under Eisenhower). During those sessions, Klein stressed the importance of the broadcast media over the more routine printed press releases, and he sought to coordinate further the flow of information from the executive branch.

As a gesture to radio, Klein saw to it that several cabinet departments installed "Spotmasters"—a sort of telephone-answering device that contained excerpts from prepared speeches given by the cabinet secretary or other officials in the department. Radio stations could access the tapes over the telephone, record them, and use them in hourly news broadcasts.[29] These excerpts (or "actualities," as they are called) served as an audio equivalent of a press release. Spotmasters were ideal for the administration, since it could thereby control which excerpts were aired by the stations utilizing the device. Use of the system also helped to ingratiate the administration to many local radio stations that could not themselves afford the luxury of sending correspondents to Washington to tape excerpts of speeches.

Through Al Snyder (a former television executive in New York), the Office of Communications coordinated television appearances by administration and proadministration officials. Snyder served as the contact point for major network news forums (such as "Issues and Answers," "Meet the Press," and "Face the Nation"), as well as for morning news and interview programs (such as "Today") and even for popular late-night talk shows. Attorney General John Mitchell, for instance, appeared on the "Dick Cavett Show," and Vice President Spiro Agnew appeared on "The Tonight Show with Johnny Carson." Klein himself appeared as cohost of the "Dick Cavett Show" and served as the guest host of radio talk shows on several occasions during the vacation season.[30]

Working through Snyder made it easier for television producers to get an administration official on the air, since all they had to do was contact the Office of Communications. It was then Snyder's responsibility to do all the legwork. When administration officials were traveling around the country, Snyder would also advise them on how and where to get the best broadcast exposure. He maintained links with local talk shows throughout the country and helped to arrange appearances by Nixon officials on these programs. As Klein once put it, "If one of our people is in Chicago, we might suggest to Irv Kupcinet [a *Chicago Sun-Times* columnist who had a television talk program] that maybe he would like to have him on the show."[31]

Nixon himself was adamant that members of his administration appear frequently on television. This was a common theme in internal White House memoranda. An early example is a memo that Haldeman sent to Klein just two months after Nixon had assumed office. In it, Haldeman wrote that the president was "especially anxious" that Klein "build a stable of television personalities from within the Administration" who would look good and could "handle the situation on TV." The goal was to get them on television as much as possible.[32] A week later, Haldeman instructed Klein that Nixon wanted administration officials to plan their schedules so that there would be "an ongoing Administration appearance day by day in the TV news."[33] Klein responded: "We will push . . . the daily TV aspect with the Cabinet members. We have been doing this considerably, particularly in connection with special trips or speeches by the members, but we will see to it that it increases."[34] A year later the same theme was being pursued. In May 1970, Haldeman said to Klein in a memo: "I know each Cabinet Officer gives several speeches a week. The problem is providing them with an appropriate forum and making sure that their speech is timely and that the coverage is right." Haldeman also said that there should be "at least one Cabinet Officer a week on television."[35]

There were, however, exceptions to Nixon's penchant for television. Initially Henry Kissinger was not allowed to go on the air because of his German accent.[36] When Kissinger expressed an interest in going on "Meet the Press" in March 1969, Haldeman sent Klein a memo expressly stating that the president did not want Kissinger to make public television appearances of that sort.[37] In the same memo, Haldeman extended the ban to all White House staff members—perhaps as a way of placating Kissinger. Exceptions included John Ehrlichman, Bryce Harlow, Herb Klein, and Daniel Patrick Moynihan, all of whom the president felt were "very effective" on television.[38] The following year, the ban was extended and White House staff members were instructed not to give press briefings or take part in any other public press appearance without approval.[39]

The coordination of speeches by cabinet members and other administration spokespeople fell under the jurisdiction of Virginia Savell. During the 1968 campaign she had managed a similar operation with Alex Troffey. Under Klein's jurisdiction, they had arranged the appearances of "surrogates"— Republican leaders who were recruited to speak on behalf of Nixon around the country. Rather like the use of Four-Minute Men during World War I, the surrogate operation worked with speechwriters and developed themes so that "each geographic area of the country . . . would hear basically the same 'party line' expressed simultaneously by a different speaker." Every day, Klein's office sent surrogates a detailed news summary by teletype. Senator John Tower (Rep.-Tex.) also took part in coordinating the program by heading an "issues office" in Washington.[40]

Once Nixon was president, Savell turned her attention to coordinating speeches given by members of the administration. The operation was a means of mobilizing public support for the administration's position on particular issues. Attention was paid both to major policy speeches that would attract the national media and to local appearances that were directed toward particular constituencies. In 1969, speakers toured the country talking about Nixon's family-assistance plan, postal reform, and proposals to eliminate the draft.[41] As Klein told an interviewer in 1970, the speeches had "regional impact. If the guy said the same thing in Washington, he'd get [only] three inches in the local paper."[42]

The speakers' operation served not only as a means of mobilizing public support for administration policy initiatives but also as a well-oiled mechanism that could be utilized in coordination with the Republican National Committee during election years. Later, Dick Howard became head of the Speakers' Bureau.[43] Charles Colson also began scheduling speakers through his separate operation (a precursor to the Office of Public Liaison), and it was he who directed the surrogates program during the 1972 presidential campaign.[44]

Efforts were also made to broaden the speaking program to include lower-level executive officials on an even more decentralized basis. Nixon himself pushed for this after being shown a memo that had been written by Marshall Wright, a forty-three-year-old career foreign service officer who had recently completed a speaking tour of Arkansas for the State Department. Wright felt that a series of such tours—coordinated throughout the country—could play a major role in rallying public support for Nixon's Vietnam policy.

Wright's memo had been written shortly after Nixon's Silent Majority speech, in which Nixon had called on Americans to support his efforts regarding Vietnam. Wright expressed the fear that the effect of that speech would gradually dissipate unless there was "a coordinated and effective follow-up at the local level." He added, "What we have got to do is get directly to the people, *without having everything colored by the lenses of the Washington and New York media communities*." This, of course, was what Nixon had been saying all along, but Wright added a twist. The point was not to send out big names but to use people that communities would trust. "Send selected Foreign Service Officers back to their own home states," he wrote. "The mere fact of being a local boy not only enhances credibility, it also reduces the average citizen's resistance to 'propaganda from Washington.' Finally, it gives the local media a hook on which to hang good local coverage." Wright also noted that the speakers should be chosen carefully—they should be "prepared to talk from personal conviction rather than canned briefing papers." Question-and-answer formats, he added, were especially good, and he stressed that the tone of the speaker should be "an easy admission of fallibility combined with a willingness to answer any question with candor." Through it all, the key was local television exposure. "In less than four days in Arkansas," Wright noted, "I had 180 minutes of television time." Nixon was highly enthusiastic and scribbled compliments in the margin: "Good"—"Excellent"—"Correct"— "This guy is smart!" He also penned a directive to Haldeman and Klein. Wright was "absolutely correct," Nixon wrote. "Let's have a program & follow-up. . . . Give me a plan for speakers to do this."[45]

Klein responded on 24 January 1970 that such a plan had been given "permanent program status" in the State Department, "with a staff officer working on it." He wrote that broadcast exposure was also being emphasized. "In the period of January 19, 1970 to March 11 a total of 14 speakers are scheduled to appear on 269 TV stations and 35 radio stations. These appearances will be in 40 cities in 24 states. . . . The State Department anticipates growth in the program during the months ahead."[46]

In February 1971, Paul Costello sent Klein a memo that summarized the publicity generated by the out-of-town speaking program of the Office of Communications. In the preceding three months (November 1970–January 1971), the office had coordinated the appearances of 465 speakers. In January, 130 speakers from 17 departments and agencies had visited 34 states, generating 43 radio interviews, 113 television interviews, 63 magazine and newspaper interviews, and 41 news conferences. Significantly higher numbers were generated during the 1970 midterm election campaign.[47]

The Office of Communications also helped to provide material for use by proadministration congressmen and senators both on and off the floors of the House and Senate. Klein and his staff maintained ties with the White House Office of Congressional Relations—initially headed by Bryce Harlow, who was succeeded by William Timmons early in 1970.[48] During his first few weeks in office, Nixon made it clear that he wanted to cultivate a congressional group that would stand up for the administration and attack the opposition. In a memo to Klein dated 9 February 1969, Haldeman wrote:

The President is especially anxious that your group, plus some of the R & W [Research and Writing] people, especially [Patrick] Buchanan and [William] Safire, set up a system of furnishing attack material on a daily basis to a group of key people on the Hill that Bryce Harlow will be lining up to be our first line of battle for the Administration.

The material always, of course, should clear through Harlow's office, and the President has asked Harlow to set up a system for handling this so that it moves fast. He is going to be expecting reports from both you and Bryce as to what is being done and what effect it is having.[49]

The responsibility for writing up that material came to rest with Lyn Nofziger, who joined the Congressional Relations staff in July 1969 as "chief wordsmith." The choice of Nofziger was made by Harlow and Klein.

Nofziger had served as director of communications to California Governor

Ronald Reagan from 1966 to 1968. He was a former journalist who, like Klein, had worked for the Copley newspaper chain in California for many years. Nofziger was described by his official White House biography as the one who stood ready "to assist Members of the Senate and House in the preparation of speeches and other written materials in support of the President's programs and policies."[50] According to Klein: "Nofziger was tough and knew how to make news. Congressmen liked and trusted him. He could attack, but within bounds of reason. He was content to stay completely in the background." Later, Nixon's aide Charles Colson—who epitomized a brand of tough pragmatic politics that came to be known within the White House as "hardball"—tried to use Nofziger for "more unsavory schemes."[51]

Colson was in charge of a White House operation that later came to be called the Office of Public Liaison. As he put it: "I was special counsel to the president in charge of relationships with groups outside of the White House— any public interest group or any special interest group. My job was to listen to them, represent their points of view at different things that went on in government, and mobilize them to get support for the president."[52] Some of the activities that Colson used to generate support among interest groups—such as direct mail and the scheduling of speeches—came to overlap with the activities of the Office of Communications. As was necessary with the Office of Congressional Relations, Klein needed to maintain links with Colson's operation. However, Klein and Colson had very different operating styles. In addition, each felt that the other was infringing on his turf. As we shall see later, this led to a major conflict between the two Nixon staff operations.

Besides maintaining links with the Congressional Relations and Public Liaison offices, Klein worked closely with the official organs of the Republican party. That link was especially important during election campaigns. In particular, Klein had close working relationships with the Republican National Committee's publications: *Monday* and *The Republican*. He was in almost daily contact with Frank Leonard of the RNC's Communications Division, letting Leonard know the week's schedule of administration news and making suggestions for items that would make good short articles. In a memo to Haldeman explaining his relationship with the RNC, Klein concluded:

> We will continue to urge the usage of material based on the Administration's programs in appealing to Republicans. . . . I have met with Jim Keogh [head of Nixon's research and writing team], Harry Dent [special

counsel to the president for political affairs], Jim Allison [deputy chairman of the RNC], and Frank [Leonard], and we have developed procedures to get additional information, particularly for the *Republican*. These will be funneled through this office to Frank, so we retain a central contact point.[53]

Haldeman was pleased with the arrangement. In a margin note, he wrote: "Klein—Great. This should really be productive over the long haul."[54]

The Office of Communications also worked with the Republican National Committee in scheduling speakers and in arranging certain sorts of direct mail operations. On at least fifteen occasions through August 1970, the Office of Communications had various presidential messages published by the Government Printing Office. These included the president's Inaugural Address, his eulogy of President Eisenhower, and his State of the Union speech, as well as longer presidential reports such as *U.S. Foreign Policy for the 1970s* (which reached nearly two hundred pages). About 75 percent of the total press run of each publication was mailed by the RNC. Depending on the nature of the publication, the cover letter included in the RNC mailings was signed by a cabinet member, the vice president, a White House advisor, or Herb Klein. There was no indication that the publication was mailed by the RNC. Envelopes and stationery for the cover letter were provided by the White House, the vice president's office, or one of the cabinet departments.

The remaining press run was distributed in a variety of other ways. Klein sent the publications to radio and television news directors, publishers, editorial page writers, Washington correspondents, and political columnists, directly from the Office of Communications. Other copies were distributed by departmental public affairs offices. Sometimes specialized individuals were targeted to receive a publication. For instance, the above-mentioned foreign policy report was sent to three hundred political science professors with a cover letter signed by Health, Education, and Welfare Secretary Robert Finch. Later, the RNC reimbursed the Government Printing Office for some of its expenses, and the White House counsel John Dean prepared new guidelines for such mailings when Jerry Landauer, of the *Wall Street Journal*, threatened to run an article charging that the Nixon administration and the Republican National Committee were engaged in "a massive political propaganda campaign financed with federal funds."[55] Still, the RNC continued to mail material that was prepared by the Office of Communications. Between 7 January and 2

November 1972, the Republican National Committee distributed 226 separate mailings to 308,009 recipients. The mailings ranged from the text of an economic speech given by Office of Management and Budget Director George Schultz (which was mailed to financial editors) to a "China Speaking Kit" (which was mailed to "Youth for Nixon" organizations in various states).[56]

Coordinating the news flow from the executive branch, scheduling interviews, organizing speaking tours, and engaging in direct mail operations were overt actions undertaken by the Office of Communications. From the start, the office also engaged in less-visible attempts to mold public opinion and highlight support of administration programs. Klein was particularly active in lobbying columnists and editorial writers. He would leak information, when appropriate, to generate a column, and he would do what he could to gain favorable editorial support for administration policies or proposals. He was particularly adept at this, since he was so well liked by journalists. Unlike Ziegler, Klein genuinely enjoyed spending spare time with newspeople over drinks or at lunch, and he developed a good working relationship with them.[57] After presidential speeches and press conferences, Klein would immediately call scores of opinion makers for their reactions. This was done partly to sound out the reviewers, but it was also an opportunity for Klein to remind these individuals of themes that he felt were particularly important for them to emphasize.

Establishing ties with small, local publications and broadcasters was also a means of generating support for the administration. Accustomed to being ignored by Washington elites, these local media were often flattered to receive a call or letter from the White House. In a summary of his office's activities, submitted to Haldeman during his first month on the job, Klein wrote of his efforts to gain editorial support and of his efforts to plant columns "on the active work in progress of the Urban Affairs Council."[58] As part of his effort to mold the outlook of editorial pages, Klein urged administration officials to write editorials suitable for publication in newspapers around the country. The Office of Communications monitored editorial pages of regional newspapers. Favorable editorials were clipped, and copies were sometimes included in mailings. For instance, Klein had the Republican National Committee mail excerpts of favorable editorials concerning Nixon's first Inaugural Address.[59]

In the first few months of its existence, the Office of Communications also began to establish an informal network to cultivate letters to the editor. This was done at the instigation of President Nixon. Such a network had existed during the 1968 campaign, and he wanted it to continue while he was in the White House. Less than three weeks after his inauguration, Nixon wrote a memo to John Ehrlichman complaining that he had not received any word as to what sort of procedure would be set up in the White House to stimulate letters to the editor and calls to television stations. As Nixon explained:

> Two primary purposes would be served by establishing such a procedure. First, it gives a lot of people who were very active in the campaign a continuing responsibility which they would enjoy having. Second, it gives us what Kennedy had in abundance—a constant representation in letters to the editor columns and a very proper influence on the television commentators. As a starter, some letters thanking those who have written favorable things about the Administration might be in order. . . . In addition, individuals can express their own enthusiasm for the RN crime program in Washington, the RN press conference technique and the Inaugural, and the general performance since the Inauguration. Later on, letters can be written taking on various columnists and editorialists when they jump on us unfairly.

> I do not want a blunderbuss memorandum to go out to hundreds of people on this project, but a discreet and nevertheless effective Nixon Network set up.[60]

Initially, letters to the editor were generated informally by the administration. As Jeb Stuart Magruder later wrote, this was done on a "hit-or-miss basis—someone would call a few friends and ask them to write letters."[61] In a memo to Haldeman dated 7 July 1969, Klein wrote that he would try to put together a network of "adept Nixon supporters in key cities across the country . . . for helping with letters to the editors, etc."[62] In September, Nixon prodded Haldeman for a report on how the plan for letters to the editor was working.[63] A few days later, Klein apologized to Haldeman: "The letter writing operation is not as efficient as it should be or will be. We have people like the [Republican] National Committee, Charlie McWhorter, Frederick Dixon, and Rose Mary Mazon working on this." He went on to point out that although letters to the editor have little influence on major newspapers, "small newspapers are different, and this is the angle Charlie is working on."[64] As we shall see, the effort to generate letters was later expanded and turned into a highly sophisticated operation.

Finally, Klein and his office were saddled with a job that they had not expected and did not want. They were assigned the responsibility for handling requests for access to government information under the 1967 Freedom of Information Act. In Klein's opinion, this was out of his purview. His job was to help *newspeople* gain access to administration officials. "I did not look at the act or my job as designed to answer voluminous requests from special-interest groups," Klein wrote, "and I was not prepared for the pressure for information that was being developed by Ralph Nader and other consumer-activist leaders."[65] The Office of Communications had neither the manpower nor the interest to handle such requests. Initially, this was the area that generated the harshest criticism of the office.

As a whole, however, Klein's operation received mainly kudos from the press during its first year of operation. For the most part, this seems to have been justified. As originally set up by Klein, the office was a primarily "professional" operation. Klein "used" the media only to an extent that may be deemed normal for a person of his position. As Nixon's first year in office progressed, however, the White House became increasingly sensitive to what it considered to be a hostile media. In the process, H. R. Haldeman began to exert more influence over the Office of Communications. This set in motion the factors that led to the politicization of the office and to the decrease in Klein's authority.

"THE PRESS IS THE ENEMY"

Richard Nixon and H. R. Haldeman shared a disdain for what William Safire (one of Nixon's speechwriters) termed "the influential, opinion-making 'Eastern Establishment' media."[66] Haldeman made this clear when he said that the president's problems were compounded, as he put it, "by the determined opposition of a large number of the press corps and establishment media who, because of their past efforts to write Nixon off, had a vested interest in his 'unsuccess.'"[67]

Concern over how to deal with the "establishment" media (which Nixon characterized simply as "The Press") became an obsession at the White House.[68] Nixon frequently referred to "The Press" as "the enemy." As Safire has written, "He was saying exactly what he meant: 'The press is the *enemy*,' to be hated and beaten, and in that vein of vengeance that ran through his relationship with another power center, in his indulgence of his most combative and abrasive instincts against what he saw to be an unelected and unrepresentative elite, lay Nixon's greatest personal and political weakness."[69]

Nixon's antagonism toward the press went back many years. He felt that the "liberal" media had turned on him in 1948 when, as a member of the House Un-American Activities Committee, he had investigated Alger Hiss. After Nixon was nominated as the Republican vice-presidential candidate in 1952, published reports that he had maintained a secret fund while he was senator reinforced this hostility. Indeed, Tom Wicker has persuasively argued that it was the trauma of the 1952 fund crisis, more than any earlier event in Nixon's life, that colored his view of the press.[70] Thus, Nixon came to the conclusion early on that "The Press" was something to be circumvented. His response to the secret fund allegations—his famous televised "Checkers" speech— showed him the potential benefits of taking messages directly to the people. Nixon's comments on that speech in his book *Six Crises* (written—perhaps significantly—after his loss to John Kennedy in 1960) reveal an astute understanding of the tactic of "going public."

> [Jim] Bassett reported the intense pressures on him as [my] press secretary to give out something in advance [of the speech]. Most of my staff urged that I do so in order to assure better press coverage. But on this issue, I overruled them all. I knew that any advance notice of what I was going to say would cut down the size of my television audience. *This time I was determined to tell my story directly to the people rather than to funnel it to them through a press account.* Consequently, Bassett made arrangements for the reporters to see my speech at television monitors in a separate room, with no advance text and with no notice of what I would say.[71]
>
> Approximately sixty million Americans saw or heard that radio-television speech. . . . [When it was over] I asked [Bassett] about the press reaction. It had been mixed, he reported. . . . But Bassett made a perceptive comment at that point. He said, *"What the reporters think about the content of the speech is not important now. That's an old story anyway. The big story now is not the speech itself but the public reaction to it."*[72] (emphasis added)

The tactic of going public became standard operating procedure when Nixon became president. It has been said that John Kennedy's televised press conferences were tailored more to meet the people than to meet the press. Nonetheless, courtesy to journalistic norms was still adhered to. Kennedy's televised press conferences were almost always held at either 11:00 A.M. or 4:00 P.M., allowing time for newspaper reporters to write about the story for the next day's edition and giving television newscasts an opportunity to give a report of the event.[73] Lyndon Johnson followed a similar practice. During his term of office, none of his televised press conferences started later than 4:50 P.M.[74] Nixon changed that. His first televised press conference as president (just one week after his inauguration) was scheduled for 9:00 P.M.—smack in the middle of prime-time viewing hours and so late that it was "nerve-rackingly difficult" for morning newspapers to cover the story.[75] The scheduling also made it difficult for the nightly television newscasts to dissect the conference, since the story was "old" by 6:30 the next evening. In fact, Nixon made it clear that his answers at press conferences were not directed to reporters but to the television audience. Haldeman put it bluntly in an internal memorandum, "The President wants you to realize and emphasize to all appropriate members of your staff that a press conference is a TV operation and that the TV impression is really all that matters."[76]

Soon, Nixon all but phased out news conferences. He was anxious to keep the press at a distance, and he apparently felt that televised speeches were a better vehicle for taking his messages to the people. During his entire time in office, Nixon had only 39 formal exchanges with reporters, excluding interviews and informal remarks at arrivals and departures. This compares with 132 under Johnson, 65 under Kennedy, 193 under Eisenhower, 160 under Truman, and 998 under Roosevelt.[77] In the meantime, Nixon's use of prime-time television speeches rose to an all-time high.[78]

The idea of taking administration messages to the people "over the heads" of "The Press" was an ever present theme in the Nixon White House. Haldeman's notes of a meeting with Nixon on 3 November 1969 bear witness to this idea:

> have hostile press—have to circumvent this
>
> should really have N go to the people
>> report every 2–3 wks
>> share the burdens & problems w/people
>> feeling of sincerity—
>>> get around hostile press
>
>> . . . . hell w/reporters[79]

Nixon's answers at press conferences were tailored for the television audience rather than the reporters asking the questions. As Chief of Staff H. R. Haldeman put it, a Nixon press conference was "a TV operation" and "the TV impression" was really all that mattered. (Courtesy Nixon Presidential Materials Project)

The most revealing statement of Nixon's personal views on the media is an extraordinary document written by Nixon in the third person and forwarded to Klein in September 1970. In that document—written not long after Nixon ordered the invasion of Cambodia by American and South Vietnamese troops—the president assessed his relationship with the media:

To the extent that the President had *any* public support during the Cambodian venture, this was a devastating indication of the lack of credibility of the national media—especially *Time* and *Newsweek*, the Washington *Post*, the New York *Times*, and the three networks. All of them opposed RN violently on this issue.

This is not something new. RN is the first President in this century who came into the Presidency with the opposition of all of these major communication powers. Since he has been in office, with only very few exceptions, he has been heavily opposed—not just editorially by these publications and networks—but primarily by the slant of the news coverage due to the attitude of reporters.

The fact that he now survives this with 55–60% approval by the people indicates not so much something about RN as it does something about the news media. . . .

In other words this is a time for soul-searching on the part of the press as to whether it is they who are out of tune with the people rather than the President. . . .

. . . When this Administration came into office a year ago, there was a credibility gap as far as the Presidency was concerned. Now, ironically, there is a credibility gap as far as the press is concerned.

The key to all this, of course, is that RN, very consciously, has taken an entirely different tact [sic] from LBJ's and a different tact than was urged upon him by some of his friends. *Instead of trying to win the press, to cater to them, to have backgrounders with them, RN has ignored them and talked directly to the country by TV whenever possible. He has used the press and not let the press use him. He has particularly not allowed the press, whenever he could avoid it, to filter his ideas to the public.* This is a remarkable achievement.[80] (emphasis added)

In that document, Nixon also revealed a strong envy of John Kennedy's success with the media. Nixon's rivalry with the Kennedys is well known. As Nixon's biographer Stephen Ambrose has written, "The way the press had fawned on Kennedy [in the 1960 campaign] had made Nixon furious and jealous; all that money and the things Kennedy had gotten away with had made Nixon resentful."[81] Nixon displayed that resentment in his memo when comparing his appearance at the annual spring dinner of the Gridiron Club with Kennedy's. The Gridiron Club is a social organization made up of the crème de la crème of print journalists, and its annual spring dinner is a private bash at which several hundred of America's most powerful gather to poke fun at each other. It is a long-standing tradition (dating back to Benjamin Harrison) for presidents to attend and join in the show. Nixon was no exception. He and Vice President Spiro Agnew brought the house down when they appeared and took part in a self-parody of their "southern strategy" in the 1968 campaign. The skit consisted of Agnew singing and Nixon accompanying him at the piano, but as the journalist Hedrick Smith wrote, "Whatever tune Nixon would start, Agnew would drown him out with 'Dixie.' "[82] For Nixon, that appearance again highlighted the difference in the ways that he and Kennedy were treated by the press:

The reaction to the coup at the Gridiron is interesting. Everytime Kennedy appeared before the Gridiron, there were reams of columns with regard to the effectiveness of the appearance, although on several of them he dropped a real bomb. It's interesting that in spite of 100% agreement by everyone there that the RN-Agnew appearance was an all time high, very little press reflected this afterwards.[83]

Elsewhere, in what appears to be a roundabout reference to Kennedy's success with television—and a jab at the fact that JFK's speeches and books were ghostwritten—Nixon wrote:

RN's effectiveness in using the television medium is remarkable. This is due, of course, to the tremendous amount of preparation that he takes before making a TV appearance. With the exception of TR, Wilson, and Hoover, RN is probably the only President in this century who still sits down from time to time and completely writes a major speech himself. This makes it possible for him to use the television medium much more effectively than anyone had before him.[84]

Nixon never forgot the actions of Kennedy and his men after the 1960 election. Nixon had lost by a mere two-tenths of 1 percent of the vote. Despite widespread charges of vote fraud, Nixon rejected the idea of a recount. It was one of Nixon's finest moments, and he was widely praised for being a good loser. Yet immediately after the election, Kennedy's "closest associates" went out of their way to tell the press that Nixon ran "one of the worst presidential campaigns." They chided him for failing to concentrate on industrial northern states, for giving up the black vote "by default," and for committing "the incredible mistake" of not adequately capitalizing on his status as protégé of the immensely popular President Eisenhower. They then proceeded to deem Nixon a less formidable opponent than Kennedy's fellow Democrats Hubert Humphrey and Lyndon Johnson, who had fought Kennedy for the Democratic presidential nomination. Their remarks stung and were widely reported by the press.[85]

Nixon was also hurt after the 1960 election by Kennedy's reported statement that Nixon had "no class" and by the fact that Kennedy never invited him to the White House after becoming president. Nixon made a point of noting in his third-person narrative that his "treatment of Johnson and Humphrey" was "180 degrees different" from the way Nixon had been treated while he was out of office. "In eight years he was never invited to a lunch or dinner at the White

House." In contrast, Nixon continued: "We have had a practice of inviting the families of all former Presidents to the White House. . . . These acts of civility are another hallmark of this President."[86]

Nixon was also angered by covert actions of the Kennedy administration to discredit him. Once Kennedy was in office, Nixon was subjected to an extensive audit by the Internal Revenue Service, and the Justice Department (led by Attorney General Robert F. Kennedy) launched an investigation of Nixon's brother Donald. As Ambrose concluded, "The probe came up empty, but Nixon naturally resented the attempt to get at him through his family, and complained about the 'abuse of the Internal Revenue Service and the Justice Department for political purposes' by the Kennedy Administration."[87] There were also widespread rumors—known to Nixon—that the Kennedy Justice Department, "through the FBI," had placed "bugs and taps on reporters, political opponents, and businessmen."[88] In 1986, Nixon's daughter Julie wrote that the "peacetime Kennedy administration had tapped more individuals, well over one hundred, than the wartime Nixon administration."[89] The Kennedy rivalry fueled particular fury for Nixon because of the public adulation of the slain Kennedy and the fact that JFK had become a constant criterion for judging presidents. As William Safire has written, "Nixon's standard as a modern President, consciously or not, was John F. Kennedy."[90]

Arguably, Nixon's feelings toward the media were exacerbated by the situation in Vietnam and his attitude that the media were undermining chances for a negotiated settlement. Yet even in the first few months of his first term, when he was the beneficiary of generally favorable media coverage, internal memoranda indicate that Nixon was extremely sensitive about the press. Nixon's barometer for how well he was being treated by the media was his "Daily News Summary," edited by Lyndon ("Mort") Allin under the supervision of Patrick Buchanan—a young (thirty-year-old) conservative loyalist who had been an editorial writer for the *St. Louis Globe Democrat* before coming to the White House as part of Nixon's research and writing team. Allin—a former social studies teacher who had been recruited by Buchanan to head Youth for Nixon in 1967—edited the "Daily News Summary" from day one of the administration. The news summary itself was not a part of either Klein's or Ziegler's operation. As Allin put it, Nixon wanted the news summary to be factual and to be independent of the White House public relations offices (which Nixon felt might be tempted to "slant or soften" the summary).[91]

Every day, Buchanan, Allin, and a staff of about four others monitored scores of publications, as well as radio and television newscasts.[92] Preparation of the summary began each day after the morning news shows on television. Work typically began in earnest around 3:00 P.M. and ended around midnight.[93] The final copy of the summary was placed on the president's desk each morning just before 8:00 A.M. The document often ran up to fifty pages and was divided into four sections. The first, prepared by Buchanan between 7:00 and 8:00 A.M., was a very brief summary of the main stories culled from the morning newspapers that were available at that hour. Buchanan also alerted Nixon's attention to the most important stories covered on the evening newscasts the day before. (This first section—Buchanan's "topper," as Allin called it—was discontinued after the 1972 election.) The second section was a compilation of all the major wire service stories that had been available before 10:00 P.M. the previous night. The third was a television and radio report, which contained a comprehensive summary of the three major newscasts and any important news stories carried by radio. The final section was a digest of columns and editorial opinions and occasional news stories culled from forty or more newspapers around the country.[94] The "Daily News Summary" was compiled six days a week and was supplemented by a weekly magazine summary that was given to the president on Mondays together with a separate weekend summary. Initially, about twenty copies of the summary were prepared for the president and selected top staffers only. After a leak occurred, the number was cut to five but later climbed to fifteen and then to thirty-five top staffers. During Nixon's second term, the summary was not so closely guarded. Selected copies were made available to the press, and the summary was distributed to some 135 members of the administration.[95]

Nixon relied heavily on the summary during his first term. He received the *Washington Post* and the *New York Times* each morning, and the *Washington Evening Star* was sent to his living quarters in the evening, but the "Daily News Summary" gave the president a much broader view of how the press covered his administration. Besides, Nixon rarely watched television news, despite the fact that he was so concerned about how the administration was being covered by the networks. So Nixon read the summary assiduously and filled his copy with margin notes and comments. Often a daily summary would generate "fifteen to twenty memos out of the Oval Office demanding followups, explanations, or action."[96]

In 1973, Fred W. Friendly, the former president of CBS News, called the summary a "faulty lens." "The tragedy of the president's dependence on this flawed filter," he said, "is not only its prejudice against all critics and its sycophantal vision of the administration's performance but, worst of all, the blurred, deformed image the president gets of the way the nation perceives him."[97] Part of what Friendly objected to were the editorial comments included in the summary and written by Buchanan and other members of the staff—for instance: "[John] Chancellor [of NBC] was determined to do a hatchet job."[98]

The summary section that dealt with network newscasts was written by Buchanan and was based on reports made by members of his staff who were assigned to watch certain broadcasts. Videotapes of the newscasts—and of virtually any appearance by administration officials on network television—were kept to be viewed by the president or other members of the administration. Nixon was particularly irked by indications from the news summary that the television networks were presenting a "biased" view of the administration. He felt that the "negative" coverage that Buchanan was pointing out to him should receive comment from the administration. Thus, Haldeman reported to Klein in March 1969 that the president wanted the Office of Communications to monitor the television news and then register its "reactions, both positive and negative, to the commentators and newscasters and networks."[99]

Two months later, Haldeman instructed Klein to establish "a Special TV News Section" within the Office of Communications.[100] Shortly thereafter, he reiterated Nixon's concern:

> The President is very concerned about the general attitude of a number of the television newscasters and commentators who are deliberately slanting their reports against the Administration's position.
>
> He would like from you immediately a report on your analysis of each of the principal network newscasters and commentators as to his basic orientation and presentation of the news. Specifically, he wants, of course, the list of those who consistently slant their reports against us, such as Terry Drinkwater and Sander Vanocur and others, but it would be helpful to try to classify all of the principal people as to their general slant so that he has a feel of which ones we can count on for reliable reporting and which ones we can count on to go the other way.
>
> He would also like the same kind of report on the principal columnists and syndicated news reporters. This is not of the same degree of urgency. You should put the television report together today and get it to Ken Cole, who will have it sent out to me by courier in California.[101]

Similar instructions were given to Ron Ziegler. Klein responded the same day with a brief three-page report.[102] In the next month, a twenty-six-page listing of media reporters and columnists was compiled based on assessments by various White House sources.[103] The names of the reporters were followed by their affiliation, a designation regarding their "slant" (e.g., "unfriendly," "neutral," "friendly"), and a brief sentence or two describing them. For instance: "RICHARD VALERIANI—NBC—Unfriendly—Valeriani, if given a chance, will go with negative slant. Must be forced to the positive."[104]

Nixon's sensitivity to individual journalists (and even entire news organizations) often led to presidential directives to cease certain relationships. For instance, on 19 May 1969, Alexander Butterfield (deputy assistant to the president) sent Haldeman a memo that stated: "The President jotted a short note to you in which he said that he had told Ron Ziegler *not* to permit our people to talk to the [St. Louis] *Post-Dispatch*, the *New York Times*, or the *Washington Post*. He directed that all contacts with these news agencies (no matter how slight or infrequent) be terminated immediately."[105] John Ehrlichman (Nixon's chief domestic affairs advisor) has written about his experiences with such directives. He noted: "Early in 1969 [Nixon] told me flatly that I was never to see 'Scotty' Reston of the *New York Times* for any reason (and I did not). When I had given interviews to Hugh Sidey of *Time* or John Osborne of *The New Republic*, Nixon would patiently explain to me that these men were not our friends; I should favor our friends and freeze out our enemies among the press."[106]

Sometimes, such directives reached the point of absurdity. In August 1970, a routine letter thanking Arthur Sulzberger of the *New York Times* for his editorial support of an administration policy was sent to the president for his signature. It was returned to Klein with a handwritten note from Haldeman's assistant, Larry Higby: "Mr. Haldeman asked that I send this back to you. He indicated that the President does *not* correspond w/the NYT."[107] Nonetheless, the president was serious. William Safire—a presidential speechwriter who, like Klein, enjoyed the company of reporters and favored a more open relationship with them—ignored most of Nixon's "freeze-out" directives. Later he wrote, "Not until mid-1973 did I realize that these contacts with the press had caused my phone to be tapped in 1969 by the FBI at the direction of a suspicious President and national security adviser [Henry Kissinger]."[108] Klein later said that he and Ziegler considered themselves to be immune from such directives, and Ziegler has tried to discount the significance of Nixon's directives. "Presidents are human beings," Ziegler has said. "If they feel they are being treated unfairly, they're going to respond that way. You know, 'Why should we let that guy go on Air Force One if he [treats us unfairly in print]?' I got a lot of those memos. But where I felt it was right, I'd still put the guy on the airplane." According to Ziegler, Nixon used those memos to "blow off steam." "So in doing history," Ziegler says, "you can either say, 'Richard Nixon sent out directives to freeze the press out.' " Or, he concludes, you can look at "reality"—"look at the press attendance list. You see the difference?"[109]

THE AGNEW ASSAULT: DISCREDITING THE MEDIA

Richard Nixon was enamored with the strategy of going public. To him, that strategy involved more than just direct appeals to the public through speeches or activities generated by the Office of Communications. It also involved managing the news, when possible, and discrediting the media when management was not possible. The latter tactic came to the fore in the fall of 1969 in the wake of the "Moratorium" (a series of nonviolent, nationwide demonstrations against American involvement in the Vietnam conflict). In Washington alone, tens of thousands of demonstrators marched. As Stephen Ambrose has written: "It was, by far, the largest antiwar protest in America's history. Altogether, millions were involved."[110] Nixon was shaken. He felt that organized opposition of that sort removed the incentive for Hanoi to sit down at a negotiating table and arrive at a settlement with the United States. His resentment toward the media was compounded because he felt that they were siding with protesters. Antiwar demonstrations and coverage of those opposed to administration policy seemed—at least to the White House—to eclipse proadministration coverage.

By October 1969, modest U.S. troop withdrawals from Vietnam were under way, and 9 October stood out as a watershed—not a single American boy had been killed in combat for a full twenty-four hours.[111] Nixon felt that these were important accomplishments. Yet media coverage of the Vietnam situation in October centered on the Moratorium. Nixon's "Daily News Summary" pointed out that all of the networks were giving play to the "escalating support of the Moratorium" while expressions of support for the administration were being downplayed. For instance, a resolution of support for the administration, prepared by Senator Robert Dole (Rep.-Kans.) and signed by thirty-three senators, was only briefly mentioned by ABC and CBS and was completely ignored by NBC. Instead, NBC ran a filmed report from Vietnam indicating that American combat operations were being carried out as usual. A U.S. battalion commander was shown saying that his orders remained the same, "to find and kill the enemy." The news summary concluded, "[The] NBC man claims our casualties are lower not because of a change in U.S. tactics, but because the enemy has not chosen to stand his ground and fight." In the margin, Nixon wrote, "Klein—give them Hell for this inadequate coverage & give me a report."[112]

In the White House, a siege mentality was developing. Indeed, there was a widespread feeling—both in and out of the White House—that the tide was turning against the president. In a column in the *Washington Post* entitled "The Breaking of the President," David Broder wrote: "The men and the movement that broke Lyndon Johnson's authority in 1968 are out to break Richard M. Nixon in 1969. The likelihood is great that they will succeed again, for breaking a President is, like most feats, easier to accomplish the second time around."[113] In a commentary on ABC's evening newscast, Howard K. Smith said that the Moratorium was yet another strike against Nixon's Vietnam policy. In the "Daily News Summary," Buchanan said that according to Smith, "[Nixon's] critics have the offensive and RN is on the skids."[114]

Nixon decided to counter that perception by going directly to the people. In a meeting with Henry Kissinger, Nixon said, "I don't know if the country can be led here, but we've got to try."[115] He then sat down and wrote a speech (without the help of speechwriters), which he delivered to the American people on 3 November 1969. In it, he asked for the support of "the great silent majority of my fellow Americans." He concluded:

> I pledged in my campaign for the Presidency to end the war in a way that we could win the peace. I have initiated a plan of action which will enable me to keep that pledge.
>
> The more support I can have from the American people, the sooner that pledge can be redeemed; for the more divided we are at home, the less likely the enemy is to negotiate in Paris.[116]

Reaction to the speech was favorable. The next day, Nixon met with William Safire to talk about the speech. Safire later recalled that the president said: "My object was to go over the heads of the columnists in this speech. We have been getting the reaction from across the country, and it's been pretty good. We've got to hold American public opinion with us for three or four months and then we can work this Vietnam thing out."[117] However, the president was upset that immediately after the speech, television commentators had engaged in "instant analysis" during which they rebutted and criticized what he had said.[118] Klein was upset too: "I listened with astonishment at the negative emotional quality of the comments. It was almost like a debate between the President of the United States and the assembled network 'experts.' The debate was heightened by the emotions that surrounded any Vietnam discussion."[119]

Within the White House, there was particular concern about ABC's treatment of the president's speech. Part of its analysis had included an interview with Averell Harriman—an outspoken opponent of Nixon's Vietnam policy— and its total commentary had lasted as long as the president's speech (roughly twenty-five minutes). In an effort to punish the networks for their treatment of the president, the White House instructed Dean Burch (who had just been appointed by Nixon as chairman of the Federal Communications Commission) to ask for transcripts of the "instant analysis." Since the FCC regulated the networks, Burch's action gave the impression that he might be planning some sort of punitive action.[120]

As a further means of retaliation, Pat Buchanan suggested that the White House respond with a tough speech that questioned the very legitimacy of the news media. Nixon embraced the idea. Without consulting with Klein, Ziegler, or Herb Thompson (the vice president's press secretary), Buchanan was assigned the job of writing the speech for delivery by Vice President Spiro Agnew. As Klein later said, "The press experts were the most surprised people in the White House when we discovered what Agnew was launching."[121] Ziegler concurs that neither he nor Klein knew about the planning of the speech.[122]

The vice president was not known for mincing words in his speeches. On 19 October, he had said that the Moratorium represented a prevailing "spirit of national masochism . . . encouraged by an effete corps of impudent snobs."[123] Buchanan took advantage of Agnew's penchant for bombastic rhetoric by drafting a pointed and hard-hitting speech. When it was completed, he sat down with the president, and together they went through every line of the speech. Nixon even added a few lines to toughen it up.[124]

The speech was set for delivery on 13 November, at the Midwest Republican Conference in Des Moines, Iowa. Every effort was made to see that it would receive the widest possible attention. In a memo written to Haldeman the day

President Nixon meets with Chief of Staff H. R. Haldeman. On the desk are telegrams supporting the president's Silent Majority speech. (Courtesy Nixon Presidential Materials Project)

before Agnew's speech, Klein outlined the strategy. Network bureau chiefs would be sent a copy of the speech on the afternoon of the thirteenth with a follow-up telephone call "suggesting that they might want to give it special attention and coverage." The text of the speech would be released to the press as a whole by 6:00 P.M. eastern time, so that the speech could be covered on the evening newscasts. In addition, Klein noted:

3. The four Chicago newspapers, which might have a special interest in this criticism of TV news handling, will receive hand delivered copies of the address.

4. Arrangements will be made with Lyn Nofziger to have the text delivered to key Congressmen and Senators and one of them will be asked to send it to Dean Burch with appropriate comment with a copy of that letter to go to network Presidents.

5. Further special distribution will be made to selected Washington sources such as *Human Events*, *U.S. News & World Report*, and key columnists who might be expected to agree with these comments.

Klein concluded that every effort would be made "to handle this through normal channels from the Vice President's office with no indication of White House involvement."[125]

Klein has since indicated that he wrote this memo without having seen a copy of Agnew's speech. He contends that he did not even receive a copy of the speech himself until Agnew was airborne for Des Moines. He later recalled that he was shocked when he saw it. "As I looked with unbelieving eyes, I was astonished. I was angry at the speech and at what I considered a sneak attack on my authority to determine press policy, particularly regarding the networks."[126]

The television networks decided to carry the speech live, but the logistics of doing so were difficult. None of the networks had facilities in Des Moines for a spur-of-the-moment national broadcast transmission. Perhaps the White House half hoped that the networks would not be able to broadcast the speech. Had that happened, Agnew and his supporters could have made the most of one particular line in the speech: "Whether what I have said to you tonight will be heard and seen by all the nation is not *my* decision; it is not *your* decision; it is *their* decision."

Luckily for the networks, an Iowa public television station was covering the speech locally. The networks made arrangements to work with that station in broadcasting the address. In the speech, Agnew said:

> The President of the United States has a right to communicate directly with the people who elected him, and the people of this country have the right to make up their own minds and form their own opinions about a Presidential address without having the President's words and thoughts characterized through the prejudices of hostile critics before they can even be digested.
>
> . . . The purpose of my remarks tonight is to focus your attention on this little group of men who not only enjoy a right of instant rebuttal to every Presidential address, but more importantly, wield a free hand in selecting, presenting and interpreting the great issues of our Nation [on the evening newscasts].
>
> . . . A small group of men, numbering perhaps no more than a dozen "anchormen," commentators, and executive producers, settle upon the twenty minutes or so of film and commentary that is to reach the public. . . . [T]o a man, these commentators and producers live and work in

the geographical and intellectual confines of Washington, D.C., or New York City. . . . [They] draw their political and social views from the same sources. Worse, they talk constantly to one another, thereby providing artificial reinforcement to their shared viewpoints.

. . . The American people would rightly not tolerate this kind of concentration of power in government. Is it not fair and relevant to question its concentration in the hands of a tiny and closed fraternity of privileged men, elected by no one, and enjoying a monopoly sanctioned and licensed by government.

The views of this fraternity do *not* represent the views of America.[127]

Afterward, Klein was upset that he was depicted by some of the media as having orchestrated Agnew's assault.[128] The Sunday after the speech, Klein was the subject of an unfavorable report on the CBS television program "Sixty Minutes." Klein later said that he considered resigning in protest to Agnew's speech but, after careful thought, decided he "could do more good by staying on and fighting the battle within the White House." Resigning would have generated short-term attention, he said, but it would not have "put a restraint on an administration which badly needed somebody who understood the real facts of the communications world."[129]

Klein has since written that Agnew's speech was "McCarthy-like."[130] Ziegler, who later said that the Agnew speech was "a mistake" and "a great disservice to the Nixon administration," categorically stated that the speech was "contrary to the very essence of Herb Klein." He added, "I know personally that he had absolutely *nothing* to do with it."[131] Still, Klein *had* been upset with the way the networks had used "instant analysis" after the president's Silent Majority speech. Thus, he appeared on television after Agnew's speech and questioned the networks' use of that kind of commentary. According to a memo that Klein wrote to Haldeman, Klein even called NBC President Julian Goodman (who had called Agnew's speech "an appeal to prejudice") and complained that his commentary after the vice president's speech "exemplified the points Agnew was making." In response, Goodman told Klein that Agnew was threatening freedom of the press through a demagogic appeal to the First Amendment of the Constitution.[132] Assuming that Klein's later assertions about Agnew's speech are accurate assessments of his true feelings, that telephone call must have been an extraordinarily difficult one for Klein to make.

Public response to the vice president's speech was overwhelmingly favorable. The networks received some 150,000 communications, running at a ratio of two-to-one in favor of Agnew's position. The vice president himself received some 74,000 letters, most of which were favorable.[133] Despite attempts by Ziegler and even Haldeman to scrap a follow-up speech that Buchanan had planned for Agnew, Nixon decided to proceed as planned.[134] The battle was under way, and the president seemed to be invigorated by it.

CREATING A TELEVISION OFFICE

The president was proud of his Silent Majority speech, and it renewed his belief in the power of television to influence public opinion. Shortly after the speech, Nixon wrote that the White House should stress "the effectiveness of RN in using the television medium." He added, "This is the point I particularly want emphasized [about the Silent Majority speech]."[135] Nixon's success with that speech also made him more conscious of the need to carefully orchestrate all of his appearances before television cameras. In a memo to Haldeman dated 1 December 1969, Nixon raised the idea of "a part- or full-time TV man on our staff for the purpose of seeing that my TV appearances are handled on a professional basis." As he put it: "When I think of the millions of dollars that go into one lousy 30-second television spot advertising a deodorant, it seems to me unbelievable that we don't do a better job in seeing that Presidential appearances always have the very best professional advice whenever they are to be covered by TV."[136]

The notion that a president should get advice about his television appearances was not new. The actor Robert Montgomery had coached Dwight Eisenhower during his 1952 presidential campaign and had served as an unpaid advisor to Eisenhower in the White House. Similarly, advice had been sought on an *ad hoc* basis during the Kennedy and Johnson administrations.[137] What Nixon wanted, however, was a full-fledged television producer who would give advice on routine appearances before television cameras as well as on important prime-time appearances. In his memo to Haldeman, Nixon noted that he had appeared before television cameras numerous times over the past week. He pointed out that he had received excellent background briefings about who would attend those appearances and—in the case of bill signings—how many pens he should use. He had received, however, "no professional advice as to where the cameras would be and how [he] could make [the] most effective use of the TV opportunity." As he concluded: "The President should never be without the very best professional advice for making a television appearance. . . . In 2 minutes, the impression of the picture is fleeting but indelible."[138] Nixon had hit upon the premise that later served Ronald Reagan so well.

Initially, Nixon had relied informally on Roger Ailes for such advice. Ailes had served as one of Nixon's television consultants during the 1968 campaign. Later, Ailes played a major role in planning the television strategy for the George Bush campaign in 1988. Ailes, however, did not have a full-time position in the Nixon White House, nor was he on the White House payroll. He merely offered advice on an "as you need it" basis—usually for major television appearances such as a nationally televised speech. In 1970, William Carruthers—a Los Angeles television producer—replaced Ailes as a part-time television consultant. Carruthers continued to live in Los Angeles but flew to Washington to advise the president whenever he made a major television appearance. That was not enough for Nixon, so in January 1971 Carruthers's consulting position was supplemented by the creation of a full-time White House Television Office. The agreement was that Carruthers would continue to serve as a consultant. He would be involved in long-range planning and be present for all of the president's major television appearances. The Television Office, on the other hand, would deal with the president's day-to-day appearances before television cameras and would be staffed by someone chosen by Carruthers and approved by the White House. That person was Mark Goode, who had worked with Carruthers in Los Angeles.[139]

The Television Office was located in the Old Executive Office Building and acted independently of both the Office of Communications and the Press Office. Goode reported directly to Haldeman, usually through Haldeman's aide, Dwight Chapin. The Television Office was a major innovation. For the first time, the president of the United States had the services of a full-time producer to plan his every appearance before television cameras. Such staging of the president's day-to-day activities was important. Television coverage of those activities on the evening news was beamed into millions of American homes and helped to determine how the public perceived Nixon's performance in office. Therefore, Nixon was eager to provide the best possible images to the television cameras. Goode was charged with doing that. His responsibilities included such things as choosing an appropriate backdrop for presidential appearances, determining where cameras would be located so as to film the event from the best angle, making sure that the lighting would flatter the president, seeing that the audio feed was clear, choosing a time of day that would maximize television coverage, and offering suggestions to the president on such things as makeup and wardrobe.[140]

Nixon recognized the importance of the "sound-bite" on the evening news, and he was determined that the visual image enhance the audio message. He also knew that by limiting presidential appearances, the White House could better control what the network newscasts would cover about the president. Nixon wanted the material that was available to the networks to be picture perfect. In short, the stage was being set for the "Rose Garden Strategy" of the 1972 election. For that matter, the stage was also being set for the success of the Reagan presidency.

A "FULL-TIME PR DIRECTOR"

Nixon's increasing distrust of the media did not help Herb Klein's stature in the White House. Klein was viewed by the president's inner circle as too "soft" in his dealings with the media—too willing to grant access and too cozy in his friendly relations with reporters. As early as 1 October 1969, Nixon conveyed a report to Haldeman that Klein was "spending too much time with the liberal press people . . . and not enough time with our friends."[141]

It was also clear that when it came to tactics, Klein exercised his independence. As John Ehrlichman put it, Klein "didn't get with the program." Rather than following Nixon's hard-line approach to the media, Klein was constantly "out talking to his old friends in the print media and appearing on television shows and announcing what the President believed or thought or desired or aspired to."[142] From Ehrlichman's perspective, that amounted to insubordination. Klein's assistant, Margita White, takes a different view of Klein's actions. According to White, "Klein's loyalty to Nixon was never in doubt."[143] On the contrary, it was precisely Klein's loyalty to Nixon that prevented him from carrying out directives that he felt might hurt the president in the long run. It was also that loyalty that persuaded him to stay in his post after Agnew's Des Moines speech and to act as a restraint against hard-line tactics coming from within the administration. According to White, Klein "followed his conscience throughout." He would not join in the "bunker mentality" shared by some other members of the White House staff.[144] Even H. R. Haldeman—who some have associated with that bunker mentality—shares that view. He agrees that Klein tried to counterbalance Nixon's "darker side." He argues, however, that Klein was not as successful as he might have been because he tried to be too much of a counterbalance. As Haldeman explains: "You can only be an effective counterbalance as long as you are available *to* counterbalance. Therefore, you've got to follow the theory of losing some of the battles in order to win the war."[145] Klein did not do enough of that and therefore was excluded from "the loop" almost from the start. According to Clark Mollenhoff, a former reporter who served in the Nixon White House for a brief time as ombudsman, "If Nixon had paid attention to Herb Klein it would have been a different Nixon presidency."[146]

Klein has written that he was distressed by the excessive emphasis placed on PR (public relations) by the White House. As he later wrote:

> From the President on down, an amazingly excessive amount of time was spent worrying about plans to conjure up better and more favorable coverage. In striving for coups with the news media, many self-designated White House experts forgot the simple fact that direct and honest dealings with the press work best, as was evident in the initial months of the Nixon administration.[147]

Klein further complained that many of those around Nixon who were dreaming up PR activities had never "had any experience in the field and most of them had never met a leading newsman before a presidential appointment."[148] Nonetheless, the impetus for PR came from the president himself. On 22 September 1969, the president sent Haldeman a memo. In it, Nixon wrote:

> In memoranda in the future, I shall use the letters PR whenever I am referring generally to a project I want carried out in the PR front. Until we get a full-time man I think we need in this field, you will have responsibility for seeing that these decisions are implemented.
>
> *PR*. Every Monday, I want a week's projection as to what we anticipate will be the major opposition attacks so that we can plan our own statements with those in mind. . . . I have reached the conclusion that we simply have to have the full-time PR Director, who will have no other assignments except to bulldog these three or four major issues we may select each week or each month and follow through with directives that I give but, more importantly, come up with ideas of his own.[149]

The next day, Haldeman received a memo from Ken Cole complaining about an NBC News story that the president had read about in his "Daily News Summary." "The President addressed the following comment to you," Cole wrote. " 'See that NBC gets a hard kick from Klein on this. And *again*, when are we going to have a system where this is automatically done and reported to me?' "[150] Haldeman attached a handwritten note stamped "High Priority" and sent the memo to Klein. Haldeman's note said, in part, "You can see the degree of concern that has developed here—and I think it is *essential* to get this going and to make sure [Nixon] knows it."[151]

That week, Haldeman took action. He hired a young aide by the name of Jeb Stuart Magruder—someone that Haldeman hoped would become that "full-time PR Director." From a PR point of view, Magruder had promise. He came from a background in advertising, where he had merchandised cosmetics, facial tissues, and women's hosiery. He had quickly moved up the corporate ladder and was, before coming to the White House, president of a cosmetics firm in California. He had a reputation for loyalty, a knack for winning people over with his friendly manner, a willingness to subordinate his own judgment to that of his superiors, and an intense ambition.[152]

Under Haldeman, Magruder put these traits to good use. He knew that the president embraced the concept of a good offense. In *Six Crises*, Nixon had written: "An attack always makes more news than defense. . . . You cannot win a battle in any arena of life merely by defending yourself."[153] And so Magruder added PO (presidential offensive) to PR and embraced the concept of "Game-Planning"—setting long-term public relations goals on major policy issues. Magruder also set up a system for a Weekly News Calendar, which outlined the major news stories coming out of the administration over the next seven days. The calendar was put together by a Planning Objectives Group, which met every Wednesday at 10:00 A.M. to discuss how best to get the administration line out to the people and to coordinate the requisite news flow. The significant thing about that group was that it was chaired by Haldeman and included four of his aides—Magruder, Dwight Chapin, Ken Cole, and Alexander Butterfield. It also included Klein, Ziegler, Safire, Nofziger, and Harry Dent (Nixon's political affairs chief).[154]

Magruder saw that Haldeman and Nixon wanted to play hardball with the press, and he was willing to accommodate. He knew that the power of those who were "soft" toward the media was in decline and that "hard-liners" were reaping the rewards of influence and status for their loyalty to the president. He later said that he had told himself at the time: "Jeb, you're not going to screw this one up. You like this job and you're going to do what they tell you."[155] This feeling was compounded when he discovered that Haldeman's wrath could be wrought by merely suggesting that one of the president's orders was unnecessary or unwise. One of Haldeman's first instructions to Magruder was to assign people at the White House to generate telegrams to three Republican senators who were opposing Nixon's Vietnam policy—Charles Goodell of New York, Charles Mathias of Maryland, and Charles Percy of Illinois. The point was to "blast them" for their "consistent opposition to the President." As Haldeman wrote, "This program needs to be subtle and worked out well so that they receive these items from their home districts as well as other points around the country." The next day Magruder reported to Haldeman that the Percy telegrams were on their way but that it was his conclusion (after consulting people with contacts in Maryland and New York) that telegrams to Goodell and Mathias would be, at best, ineffective and, at worst, counterproductive. Therefore, he concluded, "I . . . think we would do better to hold our fire in these cases." Haldeman's margin notes set Magruder aback: "*Absolutely* the wrong approach," he wrote. "See me! This is pure BS—as *excuses*. I disagree 100%—and besides, this was an order—not a question—I was told it was being carried out & so informed the P. Now let's get it carried out—and quickly." Haldeman then chastised Magruder again in a face-to-face meeting. The experience was a sobering one for Magruder, and he was determined not to repeat his mistake. As he later wrote, "After the memo and the chewing-out, I produced an avalanche of telegrams for Senators Mathias and Goodell."[156]

With Haldeman's fury still ringing in his ears, Magruder completed a memo entitled "The Shot-Gun versus the Rifle," which he sent to Haldeman on 17 October 1969 (a time that corresponded with the height of the administration's concern over press coverage of the Moratorium). In the memo, Magruder presented recommendations for how to stop "unfair coverage" of the administration by the media. As he later recalled, "I wanted to suggest that we stop 'shot-gunning' our critics with our disorganized calls and complaints, and use a focused, 'rifle' approach that might do more good."[157]

One of Magruder's recommendations was the formation of "an official monitoring system" of the broadcast media through the FCC as soon as Dean Burch was on board as chairman. He explained, "If the monitoring system proves our point [that their news coverage is unfair], we have the legitimate and legal rights to go to the networks, etc., and make official complaints from the FCC."* Magruder also suggested that the Internal Revenue Service (IRS) and the Anti-Trust Division of the Justice Department be used to intimidate the media. He indicated that even the "possible threat" of action from either government organization could force the media to portray the administration in a more favorable light.[158]**

In fact, a monitoring system of both print and broadcast media had been started just a couple weeks earlier by a Haldeman aide, Alexander P. Butterfield.[159] By 17 October, the system was up and running.[160] In December, however, Haldeman put Magruder in charge of preparing the daily "Media Monitoring Report." Butterfield conveyed the news to Magruder on 23 December and explained how the system would work:

> Under normal circumstances you will hear by 10:30 A.M. from those monitors who have information to relay—which, as you know, means that they have noted a case of "obviously unfair" reporting, and believe that the situation warrants some kind of counter action. There are times,

*Charles Colson (special counsel to the president) later advocated similar plans in a memo to Haldeman dated 25 September 1970. Such actions, he said, would "have an inhibiting impact on the networks." He also noted that the three major networks were "very much afraid of us" (see U.S. Congress, Senate, Select Committee on Presidential Campaign Activities, *Final Report*, 149).

**It seems that the Nixon administration was not hesitant about using the IRS and the Anti-Trust Division of the Justice Department for such purposes. For example, in 1971, John Dean (White House counsel) received instructions that Robert Greene (the head of an investigative team that wrote an article in *Newsday* about the activities of Nixon's friend Charles "Bebe" Rebozo) be audited by the IRS. Dean testified that he received those instructions from either Haldeman or Ehrlichman. Dean, in turn, directed John J. "Jack" Caulfield (a White House aide) to initiate the audit. Greene was audited, but the Senate Select Committee that investigated Watergate could not gain access to enough documents to determine whether the audit was a result of Caulfield's efforts.

There are also examples of attempts to use the Anti-Trust Division of the Justice Department against the media. Caulfield (with the concurrence of Lyn Nofziger) recommended to John Dean, in a memo dated 2 November 1971, that antitrust action be taken against the *Los Angeles Times*. Nothing came of the recommendation. But on 14 April 1972, the Justice Department filed an antitrust suit against the three major television networks. It is not clear whether or not the suits were motivated by the White House (see U.S. Congress, Senate, Select Committee on Presidential Campaign Activities, *Final Report*, 135–36, 145–46).

too, when a monitor will "call in" to describe a case of "especially favorable" reporting—usually by an editor or commentator known for his anti-Administration bias.[161]

The next day, Butterfield reminded Magruder that the monitoring system should continue at full speed through the upcoming holidays. The president would be looking for the reports during his stay in California.[162] After the new year, the monitoring system was enlarged. On 16 January, Haldeman wrote that the president wanted monitors to watch local television news shows in the ten major cities and prepare a weekly report. "Would you please take this on as an assignment," he wrote, "and set up the appropriate system."[163]

The following day Haldeman gave instructions to Magruder that monitors should also be watching programs like "The Tonight Show with Johnny Carson" and "Merv Griffin."[164] In October, the president had been incensed by Griffin's treatment of his guest, Senator Edmund Muskie (Dem.-Maine), who had run for vice president with Hubert Humphrey against Nixon and Agnew in 1968. In introducing Muskie, Griffin noted that the senator "had gained such popularity" during the campaign, and as he greeted him, Griffin said: "I'm so glad to meet you, Senator. . . . *Everybody's* pleased to see your latest position in the polls." When Muskie said that he was "interested in the possibility of being president" and said that he was trying to prepare himself "for any eventuality," Griffin said "Bravo!" and led the audience in applause. Pat Buchanan had seen the show and prepared a special report on it for the president. In the margin of the report, Nixon directed Klein to generate "10 calls of complaint &/or letters to CBS on this." He also wrote that Klein should "demand equal time for [Senator Hugh] Scott—or [Senator] Howard Baker—or Agnew or Finch" and prepare "a report on how these shows" had allotted time to the Democrats. He added, "See that we get the same."[165] Now Haldeman wanted Magruder to see that the monitoring team did this on a regular basis.

Haldeman was impressed with Magruder. Here was a man—unlike Klein—who followed orders and did not pander to the press. Having tried Magruder out on a trial basis as a personal aide, Haldeman decided to use him as a way to gain some control over the Office of Communications. In early 1970, Haldeman had him installed as deputy director of Klein's operation. Under the plan, Magruder would carry out the administrative duties of the office and Klein would concentrate on personal dealings with the press. Klein had been looking for a deputy for some time, but he had been overly selective and left the spot vacant. That gave Haldeman the opportunity to push for the placement of Magruder.

Klein initially resisted Haldeman's choice, recognizing it as an obvious move to undermine his authority.[166] But under the circumstances, Klein had few options. He could either accept the situation and make the best of it, or he could resign. Loyal to Nixon and eager to look out for the president's best interests, Klein stayed on. He continued to believe that he could be of better service to Nixon by remaining and acting as a counterbalance to the hardball tactics that Magruder would bring with him than he could by leaving.[167] He also recognized that it would be very difficult for anyone to have him fired. Indeed, the task of firing anybody (let alone a longtime friend and associate) was anathema to Richard Nixon. Klein took advantage of this. As John Ehrlichman later wrote, "Herb Klein survived because he insisted that Nixon personally fire him, and he figured that Nixon could never do it face to face."[168]

Still, Klein's position was an awkward one. It was clear to virtually everyone in the office that the installation of Magruder was a power play by Haldeman. Clark Mollenhoff, a special counsel to the president who acted as an ombudsman and was charged with seeking out and alerting the president to mismanagement and wrongdoing in the executive branch, later put it this way:

> Haldeman finally seized control of Klein's office by installing his protege, Jeb S. Magruder, as deputy director in charge of administration. The shift was for the ostensible purpose of freeing Klein from administrative chores so that he could more actively move toward his stated goal of "making the Nixon administration the most open in history." This excuse didn't fool anyone; even the secretaries were gossiping about Haldeman's takeover. Klein was well liked, but Haldeman was feared.[169]

There is a problem, of course, with ascribing the takeover to Haldeman and simply leaving it at that. Nixon often used Haldeman as a "cover" for his own actions, and it seems clear that Haldeman's intervention in the Office of Communications was at Nixon's behest. As Haldeman recalls, Nixon was not satisfied because of what he felt was "a lack of aggressiveness" on Klein's part in pursuing administration interests.[170] Ehrlichman concurs in the assessment that Haldeman was acting on Nixon's orders.[171] By choosing the course of action that he did, however, Nixon was turning his back on the usefulness of Klein's "soft-shoe" approach to media relations and the wealth of his extensive contacts with media representatives around the country. Virtually all of Nixon's inner circle admit Klein's strengths in those areas. As Haldeman put it, "Herb is a low-key kind of guy who's marvelous at backgrounding and maintaining relations with people at every level."[172] Likewise, Ehrlichman admitted that Klein "had a lot of very valuable friendships among the media" and that he was "a great 'shmoozer.' " "I think he was quite effective at that," Ehrlichman says, despite a certain animosity toward Klein's approach.[173] Ron Ziegler calls Klein "a decent man" who "knew how to communicate." "Herb communicated naturally—openly and honestly—all of his life as a newspaperman. Herb Klein is as much a vital part of the presidential and communications history as Jim Hagerty is."[174] Mollenhoff, who had the benefit of seeing Klein from both sides of the fence, says that Klein earned the trust of newspeople. As he explains: "There was a strong antagonism between Nixon and the press. Some of it justified, some of it unjustified. But Klein faced that reality and bent over backwards with the press generally, and was well liked by the press even when Nixon was in his deepest problems." Mollenhoff then described the Klein technique:

Herb was really the master of the "soft sell." He didn't come in and say, "You've gotta do something for us!" He'd say, "We've been watching your coverage,"—he wouldn't criticize the coverage, but he'd say, "We notice you've been giving a lot of attention to this story, and we've just got some facts here we'd like to call your attention to. We think they're quite important from our standpoint and we hope you get a chance to look at them." He'd visit with them and say, "Call me if you've got any questions. I'll be in my office." As opposed to Ziegler and Haldeman saying, "Go screw yourself. We'll call you."[175]

Even Charles Colson—who Klein later perceived as such an enemy—says that Klein was one of Nixon's most effective spokesmen. "The President used to *brag* about him. He'd say, 'I see him on television. Herb is tremendous. He can really get our line out. He does a beautiful job.' " According to Colson, the reason Haldeman put Magruder in Klein's office was because of Klein's lack of administrative skills. When it came to administration, Colson says, Klein was a "disaster."[176] Admitting that Klein was not the best of administrators, Haldeman laughed and added, "That was also true of Nixon."[177]

Whatever the precise reason for the shake-up of Klein's office, the result for Magruder was an ambiguous relationship with Klein. Although Klein was his "nominal boss," Magruder knew from day one that Haldeman was his "real boss."[178] Once installed in the Office of Communications, Magruder immediately began to expand it. He could not fire people—that responsibility belonged to Klein—but he could *hire* people. By building up a pool of loyal assistants, Magruder was able to increase his control over the office. Eventually, the number of senior assistants was built up from the four that Klein originally had, to about twelve.[179]

More and more the office came to be used as a mechanism to build public support for particular policy initiatives.[180] Nixon once complained that Ziegler's Press Office was "deficient" because it could not "sell," it could only "report."[181] Now Nixon was trying to turn the Office of Communications into a mechanism for selling himself and his administration. In short, Magruder had been installed as the "PR Director" that Nixon had been looking for.

Magruder carried out that PR function through his personal assistants, whom he called "project managers." Such assistants were invariably bright and brash and young. They included Robert C. Odle, Jr., a twenty-five-year-old law school graduate who had already been working in the Office of Communications at a low level (and who Haldeman felt had potential); Gordon Strachan, a twenty-eight-year-old lawyer who had been with Nixon's old firm in New York and who had graduated from the University of Southern California (where he had known Ronald Ziegler); and Herbert ("Bart") Porter, an ex-marine and onetime computer salesman. Their *modus operandi* was the use of "game plans." One of the project managers would be assigned a particular topic or policy initiative and would draw up a game plan for how best to publicize it. For instance, a game plan prepared by Odle and Lyn Nofziger, of the Congressional Relations Office, concerning Nixon's nomination of G. Harrold Carswell to the U.S. Supreme Court included the following points:

Description: The Senate took up the Carswell nomination last Friday.
   Debate may last for two weeks. . . .
Objective: To have Judge Carswell confirmed.
President: At this time there is no activity, but the President should
   remain in a strong pro-Carswell stance. . . .
To Date: A number of Senators have made speeches for Carswell or put
   out statements. . . .

Letters are being sent by many Americans.

. . . Carswell information has been furnished the media by Klein. [Etc.]
Follow-Up: Put together material about Judge Carswell . . . which can
be mailed by Klein. . . . Perhaps [Assistant Attorney General William]
Rehnquist's "The Case for Judge Carswell" would be good. . . .—
Nofziger.

. . . Rehnquist will supply some attack material for supplementary use
by Nofziger.

Carswell letter writing campaign.—Magruder.

. . . Enlist outside support as needed. See if the [American Bar
Association] and other legal organizations can help.—Colson.

. . . Determine whether additional help is needed from national
columnists.—Klein/Buchanan.

. . . Try to place people on television shows who can discuss the
nomination. Concentrate on talk shows in key local areas.—Snyder.

Distribute facts on the nomination to the Cabinet, their public
information officers, and speechwriters, asking that it be included in
Cabinet members' speeches.—Costello.

. . . Make Spotmasters available to radio stations in key states.—
Snyder.

Work with a committee of lawyers to place ads in such newspapers as
the *Times*, *Post*, and *Star*, on the morning the Congress first meets after
the Easter recess.—Colson.

Telephone editors, broadcasters, opinion leaders, etc., known on a
personal basis in states represented by undecided Republican
Senators.—Klein/Buchanan/Nofziger/Mollenhoff.

[Etc.][182]

With Magruder aboard, the Office of Communications became increasingly
politicized and increasingly willing to play "hardball." When Magruder sent
Haldeman a memo in early February outlining ways of discrediting NBC's
David Brinkley (who the president felt was particularly hostile), Haldeman

wrote: "Jeb, Damn good! Hack away. H."[183] To the extent that he could, Klein tried to keep Magruder from engaging in such activities. For instance, when Klein left town on one of his frequent trips he would take along the "unwanted or dangerous memos" that he had received from the White House, in an attempt to prevent Magruder from implementing them on his own. But it was an uphill battle. According to Klein, "Even on routine questions, no matter what the origin of an idea, once a PR program or project was endorsed with a Haldeman memo, it was difficult to get rid of without taking some sort of action."[184]

And so, the tactics utilized by the Office of Communications began to move away from those originally envisaged by Klein. People like Haldeman and Colson wanted to make the "fact sheets" that the office mailed to editors and broadcasters more politicized. Thus, on one occasion when Klein was out of town, Magruder—at the instigation of Colson and Haldeman—sent out a mailing without Klein's knowledge (and with Klein's name forged on the cover letter).[185] Magruder knew that Klein would not have allowed the mailing to take place. He later wrote that Klein "always insisted that [the office] mail out only factual material, not political propaganda, lest his credibility be endangered." Thus, Magruder initially had not wanted to send out the mailing. He argued against it to Colson. Then he went to Haldeman. Both insisted that the president wanted it mailed out. Finally, Magruder agreed. "Predictably," he wrote, "we were severely criticized for using our mailing program for such blatantly political purposes." Klein, of course, was furious. Rob Odle ultimately took the blame for the incident—a chore that assistants were sometimes required to do. Magruder felt that having underlings take the blame made life easier, since Klein "could write it off as a young staff man making a mistake." Otherwise, Magruder would have had to admit that "in a showdown," he "was following Haldeman's orders, not Klein's."[186]

The mailing operation was also expanded (as a precursor to the operation that Charles Colson would soon head), so that it was "an extensive, sophisticated, entirely computerized operation" that was no longer limited to media representatives.[187] Magruder had begun working on the preparations of the mailing list even before coming over to the Office of Communications. By December 1969, the White House already had access to a list of "far more than 500,000 names."[188] In addition, Magruder suggested that the names and addresses of people who sent mail to the White House be recorded and coded on computers. For instance, over one hundred thousand people wrote to the

White House after Nixon's Silent Majority speech. Their names were added to the mailing list and coded so that the administration could later determine that these were people who supported Nixon's Vietnam policy. The lists themselves were stored at the Republican National Committee.[189] Ultimately, they came to be divided by ethnic, geographical, and professional categorizations.[190]

Magruder also expanded efforts by the Office of Communications to stimulate letters to the editor. The letters themselves were written by professionals at the administration's behest and were then sent to Republican loyalists around the country, who would copy them and add their signature. Some of the letters were written by members of the White House staff (including Pat Buchanan). For instance, such letters were initiated to support the Carswell nomination.[191] Shortly thereafter, Haldeman instructed Magruder "to needle" Katharine Graham of the *Washington Post* by setting up "calls or letters every day from the viewpoint of I hate Nixon but you're hurting our cause in being so childish, ridiculous and over-board in your constant criticism, and thus [you] are destroying your credibility."[192] Magruder responded, "We have a team of letter-writers who are pestering the *Washington Post* from the viewpoint that was suggested."[193]

In May 1970—at Buchanan's suggestion—Magruder set up a "discreet" letter-writing operation at the Republican National Committee on a permanent basis, under the direction of Betty Nolan. Nolan was on the RNC payroll, but she reported to Magruder and his aides at the Office of Communications. Members of Magruder's staff generated ideas for the letters. Initially the operation sent some letters with false names and no return addresses. But by July, Gordon Strachan had helped to organize (through the Young Republicans) a network of people willing to sign the letters.[194] Magruder later wrote that the system generated fifty or sixty letters a week, of which about 15 to 20 percent were published.[195] Ron Baukol, a White House Fellow who was assigned to the letter-writing operation in early 1971, described the operation in a memo to Charles Colson on 26 April 1971:

> The current program was set up by Jeb Magruder after a couple of abortive attempts by others. The current one is a true under cover operation in which letters are printed as letters from private citizens. . . .
>
> The cost of the operation . . . is about two man-days, or $100 per letter published in the Letters to Editor column. Papers we now hit are the influential *Post*, *Times*, *Monitor*, *Newsweek*, [etc.]. . . . [A] $100 tab for a

good letter in the *Washington Post* is pretty cheap compared to what we spend on our other public efforts.[196]

Some of the letters generated by the system were particularly devious. Notable examples are letters that were sent to Hugh Sidey of *Life* and John Osborne of the *New Republic* in December 1970, at the instruction of Haldeman. As Magruder later wrote:

> These were not to be angry or critical letters. On the contrary, they were to be [from] supposed anti-Nixon liberals, thanking the two columnists for revealing Nixon as the shallow and dangerous man he so obviously was.
>
> Thus, the letter to Osborne began: "Let me begin by saying that I think you are the best political writer of our time. Your scathing attacks on President Nixon have delighted me beyond belief."
>
> To our delight, not long after this letter was sent, Osborne wrote a troubled, soul-searching column in which he conceded "a quality of sour and persistent disbelief that I did not like to recognize but had to recognize in my own work and in my own attitude toward the President."
>
> A similar letter to Sidey . . . produced not a column, but a rather defensive letter of response in which Sidey promised "to review my writings of 1970" and asserted his "fervent desire that he [Nixon] succeed in the months ahead."[197]

The letters-to-the-editor operation was only one way of trying to fabricate a mandate. According to Colson, Magruder also set up a telephone bank to generate calls of complaint to the media about their adverse coverage of the administration. The goal was to create the image of strong grass-roots support for the administration. Colson adds that the White House also rigged some local polls: "I think it was [the radio station] WTOP [that] ran a poll saying, 'Do you favor the President's bombing of Hanoi and Haiphong, and mining of Haiphong harbor on May 7, 1972?' I distinctly remember calling Magruder and saying, 'Get the phone calls in.' Six to one, the public supported it, but probably eighty percent of those calls were ones we had made."[198]

At the impetus of hard-liners on the White House staff, Magruder also became involved in the formation of supposedly independent "citizens committees," which were in fact fronts for the White House. Independent financial support for the organizations was recruited by the administration. The organizations themselves were used to sponsor proadministration advertisements that would help to generate the impression that the president was the recipient of widespread popular support. As the Senate Select ("Ervin") Committee investigating the Watergate affair later discovered, the advertisements "were edited, sometimes written, and reviewed by individuals in the White House." The public, however, was given no indication that the White House was in any way involved in either the committees themselves or their advertisements.[199] The "citizens committees" were also viewed by the White House as a way to distribute polls that were taken by the Republican National Committee and that showed support for the president. As Larry Higby (an aide to Haldeman) wrote in a memo to Klein, "In order to make [the polls] effective we need other organizations [besides the RNC] that we can hang the polls on that will have credibility."[200]

Charles Colson was highly involved in the formation of the various committees. Among the most notable of these was the "Tell It to Hanoi Committee." Formed shortly after the invasion of Cambodia in May 1970, this group supported Nixon's war policy and took aim at Vietnam protesters.[201] During its existence, the committee "placed advertisements in more than 40 newspapers and sent more than a million pieces of mail asking for public support."[202] Other organizations that the White House formed included the "Citizens Committee to Safeguard America," which was used to generate advertisements supporting the president's proposed antiballistic missile system; the "Committee for a Responsible Congress," which was used to run "negative ads" against administration opponents in Congress; and the "Committee for the Congress of 1970," which was set up to support proadministration candidates in the 1970 midterm congressional elections.[203]

Finally, as we will see in more detail in the next chapter, the Office of Communications began to exert a tougher line with the cabinet and the rest of the executive establishment. Increasingly, the office became a means of forcing other participants in the executive branch to play ball the way the White House wanted. In other words, the office came to be used to influence policy as well as to publicize it.

Magruder did not create a total metamorphosis of the Office of Communications, and the impact of some of the hard-line tactics that he implemented can be overstated. Still, the ramifications of the changes are significant. The goal of Nixon and Haldeman was to set up a sophisticated system for rallying public support around presidential initiatives. Having accepted the notion that presidential power was predicated upon public support, they set up elaborate mechanisms for circumventing other power centers and for taking their messages directly to the people. The use of television, the cultivation of ties with the local media, the reliance on direct mail, and the use of surrogate speakers were all attempts to derive a mandate from that "great silent majority" of Americans. Such is the stuff of the modern public presidency.

But Nixon went beyond that. In addition to circumventing "The Press," he tried to manage it. When it could not be managed, he resorted to attempts to attack and discredit it. In the end, when mandates could not be found they were fabricated—through administration-sponsored letters and telegrams as well as through the creation of supposedly independent citizens committees to praise administration policy. In the process, hard-liners in the administration stepped over that fine line that separates legitimate *appeals* for public support from illegitimate tactics to *induce* support. In crossing that line, this hard-line group sometimes took the Office of Communications with it.

CHAPTER FOUR

THE NIXON YEARS

A HOUSE DIVIDED

In 1969, White House observers had believed that Herbert Klein possessed more power and influence than Ronald Ziegler. By 1971, that assessment had changed. Some of that change was probably inevitable. Ziegler was far more visible than Klein. He briefed the White House press corps daily, he traveled with the president, and his office released the major announcements coming from the White House. Although Klein frequently appeared on radio and television and was in almost constant contact with broadcasters and editors, he and the Office of Communications were not as closely associated with the news that flowed from the White House as were Ziegler and the Press Office—nor was Klein in frequent contact with the individual White House reporters who wrote much of the news about the administration.

Initially, the press had exaggerated both the negative qualities of Ziegler and the positive qualities of Klein. Quite simply, they trusted Klein—a seasoned veteran with roots in the journalistic community—more than they trusted Ziegler. Klein also received a great deal of favorable publicity during his first year because of his efforts to secure an "open administration." Once that proved to be a less than acceptable policy for the president, Klein's influence waned.

In some respects, Klein's later efforts to serve as a counterbalance to hard-line factions within the White House may have been more important than his initial efforts to provide the press with access to the administration, but those later efforts went largely unseen by the media as a whole. Instead, Klein came to bear the brunt of the criticism for the very tactics that he was fighting within the administration.

And, of course, there was a real shift in the balance of power between Ziegler and Klein. Ziegler was willing to play the game the way the White House wanted; Klein was not. As a result, Klein (the longtime friend and confidant of Nixon) was increasingly distanced from the president while Ziegler was rewarded with access. By 1973—when the White House was awash in Watergate—Ziegler's conversations with the president were so intimate (and his relations with reporters so bad) that he had to relinquish most of his responsibility for press briefings to his assistant, Gerald L. Warren.

Finally, Klein's initial power was probably never as great as some in the media reported. As we have seen, the very creation of the Office of Communications was viewed by some observers as an attempt to "kick Klein upstairs." Even the physical placement of Klein's office was symbolic. Whereas Ziegler was housed in the White House itself, Klein was situated across the street in the ornate Victorian structure known as the "Old Executive Office Building" (or EOB). Although Klein occupied a prestigious first-floor corner suite that faced Pennsylvania Avenue and the White House and was just down the hall from the president's own "hideaway" office, the fact that Klein was outside the White House was construed by some observers as an indication of Klein's *lack* of power.[1] However, such hypothesizing can be misleading—the placement of Charles Colson's office on the same floor of the EOB has been cited as an indication of Colson's *strength*, since his quarters were so near the president's hideaway.[2]

Nonetheless, Nixon initially appeared to be enthusiastic about the Office of Communications. He was especially eager that it be used to influence television coverage of the administration. Indeed, one of Nixon's first tasks on entering the White House was to remove Lyndon Johnson's famous three-monitor television console from the Oval Office (which had allowed the former president to watch all three networks at once) and send it over to Klein's EOB office.

It was only after the hardening of Nixon's attitude toward the press and Klein's refusal to become Nixon's "full-time PR Director" that Klein came to be scorned by the president. As Charles Colson said in 1974, anybody on the

White House staff who got good press was automatically suspect to the president and his closest aides. They assumed that to get good press "you must have been cultivating the press, and to cultivate the press meant you had to give them something, and the whole attitude was don't give them a damned thing."[3] Yet the "soft voice" of Herb Klein persisted. He remained in his post until 1973, even after open attempts to circumvent his authority and remove him from his post. However, his survival in office led to an increased fracturing of the administration's communications operations.

AN UNEASY ALLIANCE

Despite the fact that Jeb Magruder was used by Haldeman to control the Office of Communications, Magruder and Klein eventually formed something of a truce. Klein apparently attributed many of Magruder's actions to youthful indiscretion, and Magruder became increasingly wary of the hard-line tactics that were being thrust upon him by Charles Colson. As we shall see, it was Colson (rather than Haldeman or Magruder) whom Klein perceived as his worst enemy.

Throughout 1970, Klein and Magruder worked together on a number of projects. In June, they began a series of regional press briefings that included appearances by the president. The White House press corps was excluded from participation.[4] Klein saw such briefings as yet another way of creating a more open administration by giving local media representatives access to high-level government officials. Nixon and Haldeman saw the briefings as a way to circumvent the Washington press corps. The first of the briefings was held at the president's California retreat in San Clemente. It took place at poolside and included a Mexican lunch, remarks by the president, and a foreign policy briefing by Henry Kissinger.[5] Subsequent briefings were held in New Orleans, Chicago, and Kansas City, Missouri.[6] Similar briefings for invited editors and news executives were later held in Washington, D.C., as well.

Both Klein and Magruder have expressed particular pride in a campaign that they waged against drug abuse. The campaign included highly publicized and well-attended briefings and conferences led by the president and celebrities such as Art Linkletter. The Office of Communications also worked with television producers to plan antidrug episodes on prime-time programs such as "Hawaii Five-O," "The FBI," "Room 222," "The Mod Squad," and "Marcus Welby, M.D."[7]*

One of the most important activities of the Office of Communications in 1970 was its role in the midterm elections. In many respects, the functions of the office resembled those of Klein's operation during the 1968 campaign. The difference, of course, was that in 1968, Klein's operation had been a part of Nixon's campaign apparatus, whereas in 1970 it was a part of the executive branch of government.

During the 1970 campaign, the Office of Communications served as a conduit between the Republican National Committee, the White House, and Republican members of Congress. Most notably, it scheduled campaign appearances by cabinet members and other surrogates. The Office of Communications provided such speakers with advance men, briefing books, information about the localities they would visit, and the text of the speeches they would deliver. The office also helped to coordinate the "line-of-the-day operation," in which surrogates were used to stress a single important point each day, for the benefit of the media.[8] All told, the office scheduled nearly two hundred speeches in twenty-two states between 4 September and 11 November. Most were made by cabinet members, but the speakers also included people like Senator Robert Dole (Rep.-Kans.) and members of the Nixon family.[9]

The broadcast division of the Office of Communications (led by Alvin Snyder) was also used to full advantage during the campaign. The office made a particular effort to utilize regional television so as to target specific constituencies. Between 2 September and 8 November 1970, Snyder scheduled sixty-nine election-related appearances on local news and talk shows, twenty-four of which were in prime time. At the same time, he scheduled twenty appearances on the Sunday morning network interview shows and five appearances on late-night talk shows.[10] The administration was particularly pleased with an edition

---

*Even this operation has been criticized by some. For instance, Edward Jay Epstein argued that it was an attempt to build public fear so that the public would not object to "extraordinary measures" being instituted as a part of the "War on Crime" (measures such as no-knock warrants, pretrial detention, and wiretaps). "To achieve this state of fear," he wrote, "required transforming a relatively small heroin addiction problem . . . into a plague that threatened all" (Epstein, "Peddling a Drug Scare," 51; see also Epstein, *Agency of Fear*).

of the "Dick Cavett Show" that was aired nationwide on the ABC network on 10 September. The program—with Herb Klein serving as cohost—included Attorney General John Mitchell, the presidential counselor Robert Finch and his wife, and the presidential consultant Len Garment.[11] That episode produced one of the show's best ratings—a 21 share. The show's average share, according to Snyder, was about 12. "They have sometimes gone as low as a 4 or 5," he reported enthusiastically, ". . . and sometimes pull 18 or better when they have high-powered movie stars."[12]

In the meantime, the Magruder wing of the Office of Communications was responding to pressure from Haldeman and others to wage a negative campaign against the Democrats. Charles Colson exerted considerable influence during the campaign. He convinced the president that the "Silent Majority" could be rallied around Republican candidates if their Democratic opponents were depicted as "radical liberals." As Magruder wrote, "It was a totally negative approach, one that combined the national fear of increased crime with undertones of racism."[13] Despite misgivings, Magruder gave Haldeman what he wanted. In a memo to Haldeman, he wrote, "The Democrats should be portrayed as being on the fringes: radical liberals who bus children, excuse disorders, tolerate crime, apologize for our wealth, and undercut the President's foreign policy."[14]

When it came to campaign activities, Colson rather than Haldeman usually gave Magruder his marching orders. Colson and Magruder did not get along from the start.[15] Magruder's dislike of Colson soon bordered on outright hatred, and he began to fight against his superior. According to Magruder, the "attack ads" that Colson designed for newspapers "just went too far." "It was all innuendo," he later wrote. "You questioned a man's patriotism, his intelligence, his morality, his manhood, anything you could get away with." Magruder argued against the negative ads to Haldeman, but his influence was minimal. In the end, a roughly equal number of positive and negative ads were published by the administration. All of them were placed with the advertising agency by Magruder.[16]

Despite all the efforts, the administration ended the campaign badly. On 29 October—the Friday before the election—President Nixon made a campaign stop in San Jose, California, where he was scheduled to speak to five thousand supporters inside the civic auditorium. A huge throng of angry demonstrators confronted him on the way in. They shouted obscenities and then beat on the doors of the auditorium after Nixon entered. Police pushed back the crowd and provided a protected space for the motorcade. On the way out, Nixon stepped onto his car, waved his hands in the air in his typical "victory" sign for the benefit of television cameras, and then entered the car. Nixon was in full view of the demonstrators, and they reacted with fury. They threw eggs and rocks at the motorcade as it left, smashing windows in the press and staff buses behind the president's armored car.[17]

Nixon felt that the violent display was a perfect example of the lawlessness of antiwar demonstrators, and he set out to make the most of it. Haldeman instructed the Office of Communications to "stress the San Jose incident in every possible way over the weekend."[18] The president himself released a statement saying, "The stoning at San Jose is an example of the viciousness of the lawless elements in our society."[19] Another press release called the incident "the most severe attack on a President since the assassination of John Kennedy."[20] On Sunday, the president made the incident the subject of a speech that he gave in Phoenix, Arizona.

There is no question that the demonstration was serious, but the administration's attempt to capitalize on it backfired. News reports began to suggest that Nixon had taunted the demonstrators and thereby had provoked an incident. Martin Schram, a reporter for *Newsday*, wrote that he had heard Nixon say in an angry voice when the president flashed his victory sign: "That's what they hate to see."[21] The extent to which the White House stressed the incident over the weekend further undercut the administration's credibility on the issue. As Magruder later wrote, "Left to itself, the San Jose incident might have added up to a slight plus for us, but our hard sell, plus the suspicion that Nixon had provoked the demonstrators, took the edge off it."[22]

Nonetheless, the White House decided that a tape of Nixon's Phoenix speech about the incident should be broadcast on network television on election eve. The networks provided a half hour of prime time for Nixon's speech and a response by Democratic Senator Edmund Muskie. The decision to use the Phoenix speech was an unfortunate one. The tape was in black and white, and the sound was terrible. Network executives were shocked at the quality of the tape and said that it was so poor that it should be considered unsuitable for broadcast. Nonetheless, the White House insisted on using it. The results were devastating. Not only was the quality of the tape poor, but the tone of the speech was inappropriate to the medium. The contrast of Nixon's segment to that of Muskie made the speech seem even worse. As William Safire has written, "Nixon's election eve show was 'hot'—hard-driving, angry, too political—while Muskie's speech was 'cool'—written by Richard Goodwin with a nice sense of place and contrast."[23]

In the end, the Silent Majority did not come through for the president. Although the Republicans picked up one seat in the Senate (two if a senator elected as a "Conservative" is counted), they lost nine seats in the House and—to the dismay of the White House—eleven governorships. This was a far cry from earlier White House talk of gaining control in the Senate and paving the way for a partisan realignment.[24] The incumbent party usually loses seats in off-year elections, but the White House had made the mistake of creating unreasonably high expectations. Nixon's campaigning was unprecedented for a president in an off-year election, and the Republican party had spent about $18 million on behalf of its candidates.

To offset the impression that the president had been "defeated," the Office of Communications waged a massive campaign to paint the election returns in a favorable light. Nixon claimed "victory" in front of television cameras the day after the election, but he refused to hold a press conference to discuss the results. Instead, he held a seventy-minute off-the-record briefing for nine columnists who were identified by the *Washington Evening Star* as "either Republican or conservative in their outlook, or friendly to the Nixon administration."[25] This was followed by a mailing from the Office of Communications to thirty-eight thousand opinion makers throughout the country. The mailing included a cover letter and "fact sheet" on the election by the presidential counselor Robert Finch. Robert Odle reported to Haldeman that media coverage of the mailing was "unprecedented. . . . The Finch analysis was featured on front pages [of newspapers] throughout the country and by virtually every political columnist."[26] Finch's letter said, in part:

In the wake of the campaign, the predicted has come to pass. Taking one or another item from a decidedly mixed bag, columnists and commentators are creating great myths about what occurred and structuring great predictions on what this means for the President in 1972. . . .

The inescapable conclusion I draw is that the President's campaign activity was clearly among the decisive factors in holding down the inevitable House losses and in winning Senate victories in Tennessee, Connecticut, Ohio and Maryland—which dramatically reversed the off-year trend of losses by gaining two seats politically and four states ideologically. At the national level the administration was clearly endorsed.[27]

Many of the "eastern establishment" newspapers scoffed at the Finch letter. For instance, David Broder wrote in the *Washington Post*: "It does not bother me in the slightest that the White House is laboring to portray this as the election of their dreams. . . . What does scare the daylights out of me is the possibility that the men inside the White House may believe what they are saying. . . . [I]f Richard Nixon has lost his ability to add up election returns, then the country is in worse trouble than anyone has imagined."[28] But whether or not "liberal" columnists agreed with Finch's assessment did not seem to matter much to the White House. The important thing was that they got their message across to the American people. If Republican candidates had not secured a victory in the midterm elections, the Office of Communications had.

AT WAR WITH COLSON

Charles Wendell Colson, a former assistant to Senator Leverett Saltonstall (Rep.-Mass.), joined the White House staff late in 1969 at the recommendation of Bryce Harlow. Colson was an only child, born and raised in Boston. He turned down a scholarship to Harvard and went instead to Brown University, where he was active in Republican politics, debating, and student government. He graduated with honors in 1953, served in the U.S. Marine Corps, and returned to Washington in 1956 to join Senator Saltonstall's staff and attend law school at George Washington University. He played an important role in Saltonstall's 1960 reelection campaign and then turned to a successful law practice.[29] He joined the Nixon campaign in 1968, working with Harlow as part of the "Key Issues Group," which developed policy papers and worked with special-interest groups in Washington.[30]

Colson's job in the White House was to serve as a liaison with organized groups throughout the country. The president very quickly came to like Colson because of his determined willingness to play hardball with administration opponents.[31] Nixon turned to Colson to talk about "gut politics." "That wasn't Haldeman's thing," Colson recalls. "I grew up in the school of Washington political battles and rough political campaigns in Massachusetts. Haldeman hadn't. Haldeman was a media man. Ehrlichman was an advance man. There wasn't anybody sort of skilled in the school of what I call hand-to-hand political combat in the White House except me. When Nixon would have these things he'd want to talk about, I'd be the guy he'd lean on—probably because of a similarity of views on things."[32]

Few others in the White House shared the president's favorable view of Colson. Colson and Attorney General John Mitchell, who had served as Nixon's campaign manager in 1968, had battled over competing campaign strategies for Nixon to follow in the final days of the election. After that, the two never got along. "He just didn't like me and I didn't like him," Colson says. "Nothing personal. I just thought his political judgment was very unsound."[33] Soon after Colson joined the White House, both Ehrlichman and Haldeman also developed a certain animosity toward him. In Ehrlichman's case, it was because Colson often opposed his policy views.[34] In Haldeman's case, it was because Colson had independent access to the president. "I was the only other guy on the whole White House staff that could walk into the President's office without Haldeman's OK," Colson says.[35] "I was the loose cannon. [Nixon] could give me things to do, and Haldeman would never know it. I think he was threatened. That's just an opinion." Colson goes on to say that Haldeman told him that it was his responsibility not to implement anything that was decided on at those meetings before clearing it with Haldeman—even if it was an action ordered by the president. In response Colson said: " 'Bob, I'm sorry. He got elected, not you. If he tells me to do something, I'm going to do it.' " "So," Colson concludes, "we had some uncomfortable sessions over that."[36]

Such unfettered access to the president has led to suggestions that Colson implemented actions that he should not have. Haldeman has written, "Colson encouraged the dark impulses in Nixon's mind and *acted* on those impulses instead of ignoring them and letting them die."[37] Ron Ziegler concurs. He argues that during the president's late-afternoon sessions with Colson, Nixon was "letting down his hair and sitting there and talking and blowing off steam," and that Colson would take an off-the-cuff Nixon instruction "literally and implement it . . . [even] if it was not an appropriate thing to do from the standpoint of the president's interests."[38] Asked about such statements, Colson reacted angrily:

That's part of the Ziegler/Haldeman party line, protecting themselves. . . . No question [Nixon] would let off steam with me. A *lot* of times he would let off steam and I wouldn't do the things. When he really made a point of it, I did it. But none of the things that brought the Nixon presidency down were the things that I did. So I don't know what Ziegler is talking about. Because I had nothing to do with the Watergate break-in. I didn't know about it in advance. I was not a part of the cover-up meetings. . . . So all these horrible things he told me to do in the afternoon, they're not the things that brought down the presidency.[39]

In fact, Colson has said that if "Nixon's presidency hadn't collapsed, what everybody wrote about as the dark side would have been his Machiavellian genius at manipulating situations to his advantage."[40]

Nonetheless, Colson's hardball approach earned him a dubious reputation among many people both in and out of government. The political reporter Theodore H. White once wrote, "Colson had absolutely no scruples—leaks, plants, forgeries, lies were all part of the game as he played it."[41] The *Wall Street Journal* labeled him Nixon's "hatchet man."[42] Magruder called him "an evil genius."[43] Klein called him "fanatical . . . unscrupulous . . . overly ambitious. . . . In his mind, the end justified the means. Always."[44] According to legend, Colson's favorite motto (said to have been displayed on the wall in his den) was: "When you've got 'em by the balls, their hearts and minds will follow."[45]

As we have seen, Colson played a major role in the 1970 midterm elections. By then, he had been on the White House staff for a year. During that time, he had displayed a willingness to play tough with the media. Nixon admired that. He saw in Colson the qualities that he had long wanted to see in the Office of Communications. For instance, Colson was willing to put pressure on network executives when the White House felt that their news coverage of the administration was unfair. He and Nixon were convinced that network news coverage was biased against the president. "We believed our own news summaries," Colson says. "One of my jobs was to put whatever kind of subtle, or not so subtle, pressures I could on the networks to keep them honest. See, this is where people delude themselves: I didn't feel we were doing that to unfairly bend the networks to favor Nixon. I felt we were doing it to offset their anti-Nixon bias. . . . That was one of my major assignments. I spent a lot of time at it."[46] After one meeting with executives from all three networks in September 1970, Colson wrote that the networks were "damned nervous and scared [of us] and we should continue to take a very tough line, face to face, and in other ways."[47] Colson recalls that after such meetings, he and Nixon would "sit there and laugh" about how they "had put the screws" on the networks.[48]

Such an approach was anathema to Herb Klein. He felt that it was *his* responsibility to deal with network executives, not Colson's. Such contacts led Klein to write Colson an angry memo in October 1970: "I thought we had a clear agreement you would not be calling [network executives] without consulting me. . . . Your continued calls have caused network heads to ask me privately—are you leaving? What has happened to you? With actions like this you make my work harder. Are you promoting the idea of taking over my contacts and Ron Ziegler's? They think so and tell me."[49]

In fact, Colson *was* trying to take over Klein's operation, but he was doing it at the urging of the president. "It was not my idea," Colson said. "It was Richard Nixon's idea. I didn't particularly want it, frankly."[50] William Rhatican, who worked in both the Klein and the Colson operations, agrees. "It was clear to me that it was not Chuck versus Herb. If it hadn't been Chuck there would have been someone else that they would have put in there."[51] But neither Klein nor Magruder seemed to recognize—or believe—that Colson was merely following orders from the president. They felt that he was making a power play of his own.[52]

During the 1970 midterm elections, Klein had come to Magruder's side when Colson had tried to take over his mailing operation. Soon thereafter, Colson and Magruder met at a cocktail party. "You know, Klein's got to go," Colson told him. Magruder—who now considered Klein an ally—countered that Klein could be useful if he was "properly directed." Colson dismissed Magruder's comment. Klein had to go, he repeated. "The President wants him out." Magruder thought he was just saying that. "It was classic Colson," Magruder later wrote. "If you're not pro-me, you're anti-Nixon."[53] But Colson insists that he was speaking the truth, and all indications are that he was correct. In any event, a coup was in the making. Klein and Colson were at war.

The situation reached a head in January 1971 when Colson received a copy of a memo that Nixon had written to Haldeman. Colson has paraphrased the memo this way: "Herb Klein is not really running the operation. Jeb Magruder is not able to administer it. We still don't have a Director of Communications. What I want you to do is put the job under Chuck Colson, because Chuck runs a buttoned down operation. He gets things done."[54] Colson then met with Haldeman to discuss how the transfer of power would take place. "We had a very open discussion about it," Colson recalls, "and Haldeman said, 'I've got to find some pretext because Herb Klein won't like this.' " They decided that the way to bring about the change would be to have a management study performed. "As a result of the management study, I would be assigned the Communications Department and Herb would remain Director of Communications, but I would, in fact, run the communications."[55] In short, Klein would remain as a figurehead. And so, Frederic V. Malek—the president's personnel manager—was called in to write the study. Klein was told that Malek was being brought in as "a labor arbitrator" to settle the differences that had arisen between Klein and Colson.[56]

At the time, Malek was thirty-four years old. He had graduated from West Point in 1959, served in Vietnam as a Green Beret, received a master's degree in business administration from Harvard University, and became a millionaire operating a South Carolina plant manufacturing hand tools before joining the Nixon administration in April 1969, as deputy under secretary at the Department of Health, Education, and Welfare (HEW). He succeeded Nixon's original personnel manager, Harry S. Fleming, in October 1970. Since then, he and his assistant, Daniel T. Kingsley, had restructured the personnel office and had begun the process of reviewing administration officials and getting rid of those considered "expendable." In the process, Malek had won many enemies in the administration.[57]

Colson attended the meeting in which Haldeman gave Malek his instructions. "I remember it vividly because it was a stacked deck from the beginning," Colson says.[58] Malek concurs, saying: "It was preordained by Haldeman and the president that Colson was going to get more active in this area—with or without the study. I think the study made it a little cleaner and easier to effect in a way that would be reasonably satisfactory to both Klein and Colson." According to Malek, Nixon and Haldeman felt that Klein "was a talented public relations executive who understood the media well but wasn't sufficiently assertive and aggressive." Therefore they wanted to put "more of the operating leverage in the hands of Colson, who was a real activist—a real aggressive activist." Indeed, Malek says that Colson was as tough a political operator as he had ever seen. "He was aggressive, he was totally dedicated to getting the job done, he was very bright, very determined, and he was definitely a hardball player."[59]

Magruder saw through the charade. In his memoirs he correctly conjectured that "Malek's 'evaluation' was a put-up job," although he assumed that Colson alone was responsible for it.[60] Malek sent a member of his staff to interview

Klein and Colson and members of their respective offices.[61] Klein apparently did not recognize how serious a threat Malek's evaluation was. DeVan Shumway, one of Klein's assistants, recalls that Klein downplayed Malek's intervention: "Herb said one time to somebody in my presence—'Well, if they want to bring Malek in, I can deal with that. I can deal with Malek.' Well, god, Malek and Haldeman just sort of end-runned Herb in that whole situation." Shumway had known Klein for a long time. A former UPI reporter, Shumway had come to Washington at Klein's behest to work in the press operation at HEW under Bob Finch. When Finch left HEW, Klein brought Shumway into the Office of Communications, with the understanding that Shumway would leave in a year to head the press operation at the Committee to Re-Elect the President. Shumway joined Klein's operation in December 1970—just before Malek was called in to divide the office. Shumway says that Klein was "a wonderful man—one of the world's truly great gentlemen. Everybody would say that, and it's true. But he's a pushover for a man like Colson who's ambitious and ruthless."[62]

Magruder came out squarely on the side of Klein during the evaluation, making it clear that he thought Klein should retain his powers.[63] Klein himself made his case in a memo to the president dated 3 March 1971. In it he outlined the office's functions.[64] Separate tabs were attached to elaborate each of the various functions that were outlined in the body of the memo. For instance, "Tab C" (an elaboration on the "Personal Activities of the Director") gave a detailed description of Klein's activities: he had appeared on every major television news and talk show, made 27 "major-length prime-time appearances" on network television, appeared on 152 regional television programs, made 70 speeches in and out of Washington over the past year, campaigned in 14 states during the 1970 elections, held 132 regional press conferences, and met with 50 editorial boards.[65]

The negotiations for restructuring Klein's office were long and painful. The original plan was for Colson to take charge of all the people working in the Office of Communications, leaving Klein as a sort of roving ambassador.[66] Margita White, one of Klein's chief assistants, recalls that she threatened to quit when it was suggested that she and her responsibilities be put under Colson's domain.[67] In the end, Malek suggested that Klein continue to have responsibility over media liaison and correspondence (thus leaving White and a few others under Klein) but that virtually everything else be transferred to Colson. In short, Colson would have responsibility for "day-to-day public relations activities" and would directly control cabinet department liaison,

project management, the mailing operation, the Speakers' Bureau, the scheduling department (for placing officials on television and radio), and the drafting
of "talking papers" for administration officials to use in their dealings with the
media.[68]

Klein has written that the result of the lengthy negotiations was "a secret
standoff."[69] Colson does not see it that way. He feels that for all practical
purposes, he took over Klein's operation in March 1971. Others agree. Van
Shumway says that Klein was left to "run around the country talking to
editorial boards and making little speeches and that sort of stuff, and the *real*
power in the communications operation in terms of distribution of information
was left to Colson."[70] Bill Rhatican, who had worked for Klein, echoes that
assessment. As he puts it, "We went home one evening and during the night the
building shifted and we all slid down into Colson's corner of the world." When
I asked if Klein's operation had any real power after the split, Rhatican replied,
"No." When I asked if Colson became the de facto Communications Director,
Rhatican replied: "That's right. In reality, that's what he was."[71]

Clearly, many of the most important functions of the Office of Communications were explicitly transferred to Colson under the Malek plan. But Colson
felt that even those people who technically remained under Klein's jurisdiction
were, in fact, answerable to him—much as Magruder had, in fact, been
answerable to Haldeman. For instance, part of the understanding between
Haldeman and Colson (although not a formal part of the Malek plan) was that
Jeb Magruder would leave the Office of Communications when the plan took
effect because Colson did not want to work with him. "I remember Haldeman
saying, 'We're going to put him over at the Committee to Re-Elect the
President because he can't get in any trouble over there.' Words I have never
forgotten," Colson says with an ironic laugh.[72]* Colson eventually chose
Magruder's replacement—a conservative *Washington Post* reporter by the
name of Ken Clawson. Colson says, "[He] worked for me." On an organization chart, Clawson fell under Herb Klein, and his title was "Deputy Director
of Communications," but Klein really had "nothing to say to [him]."[73] Shumway, who remained in Klein's office, says that Colson "took the ball and ran
with it." He says that Colson was constantly involving himself in what re-

---

*At the Committee to Re-Elect the President (CRP), Magruder became involved in the
planning of the Watergate break-in: an event that resulted in the collapse of the Nixon
administration.

mained of Klein's domain. Colson gave instructions to Klein's people "*all the time*," Shumway said. "Colson was *always* calling."[74]

As part of his own staff, Colson hired Desmond Barker, a public relations man from Utah, to be in charge of liaison with the domestic departments, and John Scali, an ABC News reporter, to be in charge of liaison with departments dealing with foreign affairs. The two were in daily contact with departmental public information officers (PIOs) to coordinate the release of all public statements coming from the administration. Barker also presided over a planning meeting that met three times a week in the Roosevelt Room. The meeting included representatives from the president's speechwriting team, the Press Office, the Office of Communications, and Colson's operation. The purpose was to plot communications strategies and to decide who in the administration would be saying what publicly. As such, the meeting served as a complement to the daily "line-of-the-day" meeting that was then part and parcel of the daily staff meeting led by Haldeman. Later, during the 1972 presidential campaign, Colson was put in charge of an "attack group" charged with implementing the line.[75]

Colson privately claimed victory over Klein in a June 1971 memo. He pointed out that he had taken over "the talking paper writing function, the mailing operation, the scheduling, [and] miscellaneous projects." He also added that he had "largely taken over the old [Lyn] Nofziger office function [of providing 'attack' material to friends on Capitol Hill]."[76] As we have seen, the sole remaining responsibility of Klein's operation was correspondence and liaison with columnists and local media representatives. Klein himself continued a hectic travel schedule, going from state to state to brief local editorial boards. In just five months he had held briefings in nineteen different states and had returned to states such as New York, Ohio, California, Texas, New Jersey, Illinois, and Pennsylvania several times.[77] The result was that he was seldom in his office. That, of course, was what Colson wanted. Colson rationalizes that situation: "Klein loved to travel. He loved nothing better than to call out to Andrews Air Force Base, get an Air Force plane, go somewhere, give a speech, be wined and dined, go do some television programs, [and] come back to Washington. . . . And that's not putting him down. He was good at that. He was *very* good at that. He was a great goodwill ambassador."[78] But, as Pat Buchanan put it, Klein had become "an ambassador of goodwill without portfolio." Buchanan added that Klein was "an absentee landlord, and absentee landlords around here lose their turf."[79] Klein knew that and was not

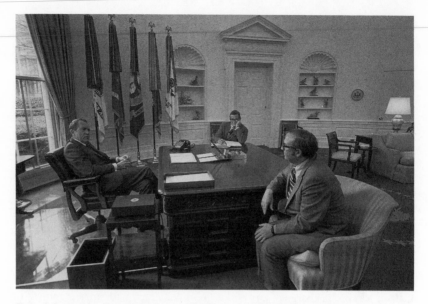

From left to right: President Nixon, Charles Colson, and Ken Clawson.
(Courtesy Nixon Presidential Materials Project)

pleased. He wanted to maintain authority over the office that he had created. In a memo to the president dated 24 June 1971, Klein alluded to the problem. "I am convinced beyond doubt that my programmed visits with media leaders across the country is working quite well," he wrote. But he added, "It also is essential that I be in Washington part of the time to be able to keep abreast of affairs, be knowledgeable and, of course, to operate the full functions of my own office."[80]

In the coming months, Klein grappled openly with Colson. For instance, Klein sent Colson a curt memo in September 1971: "In the last few weeks, I have noted a trend for some of your people to issue orders to Donna Kingswell [a member of Klein's staff] which range from acting as personal messenger to countermanding my orders on particular projects. . . . I would appreciate it if you would caution them against this."[81] Less than a month later, Klein sent Colson a detailed complaint:

> We agreed that these two offices must work closely and decided upon certain ground rules. The system is not working. Recently, there has been a steady deterioration of relations between your office and mine which has not been in the President's best interests. Basically, the problem is a lack

of coordination and, I believe, your unwillingness to cooperate. For example, I invite you to meetings, and you boycott them. Meetings you call, which I or members of my staff could contribute to, exclude this office.

. . . This last Friday at 6:30 p.m., I was handed a fact sheet on the economy which . . . had been circulated [by your office] several days before I was even aware of its existence. It was not done in a format that newspapers would respect. I therefore had to redo it myself. . . . This procedure is not good for the President. It does not represent the best use of experience and talent in the news business and only causes complications.

I was frankly upset by the orders [from your office] to my staff to call hostile newspapers after the President's Supreme Court announcement [of the nominations of Lewis Powell and William Rehnquist]. I am aware of where your instructions originated, but before instructions were given to my staff to call under my name, there should have been coordination. . . .

I deal with these news people day in and day out. I can't do this well if you are moving behind my back in each crucial moment. . . . This is injurious to the President.[82]

In his response, Colson claimed innocence: "Your memo of November 5 has hit me like a bolt from the blue. It had been my feeling that the relationships between our two offices were excellent and that we were entirely over whatever problems there had been initially when some of our respective responsibilities were changed." In the midst of his lengthy response, Colson stated that those working in the Office of Communications were not Klein's "property." Colson explained: "Rhatican, O'Donnell, Shumway, Snyder—all of them are here to serve the President. Some must take primary direction from you, others from me."[83]

John Ehrlichman claims that if Nixon had had his druthers, he would have fired Klein, but that Nixon—who loathed firing anyone—could not bring himself to do it.[84] Haldeman says that Ehrlichman's statement is too strong, but he admits that Nixon wanted to move Klein into another post.[85] A transcript of a taped conversation between Nixon and Haldeman on 23 June 1972—the "smoking-gun" tape in which Nixon approved the Watergate cover-up—contains remarks showing Nixon's displeasure with Klein. The day before, Klein had set up a meeting between the president and broadcast executives in the Cabinet Room. Klein had wanted the session to be used as an opportunity for the executives to explain to the president their problems with FCC regulations, equal time, and the like. It was yet another of Klein's attempts to provide "openness" and "dialogue." However, Colson had other things in mind. He arranged for one of the executives to stand up during the meeting and make "an impassioned address urging each of the broadcast executives to support the President in his 1972 campaign." Klein was horrified. The meeting was not the place for such an endorsement, and he could tell that the other executives did not approve of a Nixon advocate taking the floor—and taking their time—even though most of them supported Nixon. Therefore, Klein "cut off the broadcaster to avoid embarrassment for the other executives, who were not invited there to pledge political endorsements." The president was not pleased. As Klein put it, "He would have preferred hearing the words of praise instead of listening to the other executives express their complaints regarding government restrictions." Colson was not pleased either. Immediately after the meeting, he went to the Oval Office with the president and complained about Klein's action.[86]

The incident came up during the taped conversation between Nixon and Haldeman. Nixon referred to the meeting with the executives and then said: "You've just not got to let Klein ever set up a meeting again. He just doesn't have his head screwed on. You know what I mean. . . . He's just not our guy at all." Haldeman stood up for Klein. He reminded Nixon that Klein was "a very nice guy." Nixon responded, "People love him, but damn is he unorganized." The conversation turned to other topics but eventually came back to Klein. The president was again thinking about the meeting with the broadcast executives: "[Klein] just doesn't really have his head screwed on, Bob. I could see it in that meeting yesterday. . . . I don't know how he does TV so well." Again Haldeman stood up for Klein: "Well, he's a sensation on that—that goes to the [unintelligible] meaning of the thing, you know. What's his drawback is really an asset."[87]

Haldeman tries to downplay such remarks captured by the White House taping system: "They tend to sound a lot more harsh and derogatory than they really were understood to be at the time with the people in the conversation. And that's too bad. I know it hurt Herb's feelings and I can certainly understand why. But he was regarded with great affection and friendship by the president and, I think, by virtually all of us."[88]

Klein remained in his post for nearly two years after the implementation of the Malek plan, but he was less influential than ever. As John Ehrlichman graphically put it, Klein was among "the walking dead."[89] That may be something of an overstatement, but Klein's power had nonetheless waned considerably. Nowhere was that more evident than in the 1972 presidential campaign.

COLSON ASCENDANT

By 1972, Colson was the major technician for orchestrating administration PR. As such, he played an important role in the 1972 campaign against George McGovern. Klein kept a busy schedule as a roving goodwill ambassador, but it was Colson who was the real communications director. He was, however, careful to avoid publicity about it.

The year 1972 was one made for television by the White House. It was an extraordinary year of visual imagery, starting with the historic trips to China and the Soviet Union and concluding with a carefully organized "Rose Garden Strategy" in the fall campaign. Through it all, Nixon was amazingly successful at determining what the media would cover about the administration. As Colson puts it: "Nixon had a fetish about wanting to try to dominate the news from the government. He would call me in a lot and say, 'What story is going to be our story next Thursday?' And I'd say, 'Unemployment statistics,' or whatever. . . . So we kept a steady progression of administration news. I mean, it was as close to managing the news as you can do."[90]

One of those who worked with Colson during the 1972 campaign was a young White House speechwriter by the name of David Gergen, who later went on to become director of communications in the Ford and Reagan administrations. Recently, Gergen explained to Hedrick Smith how that news management worked: "We had a rule in the Nixon operation that before any public event was put on his schedule, you had to know what the headline out of that event was going to be, and what the lead paragraph would be. You had to think of it in those terms, and if you couldn't justify it, it didn't go on the [president's] schedule."[91] Gergen added that the president's goal was for the White House—not the networks—to determine what the evening newscasts would carry about the president. In other words, Gergen said, "You had to learn how to do the editing yourself."

When Nixon went out to make a statement in the White House briefing room, he insisted that he be given one hundred words [a "tight" news bite]. And we had to count 'em. We had to put up in the corner of the page how many words were on this paper. You couldn't go over one hundred. He would go out and deliver one hundred words and he'd walk out. Because he knew that they had to use about one hundred words. They had to use what he wanted to say. And if you gave them five hundred words, they would select part of it and determine what the point of his statement was. It was a very rigorous system.[92]

Each morning, Colson attended an eight o'clock staff meeting at the White House to determine the line-of-the-day. That meeting included Haldeman, Ehrlichman, and Ziegler.[93] Colson usually met with the president at nine o'clock to discuss the line with him. Colson relied on daily data from the Sindlinger polling firm to help formulate that line. In so doing, Colson was able to determine "what issues were sensitive with the public." As a result, the White House could "reflect [those issues] in the next morning's public statements. In other words, you could tell one night how people were reacting to things, and the next morning back off or intensify what you wanted to say with almost simultaneous polling."[94]

Once the line-of-the-day was determined, Colson would hold a meeting of the "attack group" from 9:15 to 9:45. That group included representatives from those parts of the executive branch and the Committee to Re-Elect the President (CRP)* that were charged with implementing the line. As Colson puts it, "The job at 9:15 was to decide who would say it and how we would get it out and who would release it and which one of the Cabinet members would go where and what kind of a surrogate program we'd have and how we would respond to attacks that might have been made upon the president by Senator McGovern or his people."[95]

Among the things that the White House scripted for television in 1972 was the Republican National Convention in Miami Beach, Florida. Nixon's televi-

---

*The CRP was a political organization that was tightly controlled by the White House. Its purpose was to circumvent the power of the Republican National Committee. Magruder made this clear in a memo to Haldeman: "The [Republican National] Committee must feel that it is in the main stream while at the same time not having actual authority or responsibility over either the campaign or, of course, the President" (memo, Jeb Stuart Magruder to H. R. Haldeman, 18 January 1971, "Klein—February 1971," Box 73, H. R. Haldeman Files, Nixon Presidential Materials Project, Alexandria, Va.).

The entertainer Sammy Davis, Jr., hugs the president at an event choreographed by Nixon's television advisors to coincide with the 1972 Republican National Convention. (Courtesy Nixon Presidential Materials Project)

sion advisors, Bill Carruthers and Mark Goode, played an important role in the production. In addition, they brought in Fred Rheinstein—a former NBC producer—to coordinate relations with the networks, and a professional art director to design the podium.[96] Above the podium were three screens, each of which was twelve feet wide and twenty-five feet tall. Whenever there was a lull in the action, slides, film, or live broadcasts were flashed on the screen. For instance, Nixon's arrival in Miami, his visit to a local rock concert, and pictures of the entertainer Sammy Davis, Jr., hugging Nixon were all beamed to those screens.[97] Whenever particularly important images were shown— such as a film chronicling Nixon's first term—the lights in the convention hall were shut off, thus forcing the television networks to carry the prepackaged material rather than their own interviews or analysis from the convention floor. The film of Nixon is said to have been so well produced that even the three thousand reporters in the press gallery—usually talkative and inattentive at such presentations—watched in silence.[98]

Nothing at the convention was left to chance. "We actually prepared, down to the minute, a script for the whole convention," Gergen said.[99] That script spelled out every single thing that would happen in the convention hall, right down to "spontaneous" demonstrations.[100] In addition, there was an "alternative script," which involved prominent individuals who "were good copy: good for television or interesting visually." Thus, if there was something dull going on at the podium, the Nixon team would turn to the alternative script and offer those individuals to the networks for interviews. For instance, they might say: "We have John Connally, the Treasury secretary, in a holding room. He's going to be coming onto the floor in just a few minutes. Would you be interested in interviewing him?"[101] As Gergen points out, the networks loved that.

Carruthers felt that such planning was absolutely essential. "In my business you don't go on television unless you have some form of a script. When you're going to be on television four nights for three hours [each] and three days for two and a half hours [each], you don't do it off the cuff. So, yeah, we scripted it, we formatted it, we counseled and coordinated the speeches and the program and the camera positions and the networks and everything else. And it was one of the best conventions ever done."[102]

Nothing—not even the Watergate break-in and subsequent allegations against White House officials in the *Washington Post*—was able to derail the streamlined Nixon operation. The public responded by giving the president a

Nothing at the 1972 Republican National Convention in Miami Beach was left to chance. Even "spontaneous demonstrations" were carefully scripted in advance. It was a television event par excellence. (Courtesy Nixon Presidential Materials Project)

landslide reelection. Herb Klein kept busy during the campaign, but it was a big step down from 1968—or even 1970. His was no longer a seat of power, and in the days after the reelection, Nixon made it clear to Klein that it was time for him to leave. Nixon facilitated the ouster of Klein and others through what soon proved to be a major miscalculation: a sort of coerced mass suicide the morning after the election at assembled meetings of the president's staff and cabinet. Those who gathered at the meetings thought that there would be victory celebrations. Instead, the meetings were set up so that Haldeman could demand resignations from everyone in the senior ranks of the administration. The timing was dreadful, leaving most of the staff angry and demoralized. Haldeman made it clear that many of the letters would be accepted. Colson claims, "The most disconsolate, dejected figure to shuffle out of the room was Herb Klein."[103] From the Office of Communications, letters of resignation were expected not only from Klein but also from his five senior assistants— Ken Clawson, Margita White, Paul Costello, DeVan Shumway, and Alvin Snyder.[104]

Later in the month, the president called Klein to Camp David to inform him of his fate. Klein was greeted by Ron Ziegler. " 'I'm not sure what is going to happen, Herb,' Ron said, 'but I want you to know I have nothing to do with it. You may not like the meeting or the President's ideas today, but whatever, I want you to know that I am not a part of the plan.' "[105] Ziegler recalls how painful that encounter was. After all, he had been in college when he first met Klein, and he had thought of Klein as a mentor.[106] After talking with Ziegler, Klein was ushered in to the president's lodge. The president told Klein that there was a great need to cut the size of the White House staff and to reorganize the executive branch. "Haldeman then interjected that a smaller White House staff would mean, among other things, that my office would be cut in size and that in the new plan it would report to [Ziegler]," Klein recalls. "That meant I had lost the power struggle. . . . I was out."[107]

Nixon then explained that they knew from Klein's own public remarks that he was planning to leave the White House within the next year or so. He suggested that perhaps Klein would like to become director of the U.S. Information Service, or even be named U.S. ambassador to Mexico. Klein replied that he had not yet decided just when to leave his post but that he would let the president know soon. As Klein has written: "The President seemed to detect by my manner that I was surprised at the direction our meeting had taken. It was as if he had believed I had had discussions of this earlier with Haldeman or someone else. Suddenly he seemed awkward and turned the conversation to the days we had spent together in Alhambra when he was a congressman. With that he stood and thanked me again for all I had done. The meeting was over."[108]

Nixon's daughter Julie has written that the president was, indeed, upset by Klein's reaction. As she put it: "My father was disappointed that Herb had not been more aggressive in his dealings with the media and hoped he would adhere to a statement he had made that fall that he would be leaving the White House sometime early in the second term. But Herb was also a good friend, one my father did not want to hurt in the process of a changeover." She says that Klein's Camp David meeting with the president lasted longer than the allotted time and that Nixon's military aide, Jack Brennan, knocked on the door to announce the arrival of New York Governor Nelson Rockefeller for an appointment. "[Brennan] could see that the President was agitated," she wrote. When Klein left, Nixon did not signal for Brennan to bring in Rockefeller. When several minutes had elapsed, Brennan went to the door to knock again. There he heard Nixon "talking angrily to Bob Haldeman: 'You told me Herb *wanted* to leave.' "[109]

Shortly thereafter, Haldeman asked Klein not to announce yet that he would be leaving "or to rush out of office." Klein wrote: "His explanation was that he wanted to be fair to me, and that he felt timing would be important to the press acceptance of my departure. I thought he also feared a negative press reaction. From that point on, I again set my own timetable, although it was clear between us that I was leaving and my office would be downgraded after I left."[110]

Initially, Klein planned to tender his resignation at the end of April 1973. Hours before he was to do so, Ziegler called and asked him to hold his announcement because of major developments that were brewing.[111] Those developments—related to Watergate—were the resignations of both H. R. Haldeman and John Ehrlichman. As a result, Klein decided to postpone his resignation. In a memo to Nixon dated 23 April 1973, Klein wrote:

> As you know, I earlier sent a memorandum to Bob Haldeman requesting a meeting with you for the purpose of discussing my resignation and forthcoming relationship with Metromedia. . . .
>
> Because of recent events, I have felt that it is of mutual interest to postpone the resignation temporarily. . . .
>
> Despite personal pressures, I do not feel it would be good for me to resign at a time when it would appear that one of your longest associates was deserting. . . .
>
> In a personal way, I do not want to be associated with any wrong doing if there has been some.
>
> I want to leave for the personal reasons you know about, and have made arrangements to do so, but I feel more that the need for loyalty during a crisis is great, and stand on this issue just as I always have.[112]

In the coming days, Klein and Ziegler drafted a memorandum to the president urging him to follow a plan of openness to counteract the Watergate debacle. They suggested that he be conciliatory and hold a televised conversation with network anchormen in which he would tell them what he knew about Watergate. They further suggested that he follow that up with a news conference and a series of meetings with columnists, television commentators, and other journalists. Needless to say, those suggestions were not followed.[113]

Finally, on 5 June 1973, Klein and Nixon exchanged letters concerning

Klein's resignation. Although it was supposed to be effective 1 July, Klein did not actually leave his office until the end of the month. With the waves of Watergate revelations and resignations, Klein's departure gave observers something good to look back on in the Nixon years. Congressmen—Gerald R. Ford of Michigan among them—stood up on the House floor to pay tribute to Klein.[114] And throughout the country, small articles appeared in the press bidding Klein farewell. Among the most poignant was one by Hugh Sidey in *Time* magazine. "His is a rather remarkable story," Sidey wrote of Klein.

> He was, these last years, abused and downgraded and ignored by Nixon and his supermen and yet he has remained loyal, kept his honor, and goes off as one of the President's few remaining displays of decency and good humor.
>
> He wasn't as efficient as the iron man H. R. Haldeman. Herb Klein kept his files in his coat pocket or somewhere, and like most ex-reporters he ignored flow charts and organization tables. What he had was an understanding that democracy and its government are untidy and considerably inefficient, and there isn't a hell of a lot you can do about that without destroying their soul.
>
> Old Herb would listen to conflicting views, now and then admit mistakes had been made and accept phone calls from critics as well as friends. He always figured it was a big wide world out there and a lot of people had something to say. . . .
>
> Last year some of us were standing in the magnificent Hall of St. George in the Kremlin on the final day of Nixon's Moscow summit. All Russia's elite were there, cosmonauts and marshalls, diplomats and artists, the Politburo and the KGB agents. . . . As the President passed, there in view across the room was Herb Klein. He looked like he had slept in his suit, or maybe hadn't slept at all in those frantic days. But his face had the same kindly look, and there was a smile and a lot of pride and warmth beneath the surface. The thought occurred to us then, and again last week, that here was one of the few men around Nixon who gave more than he took.[115]

In an "exit interview" conducted by the National Archives in July 1973, Klein expressed pleasure with what he had accomplished in his job but admitted that he looked forward to a slower pace: "skin diving and playing a little golf and," he added with a laugh, "living longer."[116] Klein's last assignment in the White House was to canvass members of the administration and other opinion makers on the president's situation in the wake of the Watergate scandal. In his report, Klein wrote: "The feeling is that the President is not showing leadership. He must be forthright, and we cannot minimize the catastrophic nature of the situation." Even in August 1973, after formally leaving his post, Klein sent a plea to Nixon that the president "go on national television and give a full exposition of Watergate to the public."[117] But once again, Klein's "soft voice" was not heard.

THE CLAWSON ERA

Ken Wade Clawson came from a working-class family in Monroe, Michigan. He attended the University of Michigan but left before graduating to pursue a career in journalism when his wife became pregnant. He worked first for his hometown newspaper, the *Monroe Evening News*, then joined the *Toledo* (Ohio) *Blade* in 1963 as a labor reporter. He amazed his superiors at the *Blade* by cultivating such high-ranking labor sources as Teamsters President Jimmy Hoffa and United Auto Workers President Walter Reuther. During the 1966–67 academic year, Clawson was a Nieman Fellow at Harvard University (among those who wrote letters of recommendation for his fellowship application were both Hoffa and Reuther), and in 1968 he joined the *Washington Post* as an editor in charge of the congressional reporting staff. Three weeks after moving to Washington, his wife committed suicide. He later became the *Post*'s Justice Department reporter and then one of its White House reporters.[118]

Clawson was always ambitious. He once said that early in his career he had "wanted to be the youngest managing editor in history."[119] The CBS reporter Fred Graham (who covered the Justice Department at the same time Clawson did) later recalled that Clawson "cultivated the law-and-order, right-of-center major figures."[120] Clawson eventually came to the attention of Charles Colson, who saw the idea of placing Clawson in the Office of Communications as a major PR coup. By hiring Clawson, the president could tout the fact that a reporter from the *Washington Post*—Nixon's journalistic archnemesis—had been placed in an important White House position. In the fall of 1971, Colson, Fred Malek, and H. R. Haldeman began courting Clawson.[121] Haldeman offered him the deputy director of communications post in December 1971, but Clawson refused. In January he was approached by Nixon himself, and this time he accepted.[122] He joined the Office of Communications in February 1972 in the position that Jeb Magruder had once held. From the start, Clawson "was given control of Klein's department (while Klein kept the title),"[123] and by autumn Colson was making the case to Fred Malek for Clawson to assume Klein's title.

Ken Clawson very much wants to succeed Herb Klein if Klein leaves. Since you are shuffling the bodies around, I simply want to strongly urge that Clawson be put into this spot. Clearly he is the best man we have for it on the White House staff. He is totally loyal and given the right kind of staff, could handle it with great skill. Since you and I are the ones responsible for bringing Ken in, I hope we can follow this through, unless the Klein situation is unsurmountable.[124]

Ultimately, Colson got his wish, although Clawson did not actually assume the title "director of communications" until 30 January 1974—six months after Klein had left.[125] In part, the delay was related to a controversy over the "Battle of the Budget" that Clawson had orchestrated from the Office of Communications in the spring of 1973. That controversy centered on a 140-page document entitled "The Battle of the Budget, 1973," which Clawson distributed to cabinet officers and other presidential appointees. The document consisted of talking points and other information that had been compiled during the preparation of the president's budget for fiscal year 1974 (FY-74). The material was meant to be used in speeches and other public statements by administration officials. Clawson described it as "a resource document" giving administration officials "an ability to explain to the public the President's position on the FY-74 Budget."[126] Forty to fifty copies of the document were prepared and distributed by the Office of Communications. An additional two hundred copies were prepared and distributed by the Republican National Committee to surrogate speakers around the country.[127]

"The Battle of the Budget" consisted of thirteen sections, including a sample speech, a collection of anecdotes and one-liners, and various "horror stories" that could be used against fifteen government programs that the president had targeted for cutbacks.[128] The document was distributed on 3 April, and the next day the *Washington Post* carried a story about it.[129] The Watergate revelations had created an intense suspicion of executive branch activities. Immediately after the budget story broke, Senators Edmund M. Muskie (Dem.-Maine) and Hubert H. Humphrey (Dem.-Minn.) ordered an investigation by the General Accounting Office (GAO) to determine if the White House had violated laws prohibiting the use of appropriated funds for lobbying or other "propaganda purposes designed to support or defeat legislation in Congress."[130] In addition, Ralph Nader's "Public Citizen" group filed a civil suit against Clawson seeking to prevent the Office of Communications from "continuing to carry out at public expense a massive publicity campaign designed to influence the passage of certain legislation pending before Congress."[131] The GAO report concluded that laws had been violated. As a result of the GAO report and the Nader suit, the Office of Communications recalled "The Battle of the Budget" in May 1973.[132] The publicity was embarrassing to both Clawson and the White House.

The delay in giving Klein's title to Clawson may also have been related to Clawson's close ties to Colson. According to one Washington journalist: "Clawson took to Colson like a duck to water. He once said that the only difference between him and Colson was that when Colson was faced with a problem, he would set off a charge of dynamite under it, whereas Ken's approach was to set off the dynamite two miles away to divert attention."[133] According to another journalist: "Clawson has always tried to play the role of Colson. He talks about Colson admiringly and at great length."[134] But with Watergate accusations swirling around the White House and Charles Colson, it was a bad time for such admiration to be known. Many reporters felt that Clawson was merely a "front" for Colson.[135] In fact, Clawson was close to Colson even after Colson left the White House. Colson recalls that Clawson "used to call me for advice a lot, and he still continued to lean on me a great deal after I left the White House—until Watergate and I became a defendant [laughs]. But we were still friends."[136]

Still, it is probably fair to say that the turbulence of the times aggravated the media's negative impression of Clawson. Klein later admitted that Clawson "could be tough almost in a Colson fashion," but he added that Clawson had "judgement."[137] Larry Speakes, who worked under Clawson in the Office of Communications and later served as press secretary under Ronald Reagan, says that Clawson served as "a lightning rod" to draw negative attention away from other parts of the White House.[138] But there were damaging accusations against Clawson. For instance, the *Washington Post* reported that Clawson had once told the reporter Marilyn Berger that he had written the "Canuck Letter"—a missive that was sent to William Loeb's right-wing newspaper the *Manchester Union Leader* during the New Hampshire presidential primary campaign in 1972 as a "dirty trick." The letter said that the Democratic candidate Edmund Muskie had used the derogatory term *Canuck* to refer to French-Canadians.[139] Muskie responded to the "Canuck Letter," as well as to allegations that had been made against his wife, from the back of a flatbed truck parked in front of the *Union Leader* building during a near blizzard on 26 February 1972. During the speech, Muskie called Loeb a "gutless coward" and reportedly broke into tears. Many observers felt that this incident played a major role in preventing Muskie from capturing the Democratic presidential nomination. Clawson repeatedly denied the *Post* report that he had authored the "Canuck Letter" and had thereby contributed to Muskie's downfall. He later said that he had told Berger, "I *wish* I'd written that!"[140] In either case, Clawson's credibility was tainted.

Originally, the president had planned to put the Office of Communications under the jurisdiction of Ron Ziegler and the Press Office when Klein resigned. But because of Watergate and the furor in the media over Ziegler's "misstatements" concerning the affair, that change did not take place. Instead, Clawson reported directly to the president's new chief of staff, Alexander Haig.[141]

As director of communications, Clawson made an effort to pacify the suspicions of the news media and tried to revive some of the access to administration officials that Klein had achieved at the outset of his tenure. In so doing, he established what came to be known as "Cocktails with Clawson." These were cozy question-and-answer sessions in which fifteen or twenty reporters chatted with Clawson and top administration officials over chips, dip, and drinks in Clawson's EOB office or its counterpart at the president's retreat in San Clemente, California. By the time Nixon resigned, Clawson had sponsored eighty-nine such sessions.[142] All were on the record and by invitation only. Some reporters, such as the *New York Times* Washington bureau chief Clifton Daniel, said that the sessions were "very, very useful." Daniel added, "I wish we were invited to every one of them."[143] Others scoffed and refused to attend, pointing out that the purpose of the sessions was to divert attention from Watergate. Larry Speakes said that "Cocktails with Clawson" was an attempt to show that the government was still functioning despite Watergate. Especially in the final months of the Nixon administration, the sessions were also an attempt to provide briefings outside the briefing room because "the atmosphere over in the West Wing [of the White House] had become so acrimonious that you could not do business there. It was just a cat fight every day in the briefing room."[144]

In those final days of the Nixon administration, the Office of Communications was divided into two sections. One—the "Government as Usual" team—orchestrated things like "Cocktails with Clawson" to show that the administration was running normally. It also continued some of the functions of the old Klein office, such as distributing op-ed pieces by administration officials and maintaining liaison with departments and agencies. The administration hoped to divert attention from Watergate in any way it could, and Speakes says that one person in the Office of Communications served as what Clawson called "the leak, plant, peddle, push man," trying to get the administration line out.[145]

The other section, called the "Watergate" team, was used to defend Nixon from Watergate charges.[146] Increasingly, the Office of Communications degenerated into a "political assault vehicle" used to orchestrate a PR counteroffensive to media reports on Watergate.[147] The office scheduled surrogate speakers to go around the country and defend Nixon. Such speakers included Rabbi Baruch Korff, the founder and president of the National Citizens Committee for Fairness to the President, and Nixon's daughter Julie.[148] Although Vice President Gerald Ford also made speeches in which he defended Nixon, Ford said that they were mostly scheduled unilaterally by his own office. Increasingly, the relations between his vice-presidential staff and the president's staff were strained. Nixon's team "didn't give us much credibility," Ford said, adding, "The White House hierarchy *really* looked upon us as sort of a stepchild." Ford pointed out that he had worked with the Office of Communications some when he was a congressman. He added: "[Klein] was a long-time very close personal friend . . . about the only one [around Nixon] that I really felt comfortable with. He was and is an outstanding person."[149]

Larry Speakes says that by May 1974, the Clawson crew also tried to provide somebody every day to go on television to "get the Watergate line out." As Nixon's resignation drew nearer, it was harder and harder to find people to do that. Speakes recalls that he got Dean Burch, the White House liaison to the Republican National Committee, to make such appearances a few times but that Burch "was absolutely *deathly* afraid of talking about [Watergate]." Speakes laughs, "You'd have to *push* him out there, you know—he'd dig his heels in."[150] One day when absolutely no one could be found, Clawson suggested that Speakes ask Father John McLaughlin, a former Jesuit priest who served as a sort of White House liaison to some religious and conservative groups, to make an appearance on the north lawn of the White House. This was the first time they had trotted him out before the cameras, and McLaughlin loved it. He was—and is—a bombastic figure (he has gone on to have some fame with his televised "McLaughlin Group"), and he made an impassioned argument that there was nothing immoral about Nixon's profanity in the edited transcripts of Watergate conversations released by the White House. As Nora Ephron later wrote, in his comments McLaughlin "invoked St. Paul, George Washington, the Judeo-Christian heritage, and the February American Bar Association *Journal*. Reporters left the briefing incredulous—one of them said afterwards that it was the first time in five years that he had longed for the comparatively clear logic of Ron Ziegler."[151] The next morning, Speakes saw a mob of reporters outside McLaughlin's EOB office. Having enjoyed the spotlight the day before, McLaughlin had now sought the cameras out on his own. Clawson was horrified. He ran to the office of Dick Moore, an old Nixon hand who had discovered McLaughlin and had brought him to the White House, and told Moore what McLaughlin was doing. "My god," Moore responded, "he's a monster and I created him!"[152]

Nixon himself used regional question-and-answer sessions to bypass the Washington press corps with increasing regularity after his notorious White House press conference of 26 October 1973, in which he lashed out at the press, saying: "I have never heard or seen such outrageous, vicious, distorted reporting in 27 years of public life. . . . [W]hen people are pounded night after night with that kind of frantic, hysterical reporting, it naturally shakes their confidence." In response to a question from Robert Pierpoint of CBS, who asked what it was about media coverage of Watergate that so angered him, Nixon replied: "Don't get the impression that you arouse my anger. . . . You see, one can only be angry with those he respects."[153]

Nixon's most infamous remark during his regional question-and-answer sessions was made before the Associated Press Managing Editors Association at Disney World in Orlando, Florida, on 17 November 1973. The appearance was part of Nixon's "Operation Candor." It was during this visit to Disney's world of make-believe that Nixon declared: "I am not a crook."[154] Similar sessions were subsequently held in Chicago and Houston.

The Office of Communication's mailing operation was also used to support Nixon during Watergate. One such mailing included five pages of quotations from members of the House Judiciary Committee, which was looking into the possible impeachment of Nixon. The quotations implied that the committee was biased against the president.[155] As late as June 1974—less than two months before Nixon was forced to resign—Clawson denounced Democrats on the House Judiciary Committee as "a clique of Nixon-hating partisans" who were engaging in a "witch hunt." He also called for the resignation of Representative Peter W. Rodino (Dem.-N.J.) as the committee's chairman.[156]

In the final days of the administration, Clawson's team closely followed the televised hearings of the Rodino committee as it debated and voted on articles of impeachment against the president. Clawson set up a room in the EOB that contained three television sets (one for each of the major networks) and two radios. Insiders called it the "Impeachment Room," but the sign on the door read "Office of Communications, Research Division."[157] There the impeachment hearings were monitored by Larry Speakes, the speechwriter Ken Khachigian, and Jack McCahill, one of Nixon's lawyers. The three men drafted rejoinders to statements and charges that were made by members of the committee. "We had immediate responses to the president's enemies down to a science," Clawson later wrote. "The responses were immediately dictated to Bill Timmon's congressional liaison staff in a room near the Judiciary Committee hearing room, and those responses would be delivered to friends on the Rodino committee to be used in defense of the president. Sometimes they were used and sometimes they weren't."[158] Speakes says that the operation was designed as a trial run for handling the floor debate on impeachment in the House of Representatives. He adds, however, that the Rodino committee rules made life difficult: "A member of the committee could only [speak] for a few minutes at a time. So if a Democratic congressman made a point and we felt it was wrong, by the time we developed a response the [allotted time] had gone from the Democrat to a Republican, and back to another Democrat, and there was no chance to get our response in. That taught us that we would have to streamline our operation before they began impeachment proceedings on the House floor."[159]

Needless to say, the glory days of good relations between the Office of Communications and the press were gone. Dan Rather, a correspondent for CBS News, called Clawson the leader of the White House "goon squad."[160] But Clawson thought Rather had it backwards. To him, the *media* was the goon squad. Clawson frequently complained of the media's biased reporting, talking to any journalists who would listen.[161] He even kept a file to support Nixon's allegation that the media engaged in vicious and distorted reporting. He spoke of the file frequently but never showed it to anyone.[162] He excoriated what he called the "Watergate syndrome," which was "a propensity to believe anything without thorough research and checking almost anything." He accused the Washington press corps of being "possessed" by that syndrome. "An exorcist is direly needed," Clawson said in exasperation. "God knows that the people who engage in that kind of crap need an exorcist."[163]

OPERATIONAL STAFF AND POLICY

S trictly speaking, the Office of Communications under Nixon was not a policy-making body. An organization chart prepared in 1970 shows two distinct tiers of White House staff. The *policy* staff included John Ehrlichman (assistant for domestic affairs), Henry Kissinger (assistant for national security affairs), and their respective staffs. Distinct from them was the *operational* staff, which included the Office of Communications, the Press Office, the Research and Writing staff, the Office of Congressional Relations, H. R. Haldeman and his deputies, and the special counsels to the president (including Harry Dent, Charles Colson, Murray Chotiner, and Clark Mollenhoff).[164]

Although operational staff was responsible for implementing rather than making policy, such staff made it possible for the president to actively pursue policy goals. In short, operational staff represented the institutionalization of the modern presidency. It made a White House–centered system of government possible. Thus, the White House used the Office of Communications as a means of strengthening the president's policy-making position vis-à-vis other governmental elites and even as a means of coercing those other elites to accept presidential policy leadership.

The Office of Communications had the potential to be a particularly effective tool of presidential power, since it could be used to increase the president's *internal* as well as *external* control over the policy-making process. It could be used to strengthen internal control of policy-making by giving the president a means of influencing which departmental policies would be publicized and what sort of "spin" would be put on that publicity. At the same time, it could be used to strengthen external control of the policy-making process by giving the president a means to rally public support for his programs. Such external support could then be used to persuade legislators to enact particular presidential policies.

As Jules Witcover wrote in 1970, the Office of Communications originally was a "rather loose superstructure."[165] Its aim was to coordinate information from the various departments, not to dictate how their individual press offices were to be run. But as the Office of Communications became more politicized, it became more inclined to dictate information policy. That shift from coordination to control reflected Nixon's reactions to the political climate of his first term. As we saw in chapter 2, Nixon faced a divided nation, a Congress that was controlled by the opposition party, a bureaucracy that he felt opposed his conservative agenda, and a press that was increasingly willing to question governmental authority. As a result, Nixon felt that his policies were thwarted at every turn.

In February 1970, Haldeman wrote Klein a memo saying that they must publicize the "great handicaps under which [Nixon] came into office—specifically, the hostile press epitomized by the *New York Times, Washington Post, Time, Newsweek*, etc., the hostile network commentators, the generally hostile White House press corps, the hostile Congress, etc."[166] Among these handicaps was what Nixon perceived to be a "Democrat-infested" federal bureaucracy[167]—a "damngovernment," as he called it, run by "damnbureaucrats."[168] As Nixon's first term progressed, he became increasingly anxious to assert control over the bureaucracy. By 1970, White House "working groups"—under the supervision of John Ehrlichman—were used to influence legislative proposals coming out of the departments. One of the earliest of these working groups was used to influence welfare policy coming out of the Department of Health, Education, and Welfare and was headed by one of Ehrlichman's assistants, Edward L. Morgan, Jr. As Richard P. Nathan has written: "The welfare working group met five to six hours a day every day over a period of ten weeks. Direct relationships were established between White House staff and agency officials well below the level of Secretary. Only the most astute cabinet member could keep on top of this policy process."[169]

Besides welfare policy, working groups dealt with "emergency labor disputes, model cities, urban-growth policy, health, revenue sharing, education, social services, and transportation."[170] The use of such working groups marked a significant change in the traditional relationship between the White House and federal departments. As John Iglehart wrote: "Presidents have always exerted some legislative initiative, particularly in areas where they have had a personal interest or when the subject has been especially sensitive. But the departments and agencies usually have developed their own legislative recommendations; the White House normally has entered the picture to approve or disapprove their proposals."[171] Through working groups, legislative recommendations became the province of the White House.

After his landslide reelection in 1972, Nixon made even more serious attempts to control the executive branch from the White House. As Harold Seidman has written:

> The bureaucracy was neutralized and isolated by (1) leaving major departments "headless" by co-opting the secretaries as assistants to the president and White House counselors, thus preventing "capture" by the natives; (2) depriving it of resources through revenue sharing and impoundment; and (3) cutting lines of communication by interposing regional councils under White House and OMB control between departments and their agents in the field. The departments were to be allowed to wither away with the White House assuming direct operational responsibility.[172]

The Office of Communications was sometimes used as a part of the White House battle to control the departments. By 1970, when Magruder joined the office, such tactics had become more commonplace. For instance, cabinet officials were viewed by the president as useful spokesmen for the administration. As a result, the Office of Communications was used to get cabinet members to deliver speeches, drafted by the White House, on matters of concern to the president. According to Magruder, cabinet members often found it to be a "rude awakening" when he called to announce, "Mr. Secretary, we're sending over this speech that we'd like you to deliver." But as Magruder observed, "That was how it was."[173] The president's desire that cabinet members promote the interests of the White House rather than the interests of their departments was made very clear in a memorandum from Haldeman to Klein, dated 19 April 1970.

> We've got to do a better job of using Cabinet Members as Administration spokesmen. We're getting them around to the various speaking opportunities very well apparently but we're not getting over to them adequately the necessity for them to recognize that *their job is to sell the Administration, not themselves or their departments.* I know that we provide them with [speech] material from Keogh, etc. that's designed towards this end, but *we've got to do more direct indoctrination that will*

result in a stronger selling attitude on the part of each of our speakers.[174]
(emphasis added)

For the departments to sell the administration rather than themselves, it was also important that their public information officers be responsive to the White House. From the start, Nixon feared that too many career press officers in the departments had been "captured by the natives." He expressed that concern in the margin of his "Daily News Summary" of 1 December 1969. Next to the summary of an article dealing with Vietnam, Nixon wrote: "This shows why Defense should reduce P.R. staffs. These guys are oriented the other way."[175] That month—at the direction of the White House—the Budget Bureau ordered a 10 percent reduction in public relations budgets throughout the executive branch, to be completed by June 1971. That meant a cut of some $10 million and the elimination of five hundred jobs. The cuts appear to have been a move by Nixon to gain more control over the press offices of the departments and agencies. Although the Office of Communications kept in daily contact with the ranking information officers in the departments and major agencies, such officers were ultimately responsible to their department and agency heads— not to the Office of Communications. Further compounding the problem for Nixon was the fact that even when ranking information officers were political appointees (as they were in the departments, as opposed to the agencies), they did not always wield real power over their own press and public affairs operations. As Dom Bonafede explained, many of those subordinate offices were "run by officials shielded by civil service."[176] That is why Nixon felt that cuts among this group would ultimately increase the power of the ranking departmental information officer and would thus increase the power of the White House.

Stephen Hess has suggested that the common White House perception that career personnel are against the interests of the White House and its departmental appointees is mistaken. He argues that suspicious political executives fail "to make a sufficient distinction between staff and line operations. Press officers perform a services function, and as staff officers they wish to develop special relationships with the supervisors on whom they must depend for advancement." Hess went on to provide an example from the Food and Drug Administration: "As the FDA press chief, a career employee, said of the FDA commissioner, a political appointee, 'the commissioner is the personification of the agency. Most of my job is to get a good press for the commissioner.' "[177]

Yet that seems to be exactly what Nixon was trying to prevent. He did not want "good press for the commissioner." That could give the commissioner an exaggerated sense of self-importance or provide him with a base of public opinion that could lead him away from White House control. What Nixon wanted was good press for the *administration*. What Nixon may have failed to recognize was that good press for the commissioner could be tantamount to good press for the administration.

Whether or not it was justified, the Nixon White House harbored a suspicion of all career bureaucrats. For instance, a White House "Talking Paper" on the IRS noted: "In brief, the lack of key Republican bureaucrats at high levels precludes the initiation of policies which would be proper and politically advantageous. Practically every effort is met with resistance, delay, and the threat of derogatory exposure."[178] That suspicion was reflected in Nixon's attempt to change substantially the relationship between the White House and the rest of the executive branch in the wake of his landslide reelection. Part of that attempt included a plan to replace career public information officers in executive agencies with White House appointees. As Joseph Spear has written:

> In various federal agencies the careerists were demoted to second-in-command positions, instructed to handle routine chores, and told to refer sensitive inquiries to their new bosses. All of the replacements possessed sound Republican credentials. The public relations director for the CRP Ann L. Dore, for example, was appointed to the top information position at the Environmental Protection Agency. Another top CRP press officer, Arthur L. Amolsch, was named director of public information at the Federal Trade Commission.[179]

Ken Clawson was very active in that endeavor. Indeed, that was his top priority from November 1972 through January 1973. He also worked to replace political appointees that Klein had chosen. He was reported to have said that many of Klein's choices were "not competent." In fact, the aim of Nixon's post-1972 efforts was to reduce the time that the Office of Communications would have to spend battling various public information offices to get them to follow the administration line. For instance, in 1970 the Office of Communications had waged a battle over the release of unemployment figures by the Bureau of Labor Statistics. The White House wanted the bureau to manipulate the statistics so as to stress the fact that the number of people holding jobs was at an all-time high (because of an expanding job market), even though the rate of unemployment did not drop. The Bureau of Labor Statistics, which had always released monthly figures indicating the unemployment rate alone, evidently felt that to accede to the White House demands would be misleading. Nonetheless, the White House eventually got its way. As a result, network newscasts began to cite the increasing number of jobs as well as the rate of unemployment.[180]

Similarly, the White House pressured the FBI to rewrite a press release dealing with crime statistics. The FBI wanted to stress the negative—that the national crime rate was up—to get more money from Congress to fund its fight against crime. The White House, on the other hand, wanted to show that the administration was achieving success in its "War on Crime." Therefore, the Office of Communications persuaded the FBI to stress two positive statistics in the lead of its press release—one indicating that violent crime had decreased, and the other that the crime rate in larger cities had decreased. As Magruder wrote, the change was an important one:

> Any reporter who wanted to play up the bad news was free to, but we knew that many reporters would follow the style of the press release. It was not an inconsequential matter. If the wire service followed our lead, newspapers across the country would be headlined "Violent Crime Drops" or "Crime Down in Big Cities." And those headlines would suggest to millions of Americans that the Nixon Administration was keeping its promise to do something about crime.[181]

On one occasion, Nixon even used the Office of Communications to discredit the Federal Reserve Board chairman Arthur Burns, who had been promoting policy that the president disagreed with. For months, Burns had been pushing the idea of establishing a wage and price control board as a way of fighting inflation. Nixon disagreed, but Burns persisted. He even testified in favor of it on Capitol Hill in February 1971. According to John Ehrlichman, Nixon ordered H. R. Haldeman to call Burns. "Tell him that the President is furious. . . . Say I'm hurt and distressed, and when [Burns] asks for a meeting, say 'The President is unavailable.' "[182] On 8 March, Nixon drafted a memo to Haldeman. He said that he had seen Burns at the White House church service that day and that Burns had requested a meeting. Nixon instructed Haldeman to drag his feet in setting it up. "I have begun taking a hard line with [Burns],"

Nixon wrote.[183] Around that time, Nixon brought up the Burns problem in one of his daily meetings with Ehrlichman. "He's still pushing that goddamned wage-price board," Ehrlichman recalls Nixon as saying. "He knows the President opposes it, but he continues to leak it and advocate it. He can't have it both ways. . . . We've been very good to Arthur; no one has taken on the Fed— yet. But I'm going to, by God."[184] In March, Ehrlichman delivered a message to Burns that Nixon was deeply disappointed in him and felt that his actions were "disloyal."[185] But the feud went on.

The controversy reached a head in July, during a cruise on the presidential yacht *Sequoia*. Among those on board that evening were the president, Colson, Budget Director Caspar Weinberger, and National Security Advisor Henry Kissinger. They were on the upper deck drinking cocktails, and Nixon turned to Colson and suggested that he leak a fabricated story that Burns was seeking a twenty-thousand-dollar salary increase for himself while simultaneously calling for a wage-price board. The point was to discredit Burns by making him look hypocritical. Colson now says that he thought Nixon's idea was a bad one because it was not true. He says he told Haldeman so the next day. According to Colson, "Haldeman chewed my ear off. He said, 'You've got an order to do that. The President knows exactly what he wants. Do it.' "[186] Haldeman does not recall the conversation with Colson. "He may be right, because I don't have a specific memory of the conversation," Haldeman says. But he adds that if Colson is right, he told Colson to do it for some reason other than that the president had simply said, during the *Sequoia* cruise, that it should be done. "I spent a lot more time *not* blindly following out the president's orders than Colson," Haldeman says.[187]

Whatever the precise details, Colson called DeVan Shumway—one of Klein's deputies in the Office of Communications—and told him to leak the story to the press. Shumway recalls that he told Colson, "This is crazy." According to Shumway, Colson replied, "Nope, we've gotta do it. The President wants it done." Klein was out of town, and Shumway tried to resist. Shumway quotes Colson as saying: "I know you don't want to do it and I didn't want to either, but it absolutely has to be done and you're the one that can do it."[188] Finally Shumway relented. So, on 27 July 1971, Shumway called Albert Hunt, an economic reporter for the *Wall Street Journal*, and told him that the president was "furious" with Burns. Shumway said that the position that Burns was taking on the wage-price board was hypocritical because of his own demands for a pay raise. Shumway also leaked the story to Norman Kempster of the UPI wire service.[189] In fact, Burns had proposed a 10 percent *cut* in the salary of all administration officials—himself included.[190] The leak backfired. "I tried to make no tracks to the White House," Shumway says, "but Al Hunt apparently dropped it—meaning that he screwed up and made it so that almost immediately there were not only tracks to the White House, but tracks to me. Norm Kempster denied that he ever let anybody know the source of it." Although the presidential speechwriter William Safire later wrote that Cap Weinberger had no recollection of Nixon's suggestion to Colson on the *Sequoia*, Shumway says that Kempster confirmed the Burns story with Weinberger before publishing it.[191]

Klein was irate about the leak, as was Safire.[192] The press, realizing that it had been duped, raised a storm of protest. Nixon was forced to issue a statement denying that Burns had requested a pay raise and calling Burns " 'the most responsible and statesmanlike' Fed chairman in memory."[193] In the end, Nixon adopted wage and price controls. Strategies to defuse the power of administration opponents do not always work.[194]

As they did with public opinion, hard-liners on the White House staff sometimes pushed the Office of Communications over the line that separates legitimate appeals for support within the executive branch from illegitimate tactics to induce it. Likewise, hard-liners sometimes politicized the Office of Communications and used it to discredit opponents. The Arthur Burns incident is an excellent example. Van Shumway was a decent man who was talked into doing something that he shouldn't have done. "It's one of those incidents that keeps coming back to haunt you," Shumway says. "I think I had good judgment when left to my own devices." According to Shumway, the incident is an example of how the Office of Communications "got off track." "I think Colson's influence in the Office of Communications was a nefarious influence," Shumway says. "Colson wanted to do a lot of really stupid things. And whether he wanted them or Nixon wanted them or Haldeman wanted them, I don't know, but they were *dumb* ideas." He adds: "I think with Herb and some reasonable people the Office of Communications made a lot of sense. The concept [of the office] was a good one. But it was misused by the Colsons of the world, or by Haldeman, or maybe by Nixon himself. Herb could have done it right, but Herb didn't move fast enough for those folks. Herb wanted to use judgment and not just say, 'Yes sir,' and salute and go forward."[195]

Despite its excesses—and even despite the fact that Watergate prevented Nixon from gaining the degree of control over the executive branch that he had hoped to achieve in his second term—the Office of Communications played an important role in the implementation of presidential policy. As an internal coordinator of information policy and an external molder of public opinion, it was a weapon of considerable strength.

CHAPTER FIVE

THE FORD YEARS

DECLINE AND RESURGENCE

Gerald R. Ford assumed the presidency under extraordinary circumstances. Watergate had taken its toll on the American psyche. It had also taken its toll on the Office of Communications and on presidential-press relations in general. Press briefings had degenerated into out-and-out verbal warfare, and Ken Clawson's communications operation had degenerated into a mechanism for warding off Watergate charges and waging public relations attacks on Nixon's opponents.[1]

President Ford immediately set out to heal the wounds. In his first public remarks as president, Ford assured the American people that he would follow his "instincts of openness and candor."[2] Later, one of his first instructions to the cabinet was to open government to the media and the public.[3] Ford also wanted to decentralize the power that Nixon had accumulated in the White House. As he later wrote: "A Watergate was made possible by a strong chief of staff and ambitious White House aides who were more powerful than members of the Cabinet but who had little or no practical political experience or judgment. I wanted to reverse the trend and restore authority to my Cabinet." Ford added that White House aides did not, in his opinion, have "the right to browbeat the departments and agencies. Nor did they have the right to make policy decisions."[4] Thus, Ford initially adopted a very decentralized approach to governing.

Ford also wanted to restore a good relationship between the White House and the media. Shortly before Nixon's resignation, Ford decided to name

Jerald F. terHorst as his press secretary when he became president. TerHorst was then the Washington bureau chief of the *Detroit News*. He had known Ford since the 1940s when Ford was a young attorney and terHorst was a young reporter in Grand Rapids, Michigan.[5]

Both Ford and terHorst were anxious to distance themselves from the Nixon approach to presidential-press relations. They wanted to depoliticize the public information arm of the White House and restore a professional relationship with the press. The result, Ford said, was that they were "not too concerned about [conveying] a rigid line or a specific message." He added, "We wanted to create the impression of an open administration in contrast to that of my predecessor."[6] That assessment is echoed by terHorst, who says that the early Ford administration was not very "programmatic" in its relationship with the media. Instead, it made every effort to provide an atmosphere of openness, to put Watergate behind it, and to make the American people believe in their president again. "That was our aegis—our reason for being," terHorst says.[7] But that aegis provided terHorst with something of a dilemma. Local media had grown accustomed to the services that the Office of Communications had initiated under Herb Klein's direction. Furthermore, President Ford wanted to maintain close ties to that constituency. "We didn't want to become a captive of the Washington press corps," Ford says. "We wanted to get our story to the local press and not be totally surrounded by the Washington press."[8] Yet the new administration was under pressure to abolish the Office of Communications—the administration's link to that constituency—because of the negative reputation it had developed near the end of the Nixon administration.

By the time Nixon resigned, the Office of Communications had developed three primary functions. First, it served as a liaison with non-Washington-based media. Second, it served as a means of coordinating the flow of information from the entire executive branch, thus providing a mechanism for centralized White House control of information policy in the departments and agencies. And third, it served as a political tool for generating public support for administration initiatives. President Ford wanted to maintain the first function but hoped to curtail—if not eliminate—the other two. The second function, when used to exercise tight control of information policy, ran counter to Ford's decentralized approach to cabinet government. TerHorst maintained PIO liaison under his jurisdiction, but the emphasis was on coordination, not control. The third function, which smacked of "the selling of the presidency," was dropped altogether. TerHorst felt that such activities did not belong in the

White House. He asked Republican National Committee Chairman George Bush if the RNC wanted to incorporate Clawson and his more political activities under its domain. Thinking back on that exchange, terHorst laughed and said that Bush's response was a quick, "Thanks, but no thanks."[9]

In fact, Clawson understood that he had to leave. According to terHorst, Clawson was "one of the few, to tell the truth, who understood that the guard had changed and that it was time to move on." Terhorst adds, "I give that to Ken's credit."[10] TerHorst then dismantled the formal structure of the Office of Communications. At the direction of President Ford, he subsumed all media outreach and public information functions under the Press Office. Thus he retained some of the core responsibilities of the Office of Communications—"the original Herb Klein format," as he put it, of "providing information [and] genuine outreach"—but he put those responsibilities in the hands of deputy press secretaries who were accountable to him and who would not draw attention to themselves.[11] Just three weeks after Ford assumed the presidency, terHorst outlined the new structure in a letter to a constituent:

> The Office of Communications which Herb Klein and Ken Clawson headed is no longer a separate entity, but the functions it filled are being continued under my direction. I've split the responsibilities between Paul Miltich [Ford's press secretary when he was House minority leader and vice president] and Jim Holland [deputy director of the Office of Communications under Clawson] who are Assistant Press Secretaries and who report to me.[12]

TerHorst never had a chance to see his plans come to full fruition. On 8 September 1974—just one month after taking office—President Ford granted Nixon a "full, free, and absolute pardon," and terHorst resigned in protest. On 20 September, Ford introduced his new press secretary, Ronald H. Nessen—an NBC News reporter who had been promoted to White House correspondent when Ford became president. Standing before the White House press corps with the president at his side, Nessen declared: "I am a Ron, but not a Ziegler. . . . I will never knowingly lie to the White House press corps. I will never knowingly mislead the White House press corps, and I think if I ever do you would be justified in questioning my continued usefulness in this job."[13]

In the coming weeks, Nessen tried to sort out the personnel and operations of the Press Office. During the transition, virtually all parts of the White House faced such problems. There were holdovers from the Nixon administration, holdovers from Ford's vice-presidential and congressional staffs, and some newcomers. As a newcomer, Nessen had to decide who should remain in the Press Office and how it should be structured. Particular care had to be taken to win back the confidence of the press corps after its stormy relationship with the White House under Nixon.

By the end of October, Nessen had made decisions about two high-ranking holdovers from the Nixon administration. He decided (with Ford's blessing) to keep Gerald L. Warren, who had been deputy press secretary under Ziegler, but he requested the resignation of Jim Holland, who had been assigned by terHorst to work with Paul Miltich in carrying out the functions of the old Office of Communications.[14] Like terHorst, Nessen decided to keep the functions of the Office of Communications under the supervision of the Press Office. In a "Talking Paper" dated 17 October, Nessen made it clear that he wanted to maintain "an office with clearly defined responsibilities for the conduct of our internal coordination of public affairs activities within the Executive Branch agencies and the external contact with the press outside Washington." Although that is exactly what the Office of Communications had done, Nessen was wary of the partisan reputation that the old office had acquired. He made it clear that he did not want to "infuse any of the more overt political aspects" of the old office into the new operation and also insisted that he wanted "to work out an appropriate title that would steer clear of the 'Director of Communications' title associated with the previous Klein and Clawson operations."[15]

Nessen chose Gerald Warren to be head of the new operation. Warren, whom Nessen described as "a slim, mild pipe-smoker,"[16] was an old friend and protégé of Herb Klein's. Warren had worked with Klein at the *San Diego Union*, where he had progressed from trainee to city editor to assistant managing editor under Klein's supervision.[17] Later, he had joined the Nixon administration as deputy press secretary. Like Klein, Warren was well liked by the media. In the last months of the Nixon presidency, he had taken over, from Ronald Ziegler, the primary responsibility for briefing the press. Even in such trying times, Warren maintained his reputation. Like Klein, he was loyal to Nixon, but it was a loyalty tempered by conscience. On the day that Nixon announced his resignation, the UPI correspondent Helen Thomas walked into Warren's office and found him in tears.[18] Warren recently said that despite all the turmoil surrounding the Watergate investigations, Nixon's resignation had still come as a shock to him and other Nixon staffers.[19]

White House press briefings during those last months of the Nixon administration were a grueling experience. Larry Speakes, who had joined the Office of Communications on 17 March 1974, later wrote that Warren looked as if he was "at death's door" even though he was only forty-three years old:

He was worn out, he had lost a tremendous amount of weight, his clothes didn't fit, there was about an inch and a half between the collar of his shirt and his neck, and there were lines in his face. After Nixon resigned I really got to know Jerry, and one time he told me, "You know, there were a lot of times during Watergate when I would drive home after a long day of press briefings and I would drive up to a red light, and I would say to myself, 'You know, if I run that red light that car coming there will hit me and I'll be injured and I'll go to the hospital, but I won't have to brief tomorrow.' " Even to recall that gives me shivers about what a tough situation Jerry was in.[20]

Others recognized the tough situation as well. Dean Burch, chairman of the FCC under Nixon, sent Warren a picture with the inscription: "Ernest Hemingway wrote the measure of a man is grace under pressure. E.H. would have been proud indeed of the way in which you handled intolerable pressure."[21] Even President Ford, who as vice president was not always happy with Nixon staffers, says that he always retained his respect for Warren.[22] Warren recalls that when Nixon resigned, there were a few people from the Nixon staff that Ford "very kindly wrapped his big arms around and said, 'Take care of these people.' "[23] Warren was one of them. He initially served as a liaison between the Ford White House and Ron Ziegler, who was with the former president in San Clemente, California. He also helped terHorst and then Nessen "get the lay of the land," as he put it.[24] Then Nessen decided to put Warren in charge of the revamped communications office. In recommending Warren for his new post, Nessen praised Warren for "the highly professional manner" in which he had conducted press briefings in the final months of the Nixon administration. "Moreover," Nessen added, "he is held in high regard by the public affairs officers in the departments and agencies, and I feel sure they would respect his judgment and advice in matters regarding their operations."[25]

Nessen, however, had to confront Paul Miltich, who had made it clear that he wanted to be head of the reorganized communications office.[26] The situation was a sticky one for Nessen. Miltich had been Ford's press secretary since 1966 and felt that he deserved an important spot in the Press Office now that Ford was president. Nessen tried to smooth over the situation by putting Miltich in charge of various "special writing projects," including the briefing books that Ford used in preparation for press conferences, and various press-related correspondences (including mailings to editors and publishers). Miltich was also given general supervision over the preparation of the "Daily News Summary."[27] His title was "Special Assistant to the President for Public Affairs."

Nessen gave the real responsibility to Warren, who became "Deputy Press Secretary for Information Liaison" on 4 November 1974. Warren was responsible for meeting outside of Washington with local editors and publishers and for setting up regional briefings for local editorial boards. He was also put in charge of coordinating the public affairs programs of the agencies and departments and of overseeing the "Op-Ed Program"—previously the domain of Miltich—in which members of the administration wrote essays for publication in the editorial pages of newspapers throughout the country.[28] Both Warren and Miltich had offices on the first floor of the EOB.[29]

Nessen was increasingly unhappy with Miltich. In January 1975, Miltich's title was reduced to "Assistant Press Secretary to the President"—one of four such commissions.[30] A month later, Miltich announced that he had decided to accept a presidential appointment to the Postal Rate Commission. When he left, Warren took over responsibility for the functions that Miltich had performed.[31] As a result, Warren's operation inherited the "Daily News Summary," which Mort Allin and Pat Buchanan had prepared independently in the Nixon administration.

Warren wanted his operation to keep a low profile. "It certainly wasn't an office when I was there that wanted to draw any attention to itself," he says. Indeed, Warren points out that the operation did not have the importance that it might have had in the early part of the Ford administration. He says that he did not want to involve himself "in any turf wars or anything like that." He was "sort of lying low and doing what was necessary."[32]

In fact, Warren was eager to return to the *San Diego Union* and the less hectic duties of private life. As Larry Speakes put it, Warren's position "was sort of a holding action for Jerry until he concluded his deal with the Copley [newspaper chain]."[33] As a result, Warren recruited Margita White to join the communications operation as his assistant, with the understanding that he would leave in six months.[34] Warren says he had decided that he did not want to go through another campaign and he knew that his office "would *have* to be part of the next campaign in terms of research and tracking and dealing with editors and publishers around the country." He adds, "And so, one, I wanted a good deputy with a lot of credibility in Washington—and that certainly was Margita; and, two, I wanted someone who could take over and be comfortable and knowledgeable about running a campaign."[35]

White had served a similar role in the Office of Communications under Klein until March 1973, when she had become assistant director of the United States Information Agency. When Warren approached her about joining the Ford administration, she was hesitant but finally agreed after meeting with Ron Nessen on 19 December.[36] Recalling her feeling at the time, White said: "I thought long and hard, because there's something about going back that you don't want to do, and because personally I had been so demoralized by the whole Watergate situation. . . . But I finally decided to go back because I wanted to contribute. It sounds corny, but that's what I wanted to do. And I'm very glad I did because President Ford certainly helped restore my faith."[37] White joined the communications operation in January 1975. She and Warren soon built up the operation so that it closely resembled the office that Klein had originally established in 1969.

THE "NEW" OFFICE OF COMMUNICATIONS

Jerry Warren left his post in July 1975 and, according to plan, was succeeded by Margita White. One of the first things she did was to recommend to Ron Nessen that her operation be renamed the Office of Communications. She further recommended that her title be "Director of the Office of Communications" rather than "Director of Communications" as it had been under Nixon. It was a subtle distinction aimed at deflecting negative publicity about the office. Her recommendations were accepted, although the Office of Communications still remained under the jurisdiction of Nessen and the Press Office.

Nessen was enthusiastic about the Office of Communications. In a memo to Donald Rumsfeld, Ford's de facto chief of staff, Nessen wrote, "I believe Margita's operation has an even greater impact than my immediate office in creating favorable press and public responses to the President."[38] When Ford first became president, Pat Buchanan had made a similar remark about the importance of the Office of Communications in a memo to Jerry terHorst. He had said that an operation such as Herb Klein's was "most valuable" because through it, the White House could "get daily press and wire coverage moving around the country, taking the President's case directly into the editorial offices."[39]

After joining the White House, Nessen came under increasing fire from the press corps. Members of the press, in the wake of their experience with Nixon, were wary of any presidential press spokesman. Nessen later admitted that he aggravated his own problems with his quick temper and thin skin. His statement, "I am a Ron, but not a Ziegler," soon haunted him. He was outspoken in his criticism of the press, and he also developed a reputation as an "intriguer" against other members of the White House staff.[40] Part of his problem lay in the fact that President Ford's honeymoon with the media ended abruptly with the Nixon pardon. Ford soon earned the reputation of a bumbler, and many in the press openly questioned his ability to lead the nation.[41] Ford was at a special disadvantage because he faced the worst recession since the Great Depression of the 1930s, along with a White House staff that was especially prone to internal bickering and backstabbing. Between 16 August 1974 and 28 March 1975, Ford's approval rating plummeted from 71 to 37 percent. His disapproval rating shot up from 3 to 43 percent.[42]

By June 1975, Nessen's relations with the press had deteriorated badly. After lashing out at the press for its "blind, mindless, irrational suspicion and cynicism and distrust" of the White House, Nessen retreated to Camp David with his staff to try to improve press office procedures and come up with a strategy for mending fences with the media.[43] Among the topics discussed at the three "Press Office Improvement Meetings" at Laurel Lodge was how to improve Ford's image for the upcoming presidential election.[44]

Clearly, the rebuilding of the Office of Communications was a part of that effort to prepare for the 1976 election. One of the first things that Warren and White did in 1975 was to revitalize the use of direct mail. On 7 May 1975, Warren and William J. Baroody, Jr. (head of the Office of Public Liaison— Colson's old operation—which maintained links with special-interest groups), wrote in a memo to Don Rumsfeld that neither office utilized "an extensive mailing operation." The memo added, "There is a continuing effort to reach the key elements of our varied constituency, but limited resources preclude the contact and outreach our offices would prefer."[45] White helped to reinstitute regular mailings of fact sheets to broadcasters and editors, although she was careful to steer clear of charges of propagandizing. "The mailings are confined to issues of primary concern, such as economics and energy," she told an interviewer at the time. "We try to be helpful to editors who have access only to the wire services [by providing them with] substantive materials. We do not send out editorials."[46] On 21 November 1975, White sent the following memo to Ford's new chief of staff, Dick Cheney:

I have sent the following mailings within the past three weeks:

To 775 editors and editorial writers: the President's remarks and question and answer session before the National Press Club.

To 325 editorial writers: the President's remarks at the New England Council Conference.

To 60 editors of the Jewish press: the President's message to Rabbi Israel Miller on the occasion of the Rally Against Racism and Anti-Semitism and Ambassador Moynihan's speech before the UN.

To 350 editorial writers and group broadcasters: the President's message to Congress, a fact sheet on the motor carrier bill, a fact sheet on the President's overall regulatory reform proposals (group broadcasters only—editorial writers received this fact sheet in an earlier mailing) and the press briefing by Secretary Coleman, Paul MacAvoy, and Ed Schmults.

To 60 editors of the Jewish press: the President's statement, a fact sheet and a memorandum to heads of departments and agencies on foreign boycott practices and anti-discrimination policy.[47]

At the top of the memo, Cheney expressed his pleasure by boldly penning one word: "*good!*"

Warren and White also revitalized the practice of regional briefings sponsored by the Office of Communications. Among the most successful regional briefings were informal meetings between President Ford and local media executives, usually over breakfast or lunch. By April 1975, such meetings had been held in Atlanta, Houston, San Diego, South Bend (Indiana), and Hollywood (Florida).[48] In a memo entitled "President's press plan for the next year," dated 12 March 1975, Nessen wrote that he strongly believed the president should continue the regional breakfasts. "I've never seen him more effective than he is at these breakfasts."[49] White reiterated that feeling: "Stories, columns, and letters about the breakfast sessions refer repeatedly to the

President's forthrightness, sincerity, candor, informality, in-depth knowledge, concern with the gravity of the problems facing the nation, and determination to solve them."[50]

Warren had initiated a similar series of presidential briefings for media groups at the White House, and this was continued under White. A typical example was a briefing and luncheon held at the White House for the officers and board of the American Newspaper Publishers Association on 11 June 1975. The ANPA represented 95 percent of the daily newspaper circulation in the United States.[51] The aim of the Office of Communications was not only to provide the ANPA representatives with substantive information about administration policy but also to entertain them in royal fashion. They were picked up from their hotel by black Cadillac Fleetwood limousines at 9:00 A.M. and taken to the White House. There they were escorted through the northwest gate to the Roosevelt Room of the White House where they were greeted by Margita White who showed them to their seats around a long mahogany table. After they were served coffee in china cups bearing the presidential seal, Warren introduced the first speaker, L. William Seidman, assistant to the president for economic affairs. From then until 12:30, they were briefed in turn by Seidman, Ron Nessen, energy czar Frank Zarb, Council of Economic Advisors Chairman Alan Greenspan, and Secretary of State Henry Kissinger. Then they were escorted to the State Dining Room for lunch, followed by a question-and-answer session with President Ford. At 2:15 they returned to the Roosevelt Room, where each one was given a copy of the president's "Daily News Summary" and a set of presidential cuff links before being escorted out of the White House.[52]

In the summer of 1975, White began a series of informal "Conversations with the President" for groups of three or more columnists at a time. The conversations lasted about an hour and were scheduled every fifteen to twenty-one days.[53] When the president traveled around the country, the Office of Communications made a point of scheduling local press conferences for him and making him available for interviews by local television anchormen. This—combined with the regional briefings by the president—was valuable to the White House. Ford points out that such contacts "worked well because, first of all, the local press enjoyed the opportunity, and secondly [the administration was] able to get a message directly to the writing and electronic press in the communities." This exposure was particularly valuable to the president as he approached the 1976 election. "I can assure you that those regional

President Ford at a regional briefing for local media executives over breakfast in San Diego, California. The Office of Communications arranged a series of these briefings around the country with great success. (Courtesy Gerald R. Ford Library)

meetings with local press were very productive," Ford said. "They developed a good rapport that, in my opinion, paid off."[54]

In addition to mailings, briefings, and contacts with regional media, the Office of Communications continued to "maintain liaison with and encourage cooperation among the public affairs officers of the departments and key agencies of the Executive Branch."[55] The office held monthly meetings with all the public information officers to get feedback from them. It also circulated fact sheets, copies of speeches, and other information on major issues to keep PIOs informed on what was going on in the White House and in other departments and agencies.[56] Likewise, it sent each member of the cabinet a weekly selection of speeches culled from those forwarded to the office from various PIOs within the executive branch.[57] In keeping with Ford's desire, the Office of Communications initially served a genuine coordination rather than managerial function.[58] That aspect was stressed in an internal memo outlining the functions of the office in July 1975. The aim of the liaison function was to "coordinate public affairs projects when programs overlap or involve several departments and agencies" and to "provide advice, guidance and direct assistance, *on request*, regarding media-related activities, including scheduling"[59] (emphasis added). Sometimes this meant that the departments and agencies did not follow the wishes of the Office of Communications. For instance, the Office of Communications continually urged PIOs to submit articles by their department heads to newspapers throughout the country for use on op-ed pages. As White explained, this was "an excellent way to provide the reading public with information about the Administration's programs and to set the record straight." Although some departments and agencies such as Treasury, Office of Management and Budget (OMB), and HEW followed her wishes, White complained that others, "despite continued follow-up calls and prodding," were less responsive.[60]

The Office of Communications continued to schedule speakers around the country and arrange for the appearances of administration officials on radio and television, and it handled all interview requests for President Ford.[61] In addition, the office supervised activities that had not been under its jurisdiction during the Nixon administration. As indicated above, it assumed responsibility for preparing the news summary (called *News and Comment*), which Mort Allin and Pat Buchanan had prepared for Nixon. Initially, Philip Warden served as news summary editor. He was replaced by James Shuman in April 1975, who, in turn, was replaced by Agnes Waldron in August 1976. The news summary itself was distributed to a much wider audience than had been the case under Nixon. Some 140 members of the White House staff received it, as did all cabinet members.[62] Under Ford, the news summary was confined to a strict summation of the news with much less editorializing than had been common under Nixon. Often Ford's summaries contained photocopies of the news articles themselves. The Office of Communications also supervised the preparation of the presidential briefing books, which were used to prepare the president for question-and-answer sessions with reporters. During his tenure as news summary editor, James Shuman also prepared the briefing books. Before him, the function was handled by Gerald Warren and Thomas DeCair.[63]

Another new function of the Office of Communications was its liaison with the press secretaries of Republican governors throughout the country. Such contact was first suggested by the Republican Governors Association in January 1975.[64] Initially, Ron Nessen rejected the recommendation. In a handwritten note to Gerald Warren, he stated: "Maybe something at the RNC is more appropriate. I'm just afraid that if this office is tainted with politics we're going to get 'Clawson Rides Again!' stories."[65] Nonetheless, Nessen eventually acquiesced. On 21 February 1975, press secretaries to Republican governors met with members of the White House Press Office in an unprecedented gathering in the Roosevelt Room of the White House. Nessen, as well as Warren and Larry Speakes of the communications office, briefed them on White House press operations.[66] Eventually, Nessen became more enthusiastic about these gubernatorial contacts. On 28 October 1975, Margita White informed Nessen that the Office of Communications had "telephoned the press secretaries to the Republican Governors about the time the grain deal was announced and briefed them on its highlights." She added, "All were delighted and we will try to do this on all major White House announcements." Underneath, Nessen wrote: "Yes. Do it each time."[67]

White's tenure as director of the Office of Communications was treated favorably by the media. News accounts often compared the politicization of the office in the latter part of the Nixon administration with its professionalism under Ford. White herself bristled at suggestions that her office was "political." "That, unfortunately, is the impression people in Washington have," she told John S. Lang of the *New York Post* in August 1975. "That is not the impression of those outside Washington whom we try to serve. [The notion that the Office of Communications is political is] one of the remnants of Watergate." "I coordinate," she concluded, "[I do] not manage."[68]

White worked hard to make sure that under her direction, the Office of Communications kept a low profile. As she recently explained: "There was tremendous suspicion of the Office of Communications in the wake of the activities of Ken Clawson, etc. And so . . . [we tried to] avoid any kind of impression that we were involved in politicizing the communications sector."[69] She was very successful. Despite the fact that the activities of the Office of Communications had grown considerably since the early days of the Ford administration, most media coverage did not note that fact. For instance, Dom Bonafede wrote an article on the office entitled "Communications Office Role Is Reduced" in the 16 August 1975 issue of the *National Journal*.[70] Nessen was pleased with the thrust of the story. He sent a copy of the article to White with the notation: "Margita, Good! RHN."[71]

In fact, the Office of Communications—as Gerald Warren had predicted—was gearing up for a major role in the 1976 presidential election. By the fall of 1975 the office was running smoothly. Its follow-up to the president's speech on 6 October 1975, announcing his tax cut and federal budget–reduction program is a case in point. The office scheduled television appearances by major administration officials to explain the president's program on shows such as "Phil Donahue," "Today," "The CBS Morning News," "Meet the Press," "Face the Nation," and "Issues and Answers." On 7 October, it mailed a transcript of the president's speech and a fact sheet describing his program to eleven hundred editors, editorial writers, television news directors, group broadcasters, and key weeklies. It scheduled a general press briefing on the program by Treasury Secretary William Simon, OMB Director James T. Lynn, and Alan Greenspan (chairman of the Council of Economic Advisors) on 6 October. It scheduled similar briefings for the public affairs officers of the departments and agencies and for the subcabinet on 8 and 10 October, as well as a briefing for eighteen key columnists by the president, Greenspan, Lynn, and Simon.[72] Over the next six weeks, the office scheduled over eighty appearances and media events throughout the country by Simon, Lynn, Greenspan, Defense Secretary Donald Rumsfeld, and White House Economic Advisor William Seidman. Attempts were made to schedule the appearances in major media markets.[73]

The gearing up of the Office of Communications reflected a realization by members of the White House staff that the president's communications operation had to be more programmatic than it had been so far. Ford's first year in office was beset by a lack of discipline within the administration itself and a laissez-faire attitude toward communications planning by the administration. Both hurt the president's image. Dick Cheney, who became Ford's chief of staff in late 1975, realized that those problems had to be corrected if Ford was to have any chance of winning the 1976 presidential election. As Cheney put it, the White House moved into "campaign mode" in late 1975: "We *had* to do better than we had done. We had to have a more disciplined system." In part, that meant doing a better job of setting the agenda for the media. Cheney sees that as one of the great lessons learned by the Ford administration. "You've got to control what you put out," he stated. "You don't let the press set the agenda. The press is going to object to that. They like to set the agenda. They like to decide what's important and what isn't important. But if you let them do that, they're going to trash your presidency."[74]

As it was, Ford faced an uphill battle. Former California Governor Ronald Reagan announced on 20 November 1975 that he would challenge Ford for the Republican presidential nomination. The Gallup Opinion Poll of 12 December 1975 showed an approval rating for Ford of only 39 percent and a disapproval rating of 46 percent.[75] The results of a comprehensive survey of public opinion by Ford's own pollster, Robert Teeter, were no more encouraging. As Ron Nessen wrote: "To the question 'What has Ford done that particularly impresses you?' 61 percent replied, 'Nothing.' The next-largest group was 4 percent, which liked the tax cut; 3 percent praised Ford's honesty and integrity; 2 percent mentioned the rescue of the *Mayaguez*."[76]

The 1976 election was in the forefront of the minds of Press Office employees who met at the White House for another "Press Office Improvement Meeting" on 18 October 1975. There it was noted: "The Office of Communications should play an important role in the advertising and public relations structure of the President's goals. We need a kind of attack group and long-range strategy—a yearly plan. . . . Everything needs to have a purpose." Nessen noted that the most immediate goal was the upcoming New Hampshire primary.[77]

Margita White had a great deal of experience with elections. She had worked in campaign press operations since 1960, and she had worked in the Office of Communications during the elections of 1970 and 1972.[78] In a lengthy memo to Ron Nessen on 26 November 1975, White suggested that the Office of Communications supervise the use of presidential surrogates during the 1976 campaign, as it had done during the Nixon administration. The memo included the following recommendations:

1. Establish a group of prominent, knowledgeable and articulate spokesmen for the President.

2. Schedule appearances by these spokesmen before important organizations in politically important areas and key media markets.

3. Arrange supporting media activities to provide maximum exposure for all such appearances.

4. Establish a briefing system to keep spokesmen fully informed of Presidential positions on key issues, [to] provide talking points on current and developing issues and to ensure that spokesmen are aware of local political information and issues.[79]

White suggested that such a program be coordinated among the Office of Communications, the White House Press Office, the White House Scheduling Office, the President Ford Committee, and the individual spokesmen and their public affairs and scheduling offices. She indicated that presidential spokesmen would include members of the White House staff, the cabinet, executive branch agencies, and Congress, as well as Republican governors and key supporters outside of government.[80]

White stressed that trips by such spokesmen "should not be perceived as campaign appearances on behalf of the President." Rather, the appearances should be presented as "government officials discussing the issues." This would allow the scheduling to be done by the White House and the arrangements for media coverage and coordination within the executive branch to be continued by the Office of Communications.[81] If it was acknowledged that the appearances were blatantly political, the involvement of White House offices in the program would be problematical under the strictures of the Hatch Act and new campaign finance laws.

The surrogate operation was designed to be a major undertaking. Spokesmen would need up-to-date issues-books, local political information for their trips around the country, briefings on new policy initiatives, and a coherent strategy for their schedules. Appearances by the spokesmen would have to be coordinated and targeted for maximum benefit. Media coverage of the appearances would be monitored by the President Ford Committee through its local organizations.

White did not stay to implement the plan. As she later put it, "I was wearing out . . . and it was really getting to me, and I thought, god, am I going to be able to make it through a fifth presidential campaign full time?"[82] She finally decided to leave after an exhausting five-day trip with President Ford to California. Her departure gave the White House an opportunity to totally revamp the communications structure of the White House. In the process, the Office of Communications was taken out from under the jurisdiction of the White House Press Office and was made a separate entity responsible for coordinating the flow of information from the entire executive branch during the campaign.

RUNNING FOR PRESIDENT

Since its inception, the Office of Communications had always played an important role in election campaigns. In 1976, that task was particularly daunting. During the primary season, the White House was unable to pull President Ford's Gallup approval rating over 50 percent, and Ronald Reagan was hitting hard on Ford's defense policy and his "giveaway" of the Panama Canal. The problem was compounded because the Ford team had no real strategy for winning the primaries. Dick Cheney remembers it as a "helter-skelter" time. "Basically what we did was just try to survive," he says. "It was a zoo—an absolute zoo."[83] Nonetheless, Ford squeaked by Reagan in the New Hampshire primary—a victory given added weight by the fact that many had thought Ford would lose.* The president went on to win in Massachusetts, Vermont, Florida, and Illinois. For a brief time it seemed that Reagan's candidacy had stalled. The morning after the Illinois primary, John Sears (Reagan's campaign manager) reportedly suggested that the Reagan camp contact Ford and tell him that its candidate was ready to withdraw gracefully.[84]

Whatever chance there was that Reagan would withdraw was quickly dissolved by the Ford organization's heavy-handed efforts to pressure Reagan out of the race. Given its string of victories, the Ford camp was beginning to show signs of overconfidence, even cockiness.[85] But that was shattered by the North Carolina primary—a stunning loss for Ford—on 23 March. As late as dinner that evening, Ford had expected to win. But by nine o'clock, Reagan had jumped out to an early lead. Although Reagan eventually won by only 52 percent of the vote, it was an important psychological victory. Ford became only the third incumbent president in U.S. history (and the first in the history of his party) to lose a primary. For Ford personally, it was his first loss at the polls in nearly thirty years. He later admitted that the experience was "jolting."[86] As it turned out, North Carolina set the stage for a string of primary losses to Reagan.

Even before the defeat in North Carolina, there had been problems in Ford's campaign organization. The president's campaign manager, Howard "Bo" Callaway, had resigned on 13 March in the midst of allegations that while serving in the Pentagon as army secretary, he had used his position to pressure the U.S. Forest Service to approve his plans to expand onto federal land a ski resort that he and his brother-in-law owned in Crested Butte, Colorado. Although Callaway steadfastly maintained his innocence and was later absolved, the post-Watergate climate did not allow for even a trace of impropriety.

For the campaign organization itself, the resignation of Callaway was probably a good turn of events. Callaway's inexperience at running national campaigns had shown, and his replacement by Rogers Morton, a former House colleague of Ford's, came with a sigh of relief from many of those around the president. The experience with Callaway demonstrated one of the problems besetting the Ford team in 1976. As Cheney said, "We were trying to run a

*Ford won by only 1,317 votes. The final tally showed 54,824 votes for Ford and 53,507 votes for Reagan.

campaign without being able to use any of the people who had won the last Republican campaign because they'd all been discredited by Watergate." In addition, the 1976 campaign was the first presidential election campaign run under the rules of the new Federal Election Commission. In short, Cheney says that the Ford campaign felt constrained by what was then thought to be "very stringent, rigid rules about what you could spend."[87]

Ford's losses to Reagan renewed the consensus that the president had to tighten the reins on both his personal and his political staffs. If there was to be any chance of winning a full term in the White House, the administration would have to close ranks. From the outset, the Ford White House had been beset by internal bickering and backbiting. In part, the problem stemmed from the unusual circumstances under which Ford assumed office. As Donald Rumsfeld put it, when Ford suddenly became president there was "no structure, . . . no organization, no platform, no nothing."[88] Thus, the task facing Ford was enormous. He had to create a team from the diverse and, at times, incompatible groups that had been thrown together when Nixon resigned. As Ron Nessen pointed out, there were carryovers from the Nixon administration, carryovers from Ford's congressional and vice-presidential staffs, a group of trusted Michigan friends from the president's native Grand Rapids, and a group of newcomers who had never worked with either Nixon or Ford.[89] These were distinct groups that never entirely coalesced into a homogeneous administration.

Ford had attempted to deal with the problem by announcing a major shake-up of his staff in October 1975, but the results had been mixed. Now, with the primary season fully under way, it was clear to Ford's advisors that power had to be centralized. This was especially the view of Dick Cheney, his special assistant David Gergen, and Michael Raoul-Duval (who began working with Cheney as "Special Counsel to the President" in April 1976). The last, better known as Mike Duval, had served in the Nixon administration as part of the president's advance team. He later joined the Domestic Council. In 1975, he was executive director of the "Intelligence Coordinating Group"—a top-level White House committee that was set up to supervise the administration's response to congressional investigations of alleged Central Intelligence Agency abuses. In 1987, Duval argued that centralization is a natural outgrowth of a mature presidency:

> When you [first] become president, your job is to decide what you should do, to create new ideas, and to come up with new programs. Then your

job becomes to implement them. And then your job becomes to maintain them and defend them. In general you create new ideas by being highly decentralized. So most administrations come in and talk about Cabinet government. . . . But then, of course, the new ideas come in and everybody's shooting at each other and nobody's paying any attention to each other and the press says it's chaos. . . . So then you start pulling together and saying, "This is my program." Then you go through implementation, which puts great stress on Hill relationships and which requires coordination. Then you go through defending and maintaining which takes a *very* tightly centralized operation. You have to be able to tell the Cabinet officers to shut up [and to tell them], "we don't want contradictions." So you go from decentralized to centralized, not so much by the style of the man as by the requirements of the job.[90]

The reorganized Office of Communications was part of that new effort to centralize control over the messages that were going out from the administration. When Margita White left, the Office of Communications was completely reorganized. It was taken out from under the jurisdiction of Ron Nessen and the Press Office, and it was made the formal apparatus for controlling the public image of the administration. David Gergen was named director of the newly structured office in July 1976. The thirty-four-year-old Gergen had served in the Nixon White House as an assistant speechwriter to Raymond Price and later as chief of Nixon's research and writing team. He was a native of Durham, North Carolina, an ex-Democrat, and an Ivy Leaguer (he had received his undergraduate degree from Yale and a law degree from Harvard). When Ford became president and Robert Hartmann took over the speechwriting team, Hartmann got rid of all holdovers from the Nixon administration. As a result, Gergen went to work at the Treasury Department as a speechwriter for Treasury Secretary William E. Simon. One of the first things that Dick Cheney did when he became Ford's chief of staff was to bring Gergen back to the White House as part of his personal staff.[91] Gergen served in that capacity from December 1975 until he was named director of the Office of Communications the following July.

During the 1972 presidential election, Gergen had worked closely with Charles Colson in planning the administration's line-of-the-day and in coordinating the flow of news from the administration. He had also been active in scripting the 1972 Republican convention. Gergen recently stated that Colson,

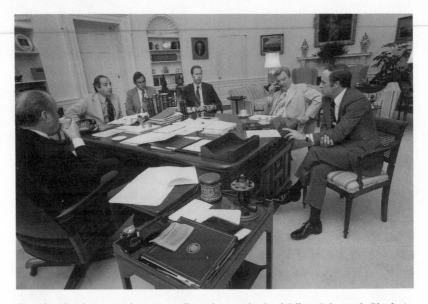

President Ford meets with senior staff members in the Oval Office, July 1976. Clockwise from the president are Press Secretary Ron Nessen, Deputy Press Secretary John G. Carlson, Communications Director David Gergen, the presidential counselor Robert Hartmann, and Chief of Staff Dick Cheney. (Courtesy Gerald R. Ford Library)

for all his negative publicity, was really very good at many of the things he did. In a sense, Gergen had learned the ropes from Colson.[92] When Gergen came back to the White House to work for Cheney, he knew that the administration would have to be more active in orchestrating the news. Therefore in April he submitted to Cheney a four-page memo that he had coauthored with Mike Duval and James Cavanaugh (another Cheney aide). In it, they suggested that a "Communications Group" be established "to develop, recommend and then to carry out approved news plans." The main purposes of the group would be

—To assist in planning of all major news announcements and newsworthy events coming out of the White House;

—To coordinate more closely the news flow from the departments and agencies which relates to the President;

—To stimulate more creative and sustained attention for Administration initiatives in areas such as the economy, crime, foreign affairs, etc.[93]

They suggested that one person on Cheney's immediate staff be "charged with the overall coordination [of communications] in the same way that [Jerry] Jones now coordinates the President's daily schedule." That person would chair the Communications Group. The rest of the group would consist of representatives from the Domestic Council, the National Security Council, the Economic Policy Board, the Press Office, the Congressional Relations Office, and the President Ford Committee. In short, "[The group] would not only coordinate what is going on in the departments but ensure that our leading spokesmen are wired in so that they can help us more effectively on the road."[94]

Duval followed up the recommendations with another memo urging that the Communications Group not be cast as a mechanism for "news management" but rather as a mechanism for coordinating "substance." He offered two reasons for this:

—If the process is presented to the Cabinet officers as a news management exercise, they are likely to assign their chief PR guy as the key White House contact point. With obvious exceptions . . . the PR guy in many departments is very weak in terms of his ability to get things done and maintain control. It seems to me as if the kind of departmental contact we're looking for is the key special assistant or the Deputy Under Secretary.

—If this process generates any criticism in the future, it's going to be a lot easier to keep the Cabinet officers in line if they can explain that it is being oriented around substance and hence removed from Hatch Act problems. It seems to me that a news control exercise is just one step closer to creating political problems.[95]

Gergen says that the plan for the Communications Group was an effort to replicate some of the things that had been done in the 1972 election. Quite simply, the plan was part of an effort to "reinvent the wheel under Ford." Gergen says that the Communications Group was put together and that it met regularly. "I think it's part of how you run a decent White House," he explains. "There are some people who think it's too political. But I think if you've got a president who's running for office, you've got to do it. It doesn't bother me in the least."[96] According to William Rhatican, who became deputy director of the Office of Communications in July, the Communications Group included Gergen, Ron Nessen, William Greener, Jr. (communications director for the

President Ford Committee [PFC]), and himself. The original idea of including representatives from all parts of the administration was abandoned because it was feared that the Communications Group would become too unwieldy. Instead, the group met at 7:15 every morning for about an hour. Individual members of the group then spread out and met with various other people, including representatives from the Domestic Council and the National Security Council (who had originally been suggested as actual members of the Communications Group). The group then reconvened briefly around 9:00 and took its recommendations to Dick Cheney around 9:15 or 9:30. As Rhatican said, "Dick would give us the go-ahead for whatever it was that we were recommending, or make whatever changes he wanted to make, and then we'd go off and do it."[97]

President Ford agreed with the assessment that the administration had to be more programmatic in its dealings with the media. He says that he and his aides recognized that a theme "was essential"and that they "tried to project that theme as uniformly as possible."[98] The Communications Group was one way of developing and projecting such themes. Throughout the primary season, concern about communications and the coordination of policy announcements surfaced again and again. For instance, Mike Duval's notes of a meeting between him and Cheney on 24 April include a list of the "goals of [the] Communications Group":

—reduce agency announcements which impact P [president].
—determine what P should announce.
—provide Q & As; fact sheet; etc. for developing news stories.
—produce basic "lines" for surrogates, etc.[99]

Later, at a meeting on 9 May of many of the top Ford strategists, including Cheney, Duval, Gergen, Cavanaugh, and John Marsh, Cheney announced the need for "creativity in how to get P's messages to people." He also announced that they needed "better control over surrogates; follow-up P's event w/surrogates, mailers, etc. in appropriate media mkt."[100] Again in July, notes of a meeting between Cheney and Duval read:

Problem: *discipline of W.H. staff system*;
leadership—energizing senior staff

Solution: Staff Secretariat
Cheney Attention.[101]

When Gergen became director of the restructured Office of Communications in July, the first task was to get Ford through the Republican National Convention. At that point it was not even a certainty that Ford would win the nomination. Gergen and his deputy, Bill Rhatican, had both worked on the 1972 campaign for Nixon. In fact, Rhatican (who, like Gergen, was then thirty-four years old) had worked in the Nixon White House under both Klein and Colson. At the beginning of the Ford administration, Rhatican went to the Treasury Department (as did Gergen), where he served as Bill Simon's press secretary. Both Gergen and Rhatican realized how important television was, so they revitalized a Television Office under the jurisdiction of the Office of Communications. Gergen says that the creation of a Television Office was one of his first commitments because the White House "simply didn't have anything in place to help supervise and choreograph what was going on. . . . [So] I went out and recruited a guy by the name of Bill Carruthers, who was somebody I had worked with in the '72 campaign and in the '72 convention."[102]

Before agreeing to join the Office of Communications, Carruthers met with Ford and Cheney and then spent a few days analyzing how prepared they were to go to the convention at Kansas City. He went back to them and said, "There's no possible way you guys are ready to go to Kansas City and win this thing." Still, Carruthers was impressed with Ford during the two meetings he had with him. He maintained that Ford had been given "a bad shuffle of the cards" in his first year and a half in the White House. "He just wasn't being taken care of," Carruthers noted. There had been little attention paid to image making during the Ford presidency, and there had been no coherent strategy during the primaries. As a result, according to Carruthers, the country began to see Ford "as some kind of buffoon when he was actually a very graceful athlete" and a man of considerable ability.[103]

The primary races against Reagan had also diminished the presidential aura that usually surrounds incumbents. As Dick Cheney puts it, "We had to go out and duke it out state by state." Instead of appearing "presidential," Ford was constantly out on the road campaigning for his political life. Cheney says that a *Time* magazine cover that came out after the Democratic convention but before the Republican convention demonstrated the problem. "It had three pictures on it—all three exactly equally: Jimmy Carter, who had just won the Democratic nomination, Ronald Reagan, and Jerry Ford. You couldn't tell who was president! His stature had been reduced by the necessity for us to go campaign in every one of those states, primary by primary."[104]

After speaking with Ford and Cheney, Carruthers agreed to direct the Television Office. He also brought in Mark Goode to work with him. This was the same team that had run the Television Office under President Nixon and scripted the 1972 Republican convention for television. As Carruthers said: "We put together a staff of people. We got it organized and we went into Kansas City and got the nomination. But I tell you, it was not easy, because the Reagan people were extremely well organized and well coordinated . . . and they didn't expect to loose the nomination."[105]

Originally, the planning of the Republican convention was to have been left up to the Republican National Committee, but Ford's own convention team unanimously felt that the RNC version was not well planned for television and would not effectively promote Ford. Dave Gergen and Jerry Jones wrote a memo to the president saying that the RNC script was "very long" and had "very little star quality." They ended up taking over the scripting of the convention. The result, as they told the president, was a script that "is streamlined, seeks to increase television appeal, and will have a more positive punch for the fall."[106]

Ford's convention team also overruled an earlier decision not to show a film about Ford at the convention. Carruthers was assigned the task of preparing the film. He did it along the lines of the extremely successful one that he had prepared for Nixon in 1972. The last-minute decision to make a film was almost thwarted by the constraints of the new campaign-financing rules that had been put in place by the Federal Election Commission. According to Cheney, the president had to sign a personal note to pay for the production of the film. "The reason we did that was because we didn't have any fall campaign funds until we won the nomination. But you couldn't spend any of the matching funds you got in the primary season for the fall campaign without violating the law. The only way that we could think of to finance that movie— which was going to be shown *after* he had the nomination, but had to be produced *before* he had the nomination—was for him to sign a personal note to finance it."[107]

In short, the Office of Communications played an important role in scripting the convention for television and in orchestrating the media coverage. In fact, the convention was one of the most important projects of the Office of Communications in 1976. The tasks mirrored those of 1972. Speeches were streamlined, interviews were arranged, stars such as Cary Grant appeared on the podium, and every effort was made to overshadow the Reagans. Rhatican says that a group including himself, Gergen, Carruthers, and Goode met for the better part of each day during the convention. They used those meetings to "sort out what it was that we wanted to see on the tube that night." The result was a script for television *coverage* of the convention that used "the events on the floor merely as a backdrop." During the convention itself, Rhatican manned a communications desk in the Ford trailer. There he had five phones— "one to the production desks of each of the three networks, one to the pool production desk, and one back to the Ford command center." From there he tried to control what the networks were showing. For instance, whenever there was no action for the networks to cover, or whenever the networks cut away from the action, Rhatican tried to determine what would appear on television. As he puts it: "I would try to sell to the networks a particular Cabinet officer talking about whatever it was that was being discussed from the podium, *or* whatever that particular network was talking about at that particular moment. So if ABC was talking about international economics, I'd try to locate Bill Simon and make him available to ABC for a live interview from wherever he happened to be. We did real well with that."[108]

Rhatican says that the battle for television coverage began the moment Ford and Reagan arrived in Kansas City. Reagan arrived early in the afternoon, but Ford's arrival on *Air Force One* was timed so that it could be covered "live" by the network newscasts. The ploy worked. In addition, Reagan spent his time that first day meeting with convention delegates in an effort to win their votes. Ford also had a group doing that, but the president himself played to a broader television audience—"post-convention America," as Rhatican puts it. Thus, Ford went straight from the airport to a hotel rally that was also carried "live" by the networks.[109]

At the convention itself, the networks paid a great deal of attention to the rival candidates' wives. On the first night of the convention, Nancy Reagan arrived early and set off a "Nancy rally" among Reagan supporters. Rhatican immediately called the Ford command center and suggested that Betty Ford go to the convention to stimulate a counterdemonstration. Rhatican recalled: "When I got the word that she was in the elevator on the way down to the car to go, I called the three networks and the pool and just reminded them that the First Lady was en route. And I think CBS went 'live'—cut away from the Nancy rally inside to have Mrs. Ford arriving in the limousine outside."[110] To prevent coverage of a Nancy rally the second night, the Ford people devised a script to focus attention on Betty. As Vic Gold has written:

Mrs. Ford would arrive at the auditorium early to take her seat in the special VIP guest box with her family and guests, among whom was Tony Orlando. At the moment Nancy arrived to take her seat, [George] Murphy would signal the convention band to break into the Orlando theme, "Tie a Yellow Ribbon Round the Old Oak Tree."

Orlando, who was to Ford at the 1976 convention what Sammy Davis, Jr., was to Nixon in 1972 (though not black, Tony was the next best thing—a show biz ethnic with a black supporting cast), had a VIP seat in the Ford family box. On cue, as the band went into his theme, he leaped to his feet, took Betty by the hand, and began dancing in the aisle.

As Carruthers had figured, the network cameras swung away from Nancy Reagan to what *Newsweek* would describe in its convention coverage as a "spontaneous" dance exhibition in the Ford section. This bit of upstaging, reported *Time*, represented a "triumph" for Mrs. Ford over "her rival." Every little contest counts.[111]

While Gergen and others had been planning the convention, Mike Duval, Jerry Jones, and Foster Chanock wrote a 120-page strategy memo that became the blueprint for Ford's general election campaign. Jones was Ford's scheduling director, and Chanock was a young aide to Cheney (Chanock died of cancer in 1980 at the age of twenty-seven). Chanock had gotten into the White House through the back door. His brother Steve had dated Rumsfeld's daughter, and when Rumsfeld was NATO ambassador, Steve and Foster visited the Rumsfelds in Brussels.[112] When Rumsfeld became Ford's chief of staff, Foster— who had just graduated from the University of Chicago—wrote a letter to Rumsfeld requesting a job and explaining why he wanted to work in the White House. Dick Cheney, who was then Rumsfeld's assistant, recalls that the "fascinating letter" was "so well done" that they decided to consider him.[113] Chanock then came to the White House and met with Rumsfeld. Rumsfeld told him that the last thing he needed was another bright young man in the White House—especially one who needed on-the-job training—but finally said that he could work for him on a volunteer basis for ninety days. If Chanock proved his mettle during that time, Rumsfeld would consider keeping him on.[114]

Chanock quickly won over everybody. Cheney recalls: "Everybody who ever met him became his friend for life. I would find him either down in the mess with the Philippino stewards who loved him . . . or he'd be over having lunch one on one with the attorney general, Ed Levi, who thought he walked on water. . . . . He was one of the brightest people I ever met."[115] Chanock stayed on after the ninety days and proceeded to develop a close relationship with Cheney. When Rumsfeld moved to the Defense Department and Cheney became chief of staff, Chanock continued working with Cheney. During that time, Mike Duval served as Chanock's mentor. They quickly became fast friends. "He was the most brilliant person I've ever known and one of the nicest human beings I've ever known," Duval says.[116] So it was that Chanock was in on the writing of the president's campaign strategy.

The memo was presented to Ford shortly before the convention.[117] Again the need for centralization was stressed as paramount. To "command and control the campaign," the Ford group needed to have "absolute control over Presidential activities and Administration officials and actions."[118] An outgrowth of this was a major shake-up of Ford's campaign staff. Rogers Morton, who had replaced "Bo" Callaway as Ford's campaign manager in March, was himself replaced by James A. Baker III in August. As Ron Nessen has written: "Morton, slow-moving, ailing, lacking administrative talents, with a penchant for saying the wrong things to reporters, just didn't fit the fast-paced, tightly organized, error-free campaign Ford needed."[119] Baker, on the other hand, had impressed everyone at the convention, where he had served as Ford's delegate hunter. "He was so damn good that I offered him the job of chairman of the campaign in Kansas City with the approval of the president," Cheney later said.[120] In an excellent move, the President Ford Committee also hired the advertising team of Doug Bailey and John Deardourff. The campaign team was rounded out with the pollster Bob Teeter and Political Director Stuart Spencer. "It was a hell of a team," Cheney recalls.[121]

Despite the good team, Ford faced overwhelmingly bad odds. Bill Carruthers has said that no one, in his or her "heart of hearts," expected Ford to beat Jimmy Carter.[122] "We were 33 points down in the Gallup Poll after the Democratic convention," says Cheney. "Carter was at his peak. As I recall in the plan, Duval had a section that talked about how many hundreds of thousands of voters you had to turn around every week [just to even it up with Carter]. The point was, obviously, [we] were going to have to rely very heavily on [a] media strategy." The trick was to find a way to make Ford look presidential while still being forceful enough to wrest votes away from Carter. In short, the Ford group had to "find some way to go on the attack and be aggressive, but still keep the president in the Rose Garden."[123]

The Ford team came out of Kansas City swinging against Jimmy Carter.

During his acceptance speech at the convention, Ford challenged Carter to televised debates. In the coming weeks the Ford team tried to portray Carter as the media manipulator and Ford as the candidate concerned with substance. Ford's campaign strategy book urged that Ford be portrayed "as Presidential and *not* as a partisan Republican," while suggesting that Carter's campaign style be characterized "as a 1976 version of the Nixon '68 campaign—a slick show done with mirrors." Carter's campaign was one waged "for power," Ford's group would argue, "not principle."[124]

Despite that, Ford ultimately waged a battle that was structurally (if not ethically) similar to Richard Nixon's campaign of 1972. Like Nixon's Committee to Re-Elect the President, the President Ford Committee (PFC) acted independently of Republican party machinery and was responsible to the White House. Like Nixon, Ford adopted a "Rose Garden" strategy in which presidential campaigning was kept to a minimum. Like Nixon, Ford used the team of Bill Carruthers and Mark Goode to script the Republican convention for television and to manage the president's television appearances in the fall campaign. Like Nixon, Ford used surrogates (called "advocates" in 1976 to avoid association with Nixon) who traveled around the country and spoke on his behalf. And like Nixon, Ford used the advertising team of Bailey-Deardourff and the polling data of Bob Teeter.[125] Stu Spencer recently said that he read one campaign account that suggested "there was a *lack* of coordination *on purpose* between the White House and the campaign because of a hangover from Watergate." He added with a laugh: "That's bull. That's bull. We were tight."[126]

The fact that the White House and the campaign committee were "tight" enabled the Office of Communications to play an important role in the campaign. Under Gergen (who reported directly to Chief of Staff Cheney), the Office of Communications served as the principal liaison among the communications efforts of the White House, the rest of the executive branch, and the PFC. The communications troika during the campaign was Gergen of the communications office, Nessen of the Press Office, and William Greener, Jr., director of communications for the PFC. Of the three, Gergen had the most important operation, and Greener appears to have had the least important. At a meeting of the White House Press Office on 6 August 1976, Nessen told the assembled group, "The PFC press office is really a creation of convenience that gives us the opportunity to not answer questions that we don't want to answer out of the White House."[127] Later in the same meeting, Gergen described the role of the Office of Communications in the fall campaign. The aim, he said, was to create "teamwork," to gear the administration activities toward the media, and to get the administration to speak with one voice. "I have never seen a place so divisive as around here," he said. "We must not be divided into different factions. . . . We are trying to build a block of activities that go together." Gergen said that Ford's old Office of Communications had not had "the resources to do that." But with a new mandate from Ford and the reorganization of the office, things had changed.[128]

The new Office of Communications was staffed by more than thirty people.[129] (See the organization chart in the Appendix.) Under its jurisdiction were four major operations: the Research Division, led by Agnes Waldron; Editorial Services, led by Fred Slight; the Presidential Spokesmen's Office, led by Hugh Cannon; and the Television Office, led by Bill Carruthers. The Research Division was responsible for preparing briefing books and the "Daily News Summary." In addition, it tried to pinpoint what sorts of subjects were of interest to particular publications.[130] By knowing that, the White House was in a better position to target things like op-ed pieces. Editorial Services was then responsible for ghostwriting those op-ed pieces, as well as magazine articles (often for publication in specialized publications). In addition, Editorial Services wrote speech inserts for surrogate speakers. Appearances by those surrogates were scheduled by the Presidential Spokesmen's Office, in coordination with the PFC. The Television Office, as we have seen, was responsible for orchestrating events for television. It played a major role in the convention. During the general election campaign, it was concerned almost exclusively with giving technical advice to the president and setting the stage for his appearances. That included the televised debates with Jimmy Carter.

Gergen and Rhatican oversaw the entire communications operation. Gergen's responsibility focused mostly on *what* was said and *how* it was said. He was involved in strategic planning. Rhatican, on the other hand, was more concerned with implementing the plan. Thus, he was responsible for *where* and *when* those things were said.[131] Surrogate speakers provided an important outlet for those messages. At a meeting of the White House communications staff on 7 August 1976, Rhatican said that he had "a small group hidden away in the EOB" that had been preparing a schedule of appearances by cabinet officers throughout the fall. "As of right now," he said, "we have every major media market [and] what we consider to be key geographic areas covered twice a week." He said that once the schedule was completed, he expected to call in the PIOs from all the departments and give it to them "as a package."[132] A plan for the implementation of the advocates program stated that the scheduling of advocates would "be split, but *fully* coordinated between the White House and PFC."[133] Thus, the Office of Communications handled the scheduling of the cabinet, subcabinet, and First Family. The PFC scheduled all other advocates, including Vice President Rockefeller and Ford's running mate, Senator Robert Dole. The only cabinet secretaries excluded from participation were those from the State and Defense departments.[134] The plan for the advocates program also stated that President Ford would have to "lay down the law at an *early* Cabinet Meeting—preferably next week—in effect a notice to the Cabinet to 'put up or get out.' " The plan also noted that cabinet members should be reminded that they would "have to assist in local Congressional fundraisers."[135]

During the week of 16 August, the Office of Communications sent out speaking schedules to all cabinet members.[136] Some members of the administration expressed concern that the Office of Communications was going too far toward politicizing the cabinet. The PFC and the White House immediately tried to squelch that impression. On 1 September, Rhatican's assistant, Bill Greener III (the son of the PFC communications director), wrote a memo to Rhatican: "I am confident that we have done nothing of even questionable legality."[137] Greener also sent Rhatican a draft of a letter to schedulers in each of the departments explaining that the Office of Communications was not trying to politicize the cabinet. The draft, which Greener suggested Rhatican send out under his name, read in part:

Let me assure you that this office has not made, and will not make any attempt to politicize the Cabinet. Neither myself [Rhatican] nor Dave Gergen will engage in *any* activity that is of even questionable legality.

I want to once again state the purpose of the White House Communications Office in scheduling—We are here to help—to help you coordinate your activities with the activities of the rest of the Cabinet. We will not dictate policy to anyone.[138]

In a memo to cabinet members on 2 September, Cabinet Secretary James Connor wrote that future political appearances would be scheduled by the PFC "in coordination with the White House."[139] Bill Greener III recently said that because of the new Federal Election Campaign Act, "everyone erred on the side of caution."[140] Rhatican agrees.[141] It was for that reason that the Office of Communications ultimately coordinated the advocates program with the PFC rather than engaging in "proactive scheduling" on its own.[142] Still, the two worked closely. For instance, if a cabinet officer was going to a particular city to deliver a speech related to official business, Rhatican would contact the PFC so that it could "build other events around the schedule that would be much more partisan and political."[143] Speech inserts were provided by the Editorial Services department of the Office of Communications no matter who scheduled the appearance. In fact, Rhatican says that Editorial Services provided "a lot of material" for politically oriented speeches.[144]

The real problem with the advocates program concerned its financing. As Ron Nessen put it, "The White House Counsel's Office ruled that the original plan—to send cabinet members around the country several days a week at government expense to speak about the president and his record—was illegal and had to be revised 'if you don't want to go to jail.' "[145] Rhatican adds that the "instructions that came out of the general counsel's office were very, very clear. There was a formula that took into account the total amount of elapsed time on the ground in let's say Atlanta, and if it were twenty hours, how much of that time was on the governmental event and how much of that was the political event—including travel time. Within, I think, 72 hours of the return of the Cabinet officer and his staff from that trip, a report had to be filed so that the Ford Committee could reimburse the government for their portion of that trip. It got to be a logistical, absolute, bloody nightmare."[146] As a result, the program was not always as successful as Nixon's efficient use of surrogates had been in 1972.[147]

Finally, the Office of Communications was involved in planning the president's televised debates with Jimmy Carter. Bill Carruthers and Mark Goode of the Television Office offered technical advice and suggestions on how Ford should look during the debates. Agnes Waldron of the Research Division supervised the preparation of the president's briefing books, and Gergen helped to plan the themes that Ford would stress in his answers. Practice sessions were held in the White House Family Theater on 19 and 20 September. The stage was set the way that it would be at the Walnut Street Theater in Philadelphia on 23 September, and Ford's responses were videotaped so that they could be analyzed and refined.[148] Ford's aides even scripted answers for "Jimmy Carter" so that Ford could practice rebuttals. After the actual debates, surrogates spoke out about how well the president had done. It was the birth of the "spin doctor."[149]

Through the course of the Ford administration, the Office of Communications changed considerably. Its powers were revitalized, and it assumed most of the important functions that it had carried out under Nixon. Ford's initial attempts at decentralization were reversed, and the Office of Communications eventually became an important tool for coordinating the administration line and for exercising tight control over information policy and public statements by administration officials. A daily line-of-the-day meeting set the agenda that the Office of Communications then played a major role in implementing.[150] As Dick Cheney recently noted, the White House decided that it had to "squeeze down pretty hard in terms of control those last few months." He added: "We stepped on a lot of toes—broke a lot of china internally. But we had to do it to get the job done."[151] In addition, the Office of Communications served as a political tool for generating public support for President Ford. It did this, for instance, through its scripting of the Republican National Convention and through its aggressive use of surrogate speakers in the fall campaign. Thus, both of the functions of the office that Ford had curtailed at the outset of his presidency were fully restored.

By increasing internal control over the administration "line" and external control over the targeting of public opinion, the Office of Communications played an important role in narrowing the gap between Gerald Ford and Jimmy Carter in the 1976 election. But perhaps the most important aspect of Gergen's Office of Communications is that it served as the prototype for Ronald Reagan's highly successful communications operation four years later. For Gerald Ford, the campaign began in 1976. For Ronald Reagan, it never ended.

CHAPTER SIX

THE CARTER YEARS

GETTING CONTROL

James Earl Carter was something of a political anomaly. Governor of Georgia from 1970 to 1974, he was an outsider to Washington politics. A populist with Southern Baptist values and simple tastes, he narrowly won the White House in 1976 by running against the Washington establishment. He harbored a deep distrust—even dislike—of the media, and yet he was in many ways a creation of the media. He is often said to have put substance over style (to his detriment), and yet style was an integral part of Carter's initial success. Ironically, it was this style that ultimately helped to break Jimmy Carter.

Like Ford, Carter entered the White House with a special desire to bring openness to government. Indeed, the beginnings of the two administrations bear a number of similarities, perhaps because each president was trying to put as much distance as possible between his governing style and that of Richard Nixon. Both Ford and Carter were remarkably accessible to the press. Both held frequent press conferences with the White House press corps and made themselves available to representatives of local media. Both wanted to decentralize the power that had accumulated in the White House, and both initially opted against a strong White House chief of staff. Both also started out with a similar approach to the workings of the Office of Communications. Like Ford, Carter initially restructured the Office of Communications so that it became part of the White House Press Office. There it fell under the jurisdiction of Deputy Press Secretary Walt Wurfel, was renamed the "Office of Media

Liaison," and was responsible for maintaining ties with non-Washington-based media. The director of the Office of Media Liaison was Patricia Bario. Carter was eager to maintain a dialogue with local media representatives. Like Ford, he recognized the value of such dialogue. As Bario recently explained, local media were important not only because they could be used to get the president's messages directly to the people but also because contact with their representatives allowed the president to learn what was on the minds of people in communities throughout the country.[1]

In keeping with his decentralized approach to governing, Carter initially downplayed the importance of using the Office of Media Liaison—or any other part of the White House—to set a public agenda and get members of the administration to promote that agenda with a unified line. In so doing, Carter ignored the lessons learned by the Ford White House. One of those lessons is that the modern presidency is much like an ongoing political campaign. As in any campaign, the president must set the agenda, maintain discipline among his spokespeople, and orchestrate media coverage of that agenda through long-term public relations planning. Yet the striking thing about the early part of the Carter administration is the lack of such planning. For instance, there was almost no effort to set a "line-of-the-day" for the administration, nor was there any real effort to get cabinet secretaries and other administration officials to articulate certain themes and otherwise "speak with one voice."

Greg Schneiders, who served as a communications advisor in the Carter White House, recently said that there was never a daily line-of-the-day meeting, as there had been under Presidents Nixon and Ford or as there later would be under Ronald Reagan. "The staff meetings at the White House tended to be much more substantive [than that]," he says. "[They were] somewhat political, but political in the sense of what was going on on Capitol Hill—a report from [Congressional Liaison Director] Frank Moore or his people about what was going on up there, a report from [Public Liaison Director] Anne Wexler on what she was doing in developing constituencies, and so forth. But *not* that very focused approach to communications: 'What's the line today?' "[2]

Likewise, there was little effort in the early part of the Carter administration to exercise control over what administration officials were stating publicly. Often the White House did not even give guidance on what to say. As a result, Schneiders notes, "Many people who wanted to support the president's programs didn't know what the right line was."[3] Walt Wurfel concurs. "We didn't do very well at coordinating the departments at all," he says.[4] Carter's speech-writer James Fallows later wrote that the result of Carter's decentralized approach was a system that gave cabinet secretaries "free rein."[5] The political observer Timothy B. Clark echoed that assessment in February 1979: "The President's mode of decision making has left him with semi-autonomous fiefdoms that quarrel among themselves and speak with different voices."[6] As a result of those conflicting voices, the media focused on policy "incoherence" in the administration.[7] For instance, one of Carter's own advisors—Nelson H. Cruikshank, the presidential counselor on aging—once testified in Congress *against* Carter's proposed social security benefit reductions.[8] There were also frequent disagreements over policy matters between Secretary of State Cyrus Vance and National Security Advisor Zbigniew Brzezinski.

Press Secretary Jody Powell did make an effort during the transition to wield some control over the selection of public information officers (PIOs) for the cabinet departments. "The President required Jody to sign off on the appoint-ment that any Cabinet [secretary] or agency head would make for the top press officer," Walt Wurfel recalls. "I remember the first gathering of the Cabinet down in Brunswick, Georgia, which I guess was in December [1976] or January [1977], and one of the items on the agenda was that they were told that they had to check these people through Jody."[9] Having done that, however, Powell did not continue to exert control over the PIOs. Wurfel presided over monthly meetings of the PIOs at the White House and tried to instill some coordination, but with little success. "Like so many of these efforts, Jody virtually never showed up at them," Wurfel recalls. "Therefore, since I was only his deputy, we didn't have as strong an iron fist as we would have if Jody had really taken part in it."[10] Similarly, Wurfel established what he called Public Affairs Advisory Groups. These were top corporate PIOs and public relations people who met for the purpose of giving advice on how to promote administration programs and improve the president's image.[11] Typically, the meetings included a dozen or so of the corporate PIOs, a couple of representa-tives from the administration (such as a cabinet secretary and a White House aide), and Wurfel. "Again, it suffered from Jody not devoting the time or actually attending the every 60 to 90 days meeting of this group," Wurfel says. "[So], they would come out with recommendations that would be heard by [the people in the room], but a lot of that stuff never got translated into action because it didn't have Jody's personal involvement."[12]

The problem of poor discipline within the administration was compounded by the fact that the president did not seem to have an agenda for the rest of the administration to rally around. During his first year in office, legislative proposals were sent to Congress with no priorities or clear-cut agenda. Carter later admitted that things could have been done better:

> With the advantages of hindsight, it now seems that it would have been advisable to have introduced our legislation in much more careful phases. . . .
>
> Now I can see more clearly the problems we created for the legislators. . . . There was really little in the list [of legislative proposals] to attract constituents, but much to alienate some of the special-interest groups that play such a key role in financing [congressional] election campaigns.[13]

The inability of Carter to predict such problems disturbed Fallows. It soon became clear to him that "Carter and those closest to him took office in profound ignorance of their jobs. They were ignorant of the possibilities and the most likely pitfalls. They fell prey to predictable dangers and squandered precious time."[14] It was not until May 1978 that Carter made a serious effort to create a coherent administration image by re-creating a formal Office of Communications under the direction of Gerald Rafshoon.

THE OFFICE OF MEDIA LIAISON

The Office of Media Liaison served as a link between the White House and non-Washington-based media. In addition to answering telephone queries from out-of-town reporters, the office also set up briefings, sent out mailings, and assisted local media when the president was traveling in their territory.[15] The office also established the practice of providing audio press releases for radio by creating the first White House radio actuality service.

The office set up briefings on request for all kinds of media groups, ranging from the National Newspaper Publishers Association to Sigma Delta Chi, the journalistic society. Sometimes the briefings were conducted by members of the Press Office staff, but often other administration officials participated. In addition, the office sometimes arranged special briefings on particular White House initiatives (such as civil service reform) for specialized Washington media who were not usually at the White House. As in previous administrations, these briefings were supplemented by ones sponsored by the Office of Public Liaison, which maintained links with special-interest groups.

The office also formalized a series of "Editors' Conferences," which had been held sporadically in previous administrations. Under Carter, these conferences took place twenty times a year. Twenty-five to thirty non-Washington-based editors and broadcasters participated in each. Different parts of the country and all sizes of media outlets were represented, ranging from small local radio stations and weekly newspapers to metropolitan dailies and top-market television stations.[16] The conferences lasted all day. The participants arrived for coffee at 8:30 in the morning and left around 4:00 that afternoon. In between, they attended a series of briefings with cabinet secretaries and other administration officials in the Old Executive Office Building, but the highlight of the day was a thirty-minute session with the president in the Cabinet Room of the White House. Participants in the briefing had exclusive use of the president's answers for one news cycle; a transcript of the session was not released to the general media until noon the next day. Immediately after the presidential briefing, participants were given forty-five minutes to file a story.[17]

In addition, the Office of Media Liaison continued the practice of mailing information to local media. These mailings included fact sheets and background reports on topics ranging from SALT to judicial reform.[18] They also included booklets (e.g., "A New Partnership to Conserve America's Communities"), summaries of significant actions taken by President Carter, compilations of presidential remarks on various subjects, and even ready-to-print articles and photographs. Some mailings were sent to the office's entire mailing list of sixty-five hundred outlets. But often specific material was targeted to specialized recipients, such as particular ethnic media, religious publications, sports publications, and so forth. Particular efforts were made to target black and Hispanic media. For instance, from February 1977 through February 1978, seventy-five special mailings were sent by the Office of Media Liaison to representatives of the black media. Subjects included civil rights reorganization, Black Press Day, and black appointments made by the Carter administration.[19] In a February 1978 memo to Wurfel and Powell, Bario reported: "Our black media mailing list currently includes 204 names—127 print and 77 broadcast. . . . We also mail to the Congressional Black Caucus and their staff (20 names) and black White House staff (23 names)." She further reported that plans were under way to send camera-ready copy—including feature articles,

President Carter at one of his regularly scheduled meetings with non-Washington-based editors and broadcasters in the Cabinet Room of the White House. Standing in the doorway to the right of the president is Communications Director Gerald Rafshoon. Standing next to Rafshoon is Deputy Press Secretary Patricia Bario, who directed the Office of Media Liaison. (Courtesy Jimmy Carter Library)

pieces for editorial pages, and even a regular column—to the black press.[20] Under Bario, precise records were kept of each month's mailings. For instance, in June 1979 there were thirty-eight sets of mailings consisting of 62,100 pieces (960 of them photographs).

Members of the Office of Media Liaison also assisted local news media during presidential trips and helped to schedule local appearances by members of the administration. As in previous administrations, the office continued to provide background material for administration speakers and to advise such officials on media contacts during their travels. In November 1978, Jody Powell reminded senior members of the White House staff that the Office of Media Liaison had an "excellent inventory of the best local media opportunities in most major metropolitan areas."[21]

As the 1980 presidential election approached, the Office of Media Liaison also followed the practice of maintaining links with the press secretaries of Democratic governors.[22] Similarly, the office served as a link to House and Senate press secretaries.[23] The office initially did not have jurisdiction over the "Daily News Summary," which the Office of Communications had had jurisdiction over during the Ford administration, but that changed in 1979.

The primary innovation of the Office of Media Liaison under Carter was the installation of a radio actuality service in the White House. As we have seen in earlier chapters, radio actualities are the equivalent of audio press releases. These short audiotapes of the president or other administration officials are made available to radio stations over a toll-free telephone line. The benefits of actualities had been known for many years. Quite simply, they are advantageous to the person providing the actualities because that person gets to choose which excerpts from which statements will be aired by radio stations utilizing the device. Moreover, many local radio stations that cannot afford the luxury of sending correspondents to Washington or other distant locales to tape such material themselves are grateful for the service and come to rely on it. As the Republican political advisor Stuart Spencer explained, "You're doing their work for them."[24]

Actuality services had been used in political campaigns for some time before the Carter administration. Both the Carter and the Ford campaigns had sophisticated actuality services during the 1976 election.[25] In addition, several cabinet departments and agencies had actuality services. Indeed, such a service had been operating out of the Agriculture Department since the 1950s.[26] When Herb Klein became director of the Office of Communications in 1969, he encouraged cabinet officers to make use of actualities (or "Spotmasters," as they were often called), but he did not formally establish an actuality service out of the White House itself. During the Watergate investigations in 1973, several members of Congress criticized government actuality services, arguing that they "constituted a propaganda mechanism for the Executive Branch to lobby for or against pending legislation."[27] In the wake of that criticism, the General Accounting Office conducted an investigation and reported various abuses of actualities by government agencies.[28] Nonetheless, the Ford administration gave serious consideration to creating an actuality service in the White House in 1975 before ultimately rejecting the plan—in part out of fear that the White House would be accused of engaging in propaganda techniques.[29] President Ford's first press secretary, Jerald terHorst, had strongly advocated the development of such a service in the White House: "It always seemed to me to be an insult to a legitimate electronic correspondent to be handed something on a piece of paper when he should have been handed something on a tape that he could really use in his own medium."[30]

The Carter administration's decision to establish an actuality service in the Office of Media Liaison was spurred in part by a letter from the Democratic mayor of Milwaukee, Henry W. Maier, to Jody Powell in October 1977. Maier explained that he had used an actuality service out of his office for some years, and he urged the White House to follow suit. "As you know, there are more than four thousand AM radio stations in the country and another three thousand FM broadcasters," he wrote. "Add to these the number of small newspapers and television broadcasters who would absorb your information and you have an opinion-making potential that would be difficult to match in any other way."[31] Maier's letter prompted Powell to consider seriously the establishment of such a service.[32] Powell asked Walt Wurfel to look into the idea. Wurfel had been aware of actualities for several years, and he was enthusiastic about establishing one in the White House.[33] In fact, radio representatives had already been lobbying Patricia Bario to establish such a service.[34] Wurfel reported back to Powell in November 1977. Although Wurfel warned that the establishment of an actuality service might generate negative publicity and be labeled a "propaganda tool," he pointed out three arguments for establishing the system: "(1) that the feeds would go out the way we want them to go out, (2) that we would be doing something specifically for radio—and local radio, at that, and (3) that we'd have an additional channel of communication operating during most of the Carter Administration, and well in advance of 1980." Wurfel added that the Democratic National Committee had a successful actuality service that had already begun providing radio cuts at least twice a week, cuts that were favorable to the White House.[35]

In the coming months, Wurfel reminded other members of the administration about the DNC's radio facilities. In a memo dealing with White House attempts to publicize its foreign aid program, Wurfel wrote, "Don't forget the DNC has a passive radio actuality service that is open from time to time to all Executive Branch agency heads."[36] In the meantime, Wurfel pursued the idea of establishing a White House actuality service. In June 1978, he estimated that the annual cost of such a service (including the equipment cost, telephone bills, and salary for one person to run the operation) would be about $70,000.[37] The next month he pointed out why such a service was needed: "The majority of the nation's 10,000 radio stations do *not* belong to a network or receive their newscasts from AP Radio or UPI Audio." He added, "We wish to get this operation functioning no later than the end of August."[38] The plan had already been delayed because the Press Office, along with the rest of the White House, was operating under a tight personnel freeze. The president was adamant that he would not expand the White House staff. Eventually a vacancy occurred in the Office of Media Liaison, and Bario reconfigured the staff assignments to make room for a new person, Richard L. Nelson, to run the actuality service.[39] Nelson, a former deputy director of Radio and Television for the DNC, had produced radio actualities for Carter in the 1976 election and for George McGovern in 1972. His White House service finally became operational in November 1978.

Nelson made two feeds available every weekday. Each feed was targeted for peak listening hours: one for the "morning drive" (when people are in their cars on the way to work) and the other for the "evening drive" (when people are in their cars returning home).[40] The feeds began with a brief description of the material on the actuality, including timings (called a "billboard") and a five-second tone signal for recorder calibration purposes. Some of the feeds included just the billboard, the calibration tone, and a sound-bite (or "cut") consisting of unedited excerpts of news events, such as a presidential speech, running up to three minutes in length. Radio stations could then edit the material as they saw fit and include it in their newscasts. Other feeds were "pre-packaged" actualities of shorter length (usually lasting no more than fifty seconds). These included not only the calibration tone and billboard but also a "voice-wrap," which framed the sound-bite much as would a news reporter.[41] The voice-wrap concluded with the following phrase: "In Washington, this is Rich Nelson of the White House Press Office."[42] Radio stations using the prepackaged feeds had the choice of airing the actuality in its entirety (including the voice-wrap) or extracting the sound-bite, editing it as they saw fit, and adding a voice-wrap by their own reporter. When there was an important ongoing news story, feeds were updated several times during the course of the day. The feeds included statements by the president and the vice president, as well as other administration officials who were testifying on Capitol Hill or making important speeches.[43]

Both Bario and Nelson stress that the actuality service was not intended to be a propaganda tool. Nelson says that he and his volunteer assistants tried to act as a mini news bureau. They were guided in their choice of material by what they knew or thought other news services would be providing. Nelson explained: "Essentially we were trying to act as a news service for stations that didn't have access to [commercial] radio actualities either through a network affiliation or some kind of Washington bureau. So if AP or UPI were leading with a particular aspect of a presidential speech or announcement, we would try to match [our sound-bite] as closely as we could."[44] Nonetheless, the operation generated criticism from the editorial pages of both liberal and conservative newspapers.[45] Some media accounts expressed fear that the White House was managing the news and that local radio stations would present the prepackaged actualities in their entirety with the implication that the reports were by independent correspondents. Some members of Congress, such as senators Ted Stevens (Rep.-Alaska) and Harrison Schmitt (Rep.-N.Mex.), also questioned the propriety of the service. The actuality service received 46,353 calls from 4 December 1978 through 22 May 1979, but the White House had no way of knowing how many of those calls were taped and used by radio stations in news broadcasts.[46] The actuality service remained in effect throughout the Carter administration and was continued by both Ronald Reagan and George Bush. A separate actuality service was also established by the Carter-Mondale Committee during the 1980 presidential campaign.

Around the same time that the Office of Media Liaison established the radio actuality service, it also established a video system that served as a primitive precursor to modern-day satellite hookups. The office arranged for representatives from local television stations around the country to conduct telephone interviews with various administration officials (not including the president). As Bario explains it, "We would book an hour of the principal's time—whether it was a Cabinet secretary, the head of some energy subdivision, or whatever—call TV stations that we thought might be interested, tell them that we have an opportunity for them to interview this person, and book four to six interviews in an hour."[47] The administration officials answered the questions in a television studio in the State Department. The officials heard the questions over a speakerphone, and the White House videotaped the answers. That raw videotape was then shipped by express mail to the television station, where it could be edited together with videotape of the interviewer asking the questions. At the request of the local station, the Office of Media Liaison could tape the interview with a special background and could orient the camera so that the local station could create a split-screen image, with the interviewer asking the questions on one half of the screen and the administration official answering the question on the other.[48] As a rule, only about one minute of each interview was actually aired by local stations.

Like radio actualities, this technology was not entirely new. Richard Nixon's press secretary, Herb Klein, had worked out a system of shipping film clips to major California cities in 1962 when Nixon was running for governor of California.[49] As Nixon's communications director in 1970, Klein rejected a proposal to provide "pro-administration, videotape, hard news actualities to the major cities of the United States."[50] Klein argued that the program's cost, which would have been in excess of half a million dollars, was simply too excessive.[51] Others, such as Charles Colson, continued to pursue the idea. In a memo to H. R. Haldeman, Colson wrote: "At a modest cost (at least compared with buying a network), we can establish a TV news service here in Washington, a private entity that will feed out TV news spots directly to licensees for use on non-network news programs. Lyn Nofziger has prepared an excellent plan which I will review with you."[52] The plan was not implemented.

Carter's video service did not consist of prepackaged video actualities. It simply provided videotapes of interviews, as described above. Nelson explains: "What we did was a precursor to what almost any television network or station can [now] do anywhere in the world. We knew that satellites were eventually going to make this much easier to accomplish."[53] The Carter campaign had provided interviews to local television stations in a similar manner during the 1976 campaign in states such as Illinois and Pennsylvania.[54] In June 1978, Walt Wurfel suggested that such interviews would be valuable in the 1980 presidential campaign and urged that the procedure be implemented in the White House as soon as possible: "I feel strongly that every possible format of getting the President together with the press/broadcast media that we want to use in 1980 should be started and operating on a routine basis by the end of 1978. That shows that the President is committed to this kind of access as a matter of regular operational policy—not just when campaign time comes around."[55] As with radio actualities, some of the media and some members of Congress raised questions about the establishment of the videotape service in the White House—particularly since it was provided at taxpayers' expense. The Office of Media Liaison responded that the costs were minimal. Existing government video equipment was used to film the three to four hours of interviews that were recorded each month. Shipping costs ranged from eight to fourteen dollars per tape, and television stations were asked to return the tapes for recycling. In the first ten months of the service, ninety-four television stations participated in such interviews.[56]

The Office of Media Liaison was not responsible for long-range communications planning, nor did it try to orchestrate the communications of the entire administration. Especially in the first year of the Carter administration, communications planning was at best a decentralized, *ad hoc* process. James Fallows later criticized that decentralization and the lack of a staff coordinator in the White House. "By the end of the first year, [the] system became more or less workable; everyone had learned whom to call to get a telegram sent, which congressmen to notify when news of a home-town project was released, what speeches were required when Carter took a trip. But a year was wasted as we blindly groped for answers and did for ourselves what a staff coordinator could have done."[57]

Carter himself once remarked, "There will never be an instance while I am president where the members of the White House staff dominate or act in a superior position to the members of the Cabinet."[58] Yet after almost two years in office, Carter tried to squelch allegations of his administration's incompetence and inexperience by centralizing control over the cabinet and the rest of the executive branch in the White House.[59] Part of this involved a reshuffling of the White House staff. Tim Kraft, who had previously been Carter's appointments secretary, was elevated to assistant to the president for political affairs and personnel. He acted as Carter's chief political advisor and also directed a personnel review of subcabinet officials (much as Fred Malek had done under Nixon).[60] The eventual result was the elevation of Hamilton Jordan to the position of White House chief of staff, a turnover of personnel in six of the twelve cabinet positions, and the replacement of some fifty subcabinet officials.[61] In the meantime, the mechanism for dealing with special-interest groups through the Office of Public Liaison was revitalized, and the Office of Congressional Relations was expanded and its strategies honed.[62] Most important for our purposes, Carter revitalized a full-fledged "Office of Communications" in May 1978 in an attempt to create a coherent media image of the administration.

GERALD RAFSHOON AND THE OFFICE OF COMMUNICATIONS

Gerald Rafshoon, the son of an air force provost marshal, was born in Brooklyn and was reared on various military bases throughout the country. He earned a journalism degree at the University of Texas, joined the navy, and eventually settled in Atlanta in 1959. There he established an advertising agency, met Jimmy Carter in 1966, and managed the advertising campaign for Carter's successful gubernatorial race in 1970.[63] Rafshoon and another young Carter aide, Hamilton Jordan, tried—unsuccessfully—to get George McGovern, the Democratic presidential nominee, to consider Carter as a running mate in 1972. Soon thereafter, they started plotting a strategy for Carter to win the White House in 1976.[64]

Rafshoon and his advertising agency played a major role in Carter's 1976 campaign, but Rafshoon has said that he never intended to work in the White House.[65] By May 1978, however, the image of the Carter administration was desperately in need of an overhaul. A CBS–*New York Times* poll showed Carter's approval rating at only 38 percent. Only 29 percent of those surveyed approved of his foreign policy leadership, and only 35 percent felt that he was "capable of restoring trust in government."[66] As the political reporter Dom Bonafede put it in the *National Journal*, "Now, after only slightly more than one and a half years in office, the Carter White House may be the first in history to look back nostalgically on the campaign as the high point of the administration."[67]

Rafshoon returned to his own business after the 1976 campaign but continued to advise Carter on an informal basis. As Carter's image problems mounted, Rafshoon suggested to the president that he appoint a communications director. As Rafshoon has put it, "There was a need to have somebody worry about long-range communications problems who wasn't mired in the day-to-day reaction problems that the Press Secretary is—somebody that could help formulate themes, formulate speeches . . . and try to sell [the president's] programs, not only to the public but to the congress."[68] Having argued for the creation of such a post, Rafshoon was approached first by Hamilton Jordan, then by the First Lady, and finally by the president himself—each arguing that Rafshoon fill the post.[69] Rafshoon agreed, and Carter announced his appointment on 18 May 1978. Rafshoon formally started his job as assistant to the president for communications on 1 July. His deputy in the new Office of Communications was Greg Schneiders, a thirty-year-old Carter loyalist who had worked in the 1976 campaign and had served as director of White House Projects from 1977 to 1978.[70]

Many of the functions that Rafshoon took charge of—such as the speechwriting operation, the press advance operation, and the television office—had previously fallen under the jurisdiction of Jody Powell. (See the organization charts in the Appendix.) Despite some efforts by Powell, there had been no concerted long-range communications planning before Rafshoon's arrival. As Greg Schneiders put it, such planning "really hadn't existed before. Jody sort of dealt with it on an *ad hoc* basis, if that's not a contradiction in terms." Schneiders then laughed and added: "As [Jody] often said himself: 'It's hard to drain the swamp when you're up to your ass in alligators.' And he was always up to his ass in alligators."[71]

Clarifying the administration's agenda, plotting long-range communications plans, and getting the administration to speak more coherently were the primary tasks of the new office. Jim Fallows, for one, felt that such actions were long overdue:

> The huzzahs that attended Gerald Rafshoon's arrival in mid-1978 as the man who was going to bring order to the process only highlighted the primitive state of affairs that had prevailed. I had no objections to Rafshoon's projects, because—contrary perhaps to the public impression—they were so elemental and so clearly needed. Soon after Rafshoon arrived, for example, Carter decided to veto a nuclear-powered aircraft carrier. Rafshoon had made sure that the speechwriters wrote up brief "talking points" about the veto, and that these were distributed to every official who had a speech to make. Six months earlier, no one would have taken the responsibility for that obviously fundamental step.[72]

In his new post, Rafshoon reported directly to President Carter. He supervised a staff of seventeen people and worked out of Richard Nixon's old "hideaway" office in the EOB. Rafshoon later recalled that he had had to get new carpeting installed to hide the wires that had been connected to Nixon's taping system.[73] An internal memo describing Rafshoon's responsibilities included the following tasks:

> —Meetings with groups such as public affairs officials, media organizations. Utilize these groups and talents to orchestrate public support for President's programs (e.g., public service advertising for Civil Service reform, *paid for by the private sector*).
> —DNC Communications. Utilizing DNC facilities to sell our programs.
> —Supervise speech writing to get smoother mode of operation and incorporate themes. . . .

—Visit editors, publishers, network executives in D.C. and throughout country.

—Speakers' Bureau: Orchestrate people to answer administration's critics; using members of the administration, *but also those outside.*

—Supervise camera crews on trips. . . .

—Work with Frank Moore to ascertain most critical [congressional] districts and monitor statements of our critics. React on local level.

—Work on PR for mid-term conference.

—Work on PR for mid-term election campaigning.[74]

Together, Rafshoon and Schneiders did most of the long-term communications planning. The "special projects" division of the Office of Communications coordinated the execution of those long-range plans.[75] The director of that division was Alan Raymond, a former press secretary to Massachusetts Governor Michael S. Dukakis. Among other things, Raymond booked administration officials on television shows, worked with the cabinet, and set up regional briefings and speeches.[76] He also sat in as Rafshoon's representative on policy meetings of the ten or so White House task forces dealing with Carter's pet policies. He then provided input about how best to "market" those policies to the American people.[77]

In addition to the special projects division, the Office of Communications also included the media advance team (led by Mike Pohl) and the speechwriting unit (led by Hendrick Hertzberg). The latter included a woman, Carol Coleman, who specialized in "non-speech writing."[78] When Coleman joined the operation in July 1978, Rafshoon wrote a memo to the senior staff:

Carol will be responsible for writing and producing material such as brochures, public service announcements, films, audio-visuals and other aids for the presentation of the President's program. Already in the works are several anti-inflation brochures (one for consumers, another for business), fact sheets on our accomplishments, radio scripts for special groups and other material on our key issues.[79]

During his tenure at the White House, Rafshoon wrote frequent memos to President Carter. In a memo outlining a "public activity plan" for the president to follow from 19 July through 30 September 1978, Rafshoon argued that the "single theme that should tie all public Presidential activity and statements together is *'getting control.'* " He wrote, "The American people want to see the government—and particularly the President—get control of the forces that affect their lives." He added: "Each appearance should reinforce the fact that you are taking, or have successfully taken, action to bring these forces under control. The theme should run *explicitly* throughout our communication."[80] Rafshoon went on to suggest that Carter concentrate on only three major priorities—economics, energy, and civil service reform. The point was to emphasize strengths rather than weaknesses. For instance, he suggested that Carter concentrate on unemployment (one area of economic success) rather than inflation and that the president keep repeating the good news of the drop in the unemployment rate at every possible opportunity.

> We should *never* tire of repeating [the fact that the unemployment rate has dropped]. One of our worst errors is that we don't utilize repetition of messages. In any kind of marketing situation you always take two or three messages and repeat them enough so that the word gets through. This is what we did with our successful TV commercials in 1976. Each commercial repeated your qualities ad nauseum so that the public—by accumulation effect—became convinced that you were a farmer, businessman, engineer, messiah, etc.
>
> You need to recognize this and constantly reiterate the good things about your administration and this country.[81]

Those themes arose again in a memo on the president's upcoming press conference. Rafshoon wrote the next day: "We want a single theme to emerge unmistakably from this press conference: GETTING CONTROL. Regardless of what you are asked you should comment on the following subjects: ECONOMICS . . . ENERGY . . . CIVIL RIGHTS REFORM."[82] Again, in September, Rafshoon wrote: "This month will be remembered as a critical one in your Presidency. . . . The all-encompassing theme is 'GETTING CONTROL.' This month, in foreign affairs, you are trying to get control of the very difficult situation in the Middle East. In domestic affairs, you will probably achieve significant victories in your attempt to get control of the areas of energy, economy, and efficiency."[83]

The same message was being given to other members of the administration. When Carter's chief domestic affairs advisor, Stuart Eizenstat, was scheduled to appear on the television program "Issues and Answers" in August, Rafshoon sent him a memo.

The important things to remember are:

1. BE THEMATIC. Don't get bogged down in details, facts and figures. Relate everything to the theme that Jimmy Carter is trying to GET CONTROL of the major problems facing our country.

2. ENERGY, ECONOMY, EFFICIENCY. You ought to say these words *together* as many times as you appropriately can. If they are picked up as our goals before the end of this session we can claim significant advances in each.[84]

An important part of Rafshoon's job was trying to get the Carter administration to speak with one voice. In August 1978, Rafshoon sent a memo to the senior White House staff and to the heads of the departments and agencies. He wrote, "One of the major reasons for establishing an Office of Communications was to provide a central point of coordination for all communications by the Administration." He added that the office was preparing a "communications budget." Rafshoon warned: "It may be necessary to recommend against Presidential involvement in some of your favorite projects. . . . [This is] a result of our attempt at more focused communication. I hope you'll support us in this effort."[85] Schneiders explains: "We used to talk about the communications budget much like the federal budget, because one of the problems we thought existed before the Office of Communications was set up was that the president was trying to communicate too many different things at the same time. . . . So we were constantly in the unpopular position of telling cabinet secretaries and agency heads that, no, the president won't be going to the Rose Garden to announce your new program, or won't have a public signing ceremony for a particular bill, or whatever." Schneiders adds that they had some success at that, but not as much as they had hoped. In part, that was because it was the nature of President Carter to be "very much involved in a whole lot of different issues." Schneiders states: "It was hard for him very often to say 'no' to people—once he had been involved in reviewing policy options, participating in the decision-making on it, and so on—when they'd say: 'Now, will you be there to make the announcement?' or sign the bill or whatever it was. I think he probably did more of that [kind of thing] than was politically healthy for him."[86] Nor was the office very successful in getting other administration officials to follow the communications budget. Rafshoon says: "Events always overtook [our] desire to just concentrate on certain things. We also had [a] situation where everybody had their pet ideas that were

a big priority to them. So controlling people from making their *own* communications budget was a difficult job."[87] Still, Rafshoon has pointed out that there
was a commitment by the president to get things "more disciplined."[88]

Rafshoon tried to instill a degree of coordination within the administration
by developing a weekly newsletter, "The White House News and Views." The
newsletter was sent to 305 executive-level personnel in the departments and
agencies and to 218 members of the White House staff. Distributed as a way of
communicating "the accomplishments and priorities of the White House," it
contained talking points for speeches, stressed the issues that the White House
wanted its spokespeople to focus on, and kept the members of the administration abreast of what was going on in the various departments and agencies.[89]
As Greg Schneiders put it, "[The newsletter] was a way of disseminating the
line we hoped people would take."[90]

The Office of Communications also began clearing television appearances
by administration officials. As Rafshoon explains: "We put in a system where
Cabinet members would check with me before they went on 'Meet the Press' or
'Face the Nation' or 'Issues and Answers.' And we tried to see that people
weren't on one network saying one thing and another network saying another
thing."[91] Schneiders adds, "I don't remember ever being in a position of
saying 'no' to someone within the administration in terms of going on a
program, but we would send them Talking Points and say, 'Here are issues that
may come up, this is what the president has been saying about these things, and
this is what we hope everybody will be saying about them.' "[92]

Rafshoon even tried to improve Carter's personal relations with members of
the elite press. He persuaded Carter to schedule a series of intimate White
House dinners for the president and important members of the news media. The
idea was not new, but before Rafshoon came to the White House, Carter had
refused to participate in such dinners.[93] As Walt Wurfel put it, Carter was "a
slow learner" on that front.[94] But once Carter agreed to the idea, Schneiders
says that the dinners were very successful. "They were all off-the-record
sessions," he recalls. "Reporters brought their spouses and had dinner in the
family quarters. The reviews were very, very positive."[95]

Rafshoon was only moderately successful at improving the president's
image. There were some early successes. Carter's triumphant Middle East
settlement at Camp David in September 1978 briefly boosted his standing in
the polls, and Carter achieved at least partial legislative victories in the areas of
energy, economy, and efficiency.[96] But, in general, Carter's standing with the

American people—and the press—continued to erode steadily in the face of an inflation rate that was nearly double the rate that Carter had inherited from President Ford and with the spring and summer gasoline shortages prompted by the Iranian revolution. Patricia Bario remembers the meeting when the domestic policy staff briefed other White House officials about the oil shortage and the resulting rise in fuel prices. "Nobody had to be in politics as long as I had to understand that it was probably going to destroy the administration," she says, "because it was totally out of our control and yet we were going to have an inflation rate that was just going to boggle your mind."[97]

In a televised interview with the PBS news anchorman Robert MacNeil after leaving office, Carter noted that there is a clear relationship between presidential popularity in public-opinion polls and press treatment of the president. That relationship, he stated, is a truism in politics: "When the president is riding high and has 50 or 55 percent favorable reaction in the public opinion polls, he's also treated with kid gloves and deference by the press. If he starts going down, though, then he's condemned by the press."[98] Even in the wake of the Camp David Accords, Carter's Gallup approval rating reached only 51 percent. By the summer of 1979, his approval rating hovered around 30 percent. A Gallup poll of 14 October 1979—just before the seizure of hostages at the American embassy in Tehran—showed an approval rating of only 13.98 percent.[99] That was the lowest approval rating of any modern president.

The Carter administration also faced other obstacles. For one thing, it had come to power with a certain contempt for all things established. It was an administration of "outsiders" whose leader had won the White House by running against the system. As a result, the Carter team failed to cultivate Washington "insiders"—including members of the establishment media. As Jody Powell has since written: "We failed to appreciate until too late the repercussions of our failure to socialize in the traditional Washington manner. We missed an opportunity to get to know Washington better. . . . We failed to establish personal relationships with individuals who could have been helpful to us professionally."[100] The outsider status, coupled with increasingly negative media coverage, led the administration to view the establishment media with a certain contempt. This ultimately contributed to the administration's undoing. As one White House official put it: "By having contempt for those establishment media people, we set a time bomb each time we ignored them. I even heard it said, 'I don't care what so and so thinks.' "[101] The problems were compounded even further by what Walt Wurfel has called a "Civil War legacy," which resulted in "the inferiority complex of the Georgians coming to Washington—undeserved, but there."[102]

Carter and his aides were frustrated by the media's negative coverage of the administration. In a 1990 televised interview with the reporter Jack Nelson, Carter spoke of that frustration. He pointed to studies that showed more negative media coverage of his administration than that of any other recent president, including Richard Nixon. "If I've had one major failure in my [political] life," Carter said, "it's a total incapacity to deal effectively with the American press, particularly the White House press when I was in office."[103]

Many Carter aides felt that his administration was treated particularly harshly because of what Powell called "the residue of cynicism" left over from the events of Vietnam and Watergate.[104] As Hamilton Jordan put it: "I believe that Watergate and Vietnam pushed the American media from wholesome skepticism and doubt into out-and-out cynicism about the American political process generally and the Presidency specifically. . . . It was against this backdrop of subtle but profound change in the media that the Carter presidency was reported and judged."[105] Rafshoon echoes those assessments. "Since Watergate, there's been a tremendous distrust of all institutions by the press," he says. "[Members of the press] exercised their strength during Watergate and they found themselves on the right side of a cause. And I'm afraid they've come to be kind of the bullies on the block since then. . . . They're going to catch you, even if there's nothing to catch you at."[106]

Aside from that, Carter was distressed by the media's tendency to substitute coverage of issues with coverage of the game of politics. As Schneiders puts it: "Jimmy Carter came to office with the view that there were right ways and wrong ways to do things in this country—there were good policies and bad policies, and that governing well was largely a matter of discerning the right policies through hard work and close study, and then persuading others that these were the right policies. I think he often felt frustrated that the media did not seem to want to be very cooperative with him in this obviously desirable effort."[107] Elaborating on the same theme, Rafshoon said: "You go back and look over the last couple of years [1978–79] of how the networks report energy. You don't see the merits of our energy program. You don't see analysis of what's in view—of what a windfall profits tax on the oil companies might buy for energy security. What you see reported most of the time is Carter having a squabble with Congress. What are the chances of it getting passed? How it affects his political fortunes for reelection." Nonetheless, Rafshoon admitted that the White House had helped to exacerbate that sort of coverage by giving the media "a free show everyday" for them to cover.[108] The cure, he felt, was not just to increase discipline within the administration but to start putting more emphasis on the stylistics of selling its programs. In the summer of 1979, Rafshoon wrote Carter a memo in which he bluntly stated that the president had to concentrate on style. "In politics—or at least 1980 presidential politics—style is everything. . . . Ideology is not the issue in 1980. . . . issues are not even that important." Rafshoon wrote that he knew that most of his suggestions were "repugnant" to Carter, but he stressed that they were "all-important." Indeed, Rafshoon argued: "Whether or not you are President for another four years does not depend so much on what you do . . . as how you do it. . . . *You're going to have to start looking, talking and acting more like a leader if you're going to be successful—even if it's artificial.*"[109]

Some have argued that Carter's poor standing with the American people was aggravated by the fact that he seemed continually to be the bearer of bad news.[110] His speeches often had a negative tone, and critics later had a field day with his "Crisis of Confidence" speech to the American people in July 1979. Schneiders has called that speech "disastrous."[111] Patrick Caddell, the Carter pollster who instigated the speech, later told the political reporter Mark Hertsgaard: "Truth is the enemy of anyone presiding over a nation in decline. Anyone who acknowledges the truth [as Carter did] is out, because it is an acknowledgment of failure. The only other option is denial. And that can only be carried off by offering a counter-reality that is further and further removed from the actual reality facing the country."[112] In a sense, Ronald Reagan created that sort of counter-reality during his administration. As Carter put it in 1989: "I think that [Reagan] has given the public an image of a strong leader who sees in our country nothing but good, and who has convinced the American people that everything is okay. . . . I think if something has a connotation of disappointment or failure or unpopularity, he has very adroitly stayed personally aloof from that particular news item. But if something is popular, he's associated himself with it. . . . So I think his aloofness from the press and his ability to orchestrate the daily news item has been remarkably successful." In contrast, Carter added with a laugh, "I never was able to orchestrate any news, and [I] had a very unsuccessful relationship with the press."[113]

Much of Carter's failure is attributable to external factors such as the oil shortage, inflation, and the hostage crisis in Iran. The media also exposed Rafshoon's attempts to sell administration programs. If anything, Rafshoon

The Oval Office is transformed into a television studio for a presidential address to the nation. Communications Director Gerald Rafshoon is standing in the doorway overseeing the operation. (Courtesy Jimmy Carter Library)

and the Office of Communications were the subject of exaggerated criticism by the media. In part, that was because the Carter administration had not originally tried to control either what its officials were saying or what the media were reporting about it. Rafshoon concedes that this was a mistake.[114] Greg Schneiders concurs and adds that the original operating style of the administration allowed the media to focus more attention on Rafshoon's efforts than the press otherwise would have. "I think because we started off with very little of that kind of control, the media had grown accustomed to one style of operation at the White House. And when Rafshoon came in and tried to establish some of these things, the media balked and we tended to be defensive about it."[115]

In short, Carter violated an old Nixon maxim that presidents must manipulate the media while avoiding at all costs the *charge* of manipulating the media.[116] Patricia Bario feels that Rafshoon and the Office of Communications ultimately became a handicap because of just such charges. "The media invented this word 'Rafshoonized,'" she says. "And so everything that the

President did or the administration did that looked like it was slick—the kind of thing that [Michael] Deaver might do [in the Reagan administration]—became [the] 'Rafshoonizing' of the President, you know, and it was a negative word."[117] "Yeah," Schneiders added with a smile, "Rafshoonery."[118] Rafshoon agrees that his "high profile" led to accusations that he was packaging the president.[119] In fact, so much media attention was focused on him that his efforts were almost counterproductive. Even Barry Jagoda, Carter's first television advisor, later lamented, "In my view, Carter would have been much better off in his last two years if he had continued to have what was called an 'open presidency' instead of the 'selling of the presidency.' "[120] Schneiders does not agree with that assessment: "The selling of the presidency is not, in any sense, a closing down of that openness. The main things we were trying to do were, with hindsight, charmingly fundamental—almost naive compared with what we're seeing in the Reagan years. . . . We were primarily concerned with just making a more orderly process in terms of the President's involvement [in communications]: when he was going to go on television, when he was going to have press conferences, what issues he would focus on in terms of his public involvement."[121] Rafshoon concurred. "To say that I'm an image-maker is just false," he said in 1979. "It also tends to impugn the President's motives. . . . All I do is try to define what he is; to sharpen, to clarify."[122]

SELLING SALT

The effort to mobilize public support for the Senate ratification of the SALT II treaty with the Soviet Union serves as an excellent example of how the Office of Communications tried to sell administration programs. The only comparable campaign by the Carter White House was its attempt to build public support for the Panama Canal treaties in early 1978—before the establishment of the Office of Communications. That effort was coordinated by Hamilton Jordan on an *ad hoc* basis. The Panama Canal campaign was successful, but the SALT II effort was not.

Rafshoon directed the efforts to sell SALT. In October 1978, Rafshoon wrote that there were only two "priority issues" for the Office of Communications for the next six months: inflation and SALT. The selling of SALT would be achieved through coordination with the Office of Media Liaison, the Office of Public Liaison, and the Speakers' Bureau. Rafshoon then listed a number of activities to be undertaken by the Office of Communications on behalf of SALT:

—We will develop theme papers, talking points, speeches, and speech inserts.

—We will develop a kit which will include film, TV spots, radio spots, newspaper and magazine ads, pamphlets plus "how-to" manuals for use by state Committees (committees should exist in every state with emphasis on targeted states).

—We will consider a cross-country "whistle-stop" tour for the President.

—We will arrange other Presidential activity to raise awareness— speeches, news conferences, statements, appearances, etc.

—We will promote media events—including: television specials, televised debates, White House events.

—We will coordinate media appearances; work with principal spokespersons; arrange scheduling.

—We will work with "outside" spokespersons to insure maximum coordination and encourage statements of support.

—We will work with the Media Liaison Office on mailings to out-of-town editors.

—We will arrange one-on-one columnist briefings.

[Etc.][123]

In December 1978, Rafshoon wrote a lengthy memo to Carter outlining ways of developing public support for a SALT II treaty. One of his overarching concerns was to develop a consistent theme for explaining SALT to the public. It was important, Rafshoon said, not to deviate from that theme.

SALT is very complex. There may be twenty or thirty good reasons why the public should support ratification. If the White House does not exert some discipline, Administration spokespersons will be developing all of those themes, reacting to every criticism, and leaving the public with no clear idea of why SALT deserves support.

The themes we settle on must be *simple and easily understood*. They must appeal to *common sense* and strike a *"responsive chord"* in the public. They should *not try to educate* the public either about the complexities of strategic planning or the details of the treaty. The themes should be compelling and general. Wherever possible, they should be related to what is *current and immediate* in people's lives.

It's useful to look at some of our recent experiences in developing themes to support our positions. There were many good arguments for the veto of the Defense Authorization Bill, but we focused on a "two billion dollar boat" that we didn't need. The Public Works veto could have been presented in terms of water policy, environmental concerns, or legislative process, but we focused on inflation and made the veto stick. Finally, there is the history of the energy bill. When we tried to sell it as the "moral equivalent of war," people didn't believe it. But when we changed the theme and tied energy to the sinking of the dollar, inflation, and national will, it was far more compelling. Each successful theme has been simple, immediate, and has appealed to common sense.

Our central theme—and the theme which should be used consistently when this Administration talks about the desirability of SALT II—is that SALT II maintains the strategic balance and nuclear deterrence *without* a wasteful and inflationary new arms race that would in no way buy us *more* security and which might very well *threaten* the peace and security we have maintained for the last thirty years.

The second, related theme is that defense funds are sorely needed to bolster our conventional military forces and to strengthen NATO. A renewed nuclear arms race would unnecessarily hinder that effort.[124]

In the margin, Carter wrote "OK," and at the end of the memo he checked the "approve" box and initialed it. In a postscript, Rafshoon suggested that consideration should also be given to working with independent "citizens' committees" to support SALT. He pointed out that if conservative activists, such as Richard Viguerie, conducted a major media campaign against the treaty, "the citizens' committees could counter with film, television, radio, print and direct mail which could be developed nationally and paid for locally." In the margin, Carter wrote: "should do."[125] Greg Schneiders later said that the White House encouraged any effort by outside groups to support SALT. However, he said that the White House was very careful not to lend financial support to such groups because of restrictions on the use of appropriated funds for lobbying Congress.[126]

Rafshoon worked closely with a SALT II task force, chaired by Hamilton Jordan. The task force included representatives from the State Department, the

National Security Council, the Defense Department, the CIA, and the White House.[127] In addition, Rafshoon worked on media strategy with a subgroup that included Jody Powell and the PIOs from the Defense and the State departments.[128] For instance, the State Department sponsored numerous citizens' conferences around the country to advocate the SALT II treaty.[129] Paul Warnke, director of the Arms Control and Disarmament Agency, was a frequent participant in those conferences.[130]

Members of the Office of Communications soon found that limiting the public discussion of SALT to consistent themes was easier said than done. On 6 February 1979, Special Projects Director Alan Raymond wrote: "I was surprised that the SALT task force seems to be in the process of developing new SALT themes when I thought we had reached some consensus about what they should be. . . . With State continuing to develop themes and NSC probably doing the same, I think we need to reach some agreement about what the themes will be and how they will be used. Someone will have to lay down the law."[131]

As the actual signing of the treaty approached, the Office of Communications stepped up its efforts to counter criticisms of SALT II. For instance, Rafshoon developed a program called "Operation Response," which was designed to be a mechanism for responding quickly and efficiently to such criticism. In his office Rafshoon set up a file that matched "important administration issues with potential spokespersons both inside and outside government." As he put it, these spokespeople could then "be called upon to respond to statements, columns, or news stories which need to be corrected quickly and authoritatively."[132] Rafshoon described the operation in more detail in a memo to the senior White House staff on 27 March:

We will establish a file based on the major issues on which we may want to respond to criticism. . . . Under each issue category we will file cards for each of the major responders. These names will be drawn from the Administration, the Congress, the Democratic Party, State and Local Government, Special Interest Groups, Business and Labor. . . .

Each morning this office will review the news summary, the network summary, the *Post*, the *Times*, the *Wall Street Journal*, and the *Star* (and the magazines weekly) for stories of major criticism. For each criticism requiring a response we will identify the most appropriate responder. We will then call the staff contact (someone who has a continuing relationship with the responder) and ask them to request the response. We may or may not suggest the general line of the response depending upon the circumstance.[133]

In the memo, Rafshoon also outlined some general principles to be followed in the program. He stressed that the administration should not overrespond. "A blatantly partisan and/or unfounded charge should be allowed to fall under its own weight." He also stressed that there should be "general symmetry to the criticism and response." In other words, the response should "come from the same sector and be at roughly the same level" as that of the critic. Finally, he stressed that the response should come quickly. "No more than 24 hours should elapse between criticism and response."[134] The *New York Times* revealed the existence of the operation in an article by Terence Smith on 3 May 1979. When asked by Smith who was on the list, Rafshoon refused to say. " 'They'll become obvious as they speak out,' he said, adding that they included 'consumer advocates and business people.' " Another White House official said: "We all feel that we failed in the past to challenge sufficiently the criticisms of the President and the Administration. Now, at least, we are geared up to give our side of the story."[135]

President Carter launched his own public offensive on behalf of SALT II at a speech in New York to the American Newspaper Publishers' Convention on 25 April 1979. The treaty itself was signed in Vienna on 18 June 1979, by Carter and the Soviet leader Leonid Brezhnev. But Carter knew that achieving ratification of the treaty by the U.S. Senate would be as difficult as it had been to negotiate the treaty with the Soviets.[136] As he later wrote: "The lobbying campaign we mounted throughout the nation during the next few months made the Panama Canal treaties effort pale into relative insignificance. Thousands of speeches, news interviews, and private briefings were held. The personal and political interests of each senator were analyzed as we assessed the prospects of the ultimate vote for SALT II. It was obvious that we faced formidable opposition."[137]

In the end, the efforts were for naught. Any hopes that the SALT II treaty would be ratified were dashed when Soviet troops invaded Afghanistan on 27 December 1979. The treaty never went to a Senate vote, but both the United States and the Soviet Union continued unofficially to honor the terms of the treaty. Once again, events had intervened to prevent Carter from achieving victory. He later wrote that the failure to ratify the SALT II treaty "was the most profound disappointment" of his presidency.[138]

THE FINAL DAYS

The formal Office of Communications was disbanded in August 1979 as the administration prepared for the 1980 presidential election. Both Rafshoon and Schneiders left to work at Rafshoon's advertising firm, where they produced Carter's campaign commercials and plotted communications strategies, much as they had done at the White House. Rafshoon worked closely with the pollster Patrick Caddell. He also maintained in his Atlanta office a forty-person staff that was responsible for the "planning, buying and marketing work" involved with Carter-Mondale advertisements.[139] Eventually, White House Chief of Staff Hamilton Jordan also left the White House and joined the reelection effort. As Rafshoon told him at the time: "You can't run the campaign from the White House, but maybe you *can* run the government from the campaign!"[140]

The decision to disband the formal structure of the White House Office of Communications was made for pragmatic reasons. Schneiders says that Carter's inner circle decided it would be easier to divide up the communications functions among other existing offices than to recruit replacements for the Office of Communications. For that sort of communications function to work, he says, it "has to be headed up by someone who is very much in the loop and is able to exercise some discipline as much as anything else." To have brought someone in from the outside to head up the Office of Communications would have been fruitless "given the circumstances of the time—the pressures that were on the administration and the fact that it was still a very tight knit group of people making the decisions."[141] In fact, long-range communications planning was soon rendered all but meaningless by day-to-day crisis management as the administration tried to secure the release of some sixty-five Americans taken hostage by Iranian militants on 4 November 1979.[142] The Americans were held hostage in the U.S. embassy in Tehran for the next 444 days.

In addition to the work by Rafshoon and Schneiders, there was a formal communications apparatus at the Carter-Mondale committee, run by Linda Peek. Her operation was a microcosm of the Office of Media Liaison (where she used to work) and Rafshoon's old Office of Communications. Peek and her assistant, Scott Widmeyer, supervised a staff, including volunteers, of about thirty. Her office mailed fact sheets to opinion makers, prepared briefing papers, compiled a news summary, arranged press conferences and news briefings, provided a radio actuality service, and supervised a "special projects" division. She also worked closely with the White House Press Office and the Office of Media Liaison. Indeed, Peek admitted that her operation was "an extension" of those sister operations.[143] At the same time, the Office of Media Liaison was enlarged and given more authority. Alan Raymond, who had headed the special projects division of the Office of Communications, was transferred to the Office of Media Liaison, where he continued to perform the same functions that he had under Rafshoon.

Carter's communications apparatus did little good in helping him to secure victory in the November election. The president had already waged a divisive battle with Senator Edward M. Kennedy (Dem.-Mass.) for the Democratic presidential nomination, and his efforts in the fall were further undermined by his apparent ineffectiveness in securing the release of the hostages.

As a result of the hostage crisis, the surrogate speakers program became a major element of Carter's campaign. When he first announced his candidacy on 4 December 1979, Carter said that he would engage in no active campaigning until the hostages were released. As a result, all of the early campaigning for his nomination was carried out by surrogates.[144] In March 1980, the Speakers' Bureau was reorganized and placed under the direction of Jay Wade. According to Jim Purks, of the Office of Media Liaison, the reorganized bureau was a "major priority." Purks noted that speeches drafted for use by surrogates went through "a very exhaustive clearance process."[145] Among those helping in the scheduling of surrogate speakers were Patricia Bario, of the Office of Media Liaison, and Anne Wexler, of the Office of Public Liaison.[146]

By the end of the Carter administration, there was no lack of "Rafshoonery" in the White House. But it came too late, drew too much attention to itself, and was further impeded by the external crises that mired the administration. Rafshoon later admitted that it had been a serious mistake not to have a full-fledged Office of Communications from the outset of the Carter presidency.[147] In many respects, the Carter administration learned the same lessons that the Ford administration had learned before. Both administrations started out with a decentralized "spokes of the wheel" system of cabinet government. Neither started out with a formal White House chief of staff. Neither engaged in proactive attempts to shape media coverage of the administration. Both pledged an "open administration." And both were forced to change from that initial approach.

As we have seen, Ford's chief of staff, Dick Cheney, argued that any White House must have a disciplined system for controlling what administration officials are saying and for setting the media's agenda. It is essential, he said, for the White House to set the agenda rather than to let the media set the agenda for the administration. He also argued for a strong White House chief of staff. Hamilton Jordan, who became Carter's chief of staff in 1979, later wished he had listened to such advice. Shortly after becoming chief of staff, he penned Cheney a quick note:

> Dick—
>   If only I'd listened to you—
>   A Former spoke.[148]

CHAPTER SEVEN

THE REAGAN YEARS

PERFECTING THE ART OF

COMMUNICATION

Ronald Reagan has often been referred to as "The Great Communicator." As a former Hollywood actor, Reagan knew how to
follow a script. But he was aided immeasurably by a staff that knew how to set
the stage. In stark contrast to Jimmy Carter, Reagan came across as a decisive
leader. He shrewdly transformed his landslide victory over Carter into a
"mandate" for his political agenda. He then proceeded to present to Congress a
tightly constructed legislative package with clear-cut priorities and no excess
baggage.[1] Unlike both Ford and Carter, Reagan did not come into office with a
promise for an open administration. Furthermore, he set clear lines of authority
in the White House, and he and his staff wielded considerable control over the
flow of news from all parts of the executive branch.

Reagan's choice as his chief of staff was James A. Baker III, who had served
as Gerald Ford's campaign manager in the 1976 general election campaign.
During that campaign, Baker had worked closely with David Gergen—Ford's
communications director. They worked together again when Baker managed
George Bush's unsuccessful bid for the Republican presidential nomination in
1980. When Bush became Reagan's running mate, Baker joined the Reagan
fold. There he argued strongly that Reagan should debate Carter—something

that other key advisors opposed.[2] Baker's argument prevailed, and he directed Reagan's preparation for the debate. Gergen joined him in that effort. Reagan's performance in the debate was a resounding success, and Baker's stock rose. Nancy Reagan was impressed.[3] So too were Reagan's close advisors Michael Deaver and Stuart Spencer, who were already maneuvering to keep Reagan's campaign manager and longtime crony, Edwin Meese III, from becoming White House chief of staff. Deaver and Spencer promoted Baker for that post. Much to the consternation of Meese and other conservatives, that maneuvering was successful. One week after the landslide victory over Carter, Reagan announced his choice of Baker—a moderate and a Washington insider. Meese was made counselor to the president and given cabinet rank.[4] Deaver was named deputy chief of staff. The new White House would be run in unique fashion—by this troika of presidential advisors.

Meese was the formal director of Reagan's transition team, but Baker wielded much of the power (just as he later did in the White House). During the transition, Baker surrounded himself with other Washington insiders, including Gergen. Both Baker and Gergen were keenly aware of the mistakes that Ford and Carter had made at the outset of their administrations and were determined to avoid repeating these mistakes under Reagan. In particular, the two advisors were eager to set a clear agenda for the administration. To promote that idea, Gergen prepared a study that compared the first one hundred days of every administration since that of Franklin Delano Roosevelt. He showed that the successful presidents were those who immediately established a clear and simple agenda.[5] Baker and Gergen also took care to screen candidates for public affairs posts in the agencies. The committee that did the screening consisted of Gergen, Bill Rhatican, Larry Speakes, and Michael Baroody.[6] All except Baroody had previously worked in the Office of Communications. And, of course, Baker and Gergen recognized Reagan's skills as a communicator. "We think we have the best communicator president since John Kennedy," Baker said at the time. "We want to husband that resource. We want to use it properly."[7]

During the transition there was some controversy over the choice of a White House press secretary. Meese was anxious to downgrade the importance of that post.[8] He suggested that there be four assistant press secretaries—each one responsible for a particular area of expertise—rather than the one traditional press secretary. Recently, Gergen called Meese's plan "a bizarre idea." Gergen added: "It illustrated the fact that he was interested in having essentially functionaries as press secretaries. Then *he* would be the spokesman—or others like him would be the chief spokesmen for the administration. But the idea went down in flames."[9] Lyn Nofziger, who had been Reagan's press secretary during the campaign, took himself out of the running for the position of White House press secretary—some said at the instigation of Nancy Reagan—and instead became Reagan's political affairs advisor.[10] Earlier, Nofziger had served as director of communications when Reagan was governor of California and as a member of Nixon's congressional relations office.

When Nofziger took himself out of the running, moderate and conservative factions of the transition team battled over who should be press secretary and how the press office should be structured. The final choice was something of a compromise. James Brady, who had served as a press spokesman for Reagan during the campaign and then as the spokesman for Reagan's Washington transition headquarters, was named press secretary, and Karna Small was named deputy press secretary. Small, who came from a background in television and radio reporting, was recommended by Pat Buchanan. Her appointment helped to mollify the conservatives. Brady, on the other hand, was the choice of Baker and Deaver and was viewed as a moderate.[11] On 6 January, Reagan—who had not appeared at the announcements of any other high-level appointments—personally announced the Brady and Small appointments.[12] The appearance by Reagan was a symbolic gesture to show that the press secretary role had not been downgraded. Nonetheless, Gergen says that there was some carryover of Meese's intention to reduce the power of the press secretary. He points out that when Reagan first became president, Brady did not have a lot of access to his superiors, nor was the overall communications operation fully up and running.[13] After the announcement of the Brady and Small appointments, Larry Speakes was chosen as a deputy press secretary.

There was also some confusion during the transition about how to structure the Office of Communications. Originally, Baker planned to structure a communications apparatus closely resembling the one that had existed in the Ford White House during the 1976 campaign. The idea was to have the press secretary and the director of communications share equal rank as assistants to the president. Gergen suggested that the communications post be given to William H. Carruthers, a California television producer.[14] Carruthers had been a television advisor to Presidents Nixon and Ford, and Gergen had worked with him in both capacities. In fact, it had been Gergen's idea to make Carruthers a part of the Office of Communications in 1976. More recently, the two had worked together on the unsuccessful Bush primary campaign and on Reagan's general election campaign. Baker offered Carruthers the job during the transition. Carruthers turned it down, partly because of financial reasons and partly because of personal conflicts with Mike Deaver. He did agree to do some informal television advising at the White House, but even that soon ended.[15]

By the time Reagan was sworn in, there still was not a director of communications, and Reagan's advisors decided to downgrade the post. Instead of being an assistant to the president on a par with Press Secretary Brady, the communications director would be a deputy assistant reporting to Baker through Gergen, who had joined the White House as staff director.[16] Gergen had accepted that post somewhat reluctantly, with the understanding that he would stay in the White House only six months. The job he had really wanted was the directorship of the U.S. Information Agency, a position that went to Charles Z. Wick.[17]

Despite the staff director title, Gergen was deeply involved in communications from the start. Not only did the Office of Communications report to him, but so did the speechwriting team. Gergen had experience in both of these areas, as communications director under Ford and as the director of Nixon's research and writing team. Until Frank A. Ursomarso was chosen as Reagan's communications director in February, Gergen basically ran the Office of Communications himself. As Ursomarso recently put it: "Before I actually set foot, he had done a lot of work in trying to set up the communications strategy [for the administration]. So I merely picked up the pieces and tried to implement them." In fact, Ursomarso felt that Reagan's early success in setting the agenda "was a direct result of the work that David did." In addition to communications planning, Gergen also regularly talked to the press on a background basis. Gergen "liked the members of the press immensely," Ursomarso recalled. "His intellectual abilities were absolutely unlimited, so he enjoyed the verbal back and forth with the press. It would be enjoyable for him, for example, to take [CBS reporter] Leslie Stahl and say, 'Well, come into my office and we'll spend twenty minutes,' which would go on to an hour and twenty minutes because he absolutely loved the interaction, and he loved the contact, and he loved the press." The purpose of Gergen's backgrounders was "to try and tone out the various [administration] themes and stories." According to Ursomarso, that is "a very difficult and artful task which requires a lot of time, a lot of patience, and a lot of skill."[18] Gergen and Brady were at the same rank: assistant to the president.

Initially, the Office of Media Liaison continued to exist, separate from the Office of Communications, as part of the Press Office. Thus, the formal structure basically followed that of the Carter administration. The Office of Media Liaison was run by Lou Gerig, a friend of Brady's who had previously served as press secretary to Senator Richard Lugar (Rep.-Ind.). As before, the office maintained links with local media throughout the country. Gerig led a staff of about seven people. They held briefings at the White House for out-of-town media representatives, mailed fact sheets to editors, and arranged telephone interviews with the president and other key administration officials for local radio and television stations. Gerig's office was more explicitly designed to further specific administration goals than its previous incarnations. "Reagan was much more proactive than Carter," Gerig says. "We really tried to define the agenda every day. . . . We were more focused."[19] In particular, the office worked closely with Reagan's congressional liaison team in an effort to win support for the president's legislative initiatives. For instance, out-of-town media representatives were not chosen randomly to attend White House briefings. Instead, the choices were made carefully, and the briefings were clearly designed to build support for administration proposals. As Gerig explained, the media representatives invited to attend the briefings were from those legislative districts that the administration needed support from—the districts "where we had a congressman that was leaning our way, or a congressman who might have needed some support [from his district]. It was targeted. On key issues, we would bring in reporters from swing districts [because] we needed their vote."[20]

Other parts of the White House also worked in concert to build legislative victories. For instance, Bill Hart, who ran the radio actuality service out of the White House, took advantage of the Senate's television studio. When important votes were looming, senators were filmed answering questions about the proposed legislation. Sometimes the questions were asked by staffers as if they were reporters. Hart's office then telephoned all of the television stations in that senator's state to inform them of the availability of the senator's message via satellite.[21] Again, the point was to build grass-roots support for the president's programs. In addition to the Office of Media Liaison, the Advance Office, the Photographic Office, the news summary, and the radio actuality service all fell under the jurisdiction of the Press Office.[22]

THE OFFICE OF COMMUNICATIONS UNDER FRANK URSOMARSO

Frank Ursomarso, who finally filled the director of communications post in February 1981, was a Republican television consultant who had worked in the White House Advance Office in the Nixon and Ford administrations. He had worked closely with Bill Carruthers and Mark Goode and had been part of the Reagan debate team in the 1980 campaign. As director of communications, Ursomarso was responsible for long-term communications planning and for coordinating the communications that came out of the departments and agencies. Under Ursomarso's jurisdiction was the Speakers' Bureau run by Judy Pond, the Television Office run by Mark Goode, and a research and writing section run by Michael Baroody (the last department prepared "fact sheets" and "talking points" for administration officials, as well as briefing books for the president's press conferences).[23]

As planned, Ursomarso was a deputy assistant to the president and reported to Chief of Staff Baker through Staff Director Gergen. Although that chain of command sounds simple enough, Ursomarso's life was complicated by the fact that the White House was run by the troika of Baker, Meese, and Deaver. "The trouble was that those three people wore many of the same hats. And so, while I was nominally reporting to David Gergen, I was in fact doing work for all three of those [other] men, which meant that I was working for four people," Ursomarso said with a laugh. "These men had different priorities, they had different ideas, and what was of importance to one was of no significance to another. If you have four balls that you're juggling in the air, it's sometimes difficult to keep them all up there at the right height and right speed to satisfy everyone."[24]

Ursomarso feels that one reason his title was downgraded to deputy assistant was because neither Meese nor Deaver wanted a communications director who would command a wider visibility than either one of them. "They wanted a staff person in press communications, not an equal, because they felt that they were the superior people and they were concerned about their public standing, so to speak."[25] Deaver, in particular, was quite active in the president's communications agenda. He was a longtime Reagan aide who had also served as deputy chief of staff under William Clark when Reagan was governor of California.[26] And he was a skilled publicist, having run the public relations firm of Deaver and Hannaford in Los Angeles through much of the 1970s. But Meese was also active. One of the people on his staff was a pollster, Richard

Beale, who worked with the Republican National Committee pollster Richard Wirthlin to determine priority issues that the administration should concentrate on. Based on their polling data, the Office of Communications prepared a document that "determined what issue would be top priority, second priority— what the visibilities would be for the various themes." If the top priority was a theme dealing with the Justice Department, Ursomarso explained: "Then I would have to get together with the fellow at Justice and say, 'Look, this is the priority that we're going to be working on, and this is what we're trying to do. Now, how can you help and what can we do together and what do you know?' " Together they would develop that theme, prepare background material so that either Press Secretary Brady or the Office of Communications could brief on that subject, provide background sessions, and "somehow move that issue and keep the visibility up." To determine their success, Ursomarso instructed Beale to set up a tracking system for the network news. "He would generate graphs from his computerized system showing the number of minutes devoted to various stories," Ursomarso recalled. "We would use those graphs to determine, in part, how well we were doing."[27]

Part of Ursomarso's efforts at coordination involved a daily conference call concerning foreign affairs. Each morning he and Lyndon "Mort" Allin, from the Press Office, got on a secure telephone line with the public affairs officials in the State and Defense departments, the Central Intelligence Agency, and the National Security Council. Allin, who had run the "Daily News Summary" in the Nixon administration, was in charge of foreign policy issues for Brady. During the conference call, they discussed the issues that might come up at the press briefings that day. Allin then used that information to prepare Brady for his daily press briefing, and Ursomarso made sure that there was a unified line coming from the various public affairs offices. "What we were primarily trying to do was to make sure that we did not get caught off guard with something that was occurring or something that was brewing," said Ursomarso. Later in the administration, Michael Baroody—by then the director of the Office of Public Affairs—made a similar conference call to key domestic departments.

White House officials tried to make it clear to the departments that Ursomarso should command respect. For instance, Meese invited him to cabinet breakfasts and regular cabinet meetings in an effort to show that he was in the loop. "That sort of identified me as someone who was 'okay,' " Ursomarso explained. "[Therefore], if I said something, I should be listened to—which is important in that position."[28] Walt Wurfel, trying to coordinate the activities of public affairs offices during the Carter administration, had not commanded that authority and thus was often less effective than he should have been.

Ursomarso's efforts at coordination also included screening the appearances of cabinet officials on television programs such as "Meet the Press." However, the networks did not schedule the appearances through the Office of Communications. Instead, they scheduled the appearances by contacting the public affairs office of the cabinet member that they wanted. The public affairs person then cleared the appearance with Ursomarso, who decided whether or not that official should be on. "I did not want the people at the [network] booking desks to realize that I was involved in that process," Ursomarso explained. Although much of his involvement was for purposes of coordination, he also performed an explicit clearance function that he feels was about 90 percent effective. For instance, Ursomarso notes, "There was a period of time when we did not want as high a visibility for [Secretary of State] Alexander Haig as he wanted to have, so we were trying to juggle those priorities."[29] The problem with Haig was that he was diverting public attention away from the Reagan administration's top priority—economic policy—by his strong rhetoric about the threat of communism in Central America. Haig's visibility reminded people about the charges, made during the 1980 presidential campaign, that Reagan was "trigger-happy." Beale's tracking studies of the network news showed that domestic policy issues were no longer dominating the news, as they had been in the early weeks of the new administration, and Wirthlin's polls showed that Reagan's popularity was slipping. "We were losing control of the agenda," Gergen told Hedrick Smith. "We had a different game we wanted to play. Important as Central America was, it diverted attention from our top priority, which was economic recovery, which we wanted to be our only priority. Haig didn't understand that. We decided to cut off his story."[30]

Aside from coordinating communications from the departments, Ursomarso's other major responsibility was long-term planning. Gergen, in particular, stressed the importance of planning. "David used to keep yelling at me," Ursomarso recalls. "He said, 'Frank, you've gotta be focused on the future. You've gotta be out there.' And I'd say, 'Well, I'm out there thirty days.' And he'd say, 'That's not enough.' And I'd say, 'Well, I'm out there ninety days.' And he'd say, 'That's not enough. You've got to be out there six months.' So he was constantly pressing me to push the envelope out into the future."[31] That was easier said than done, since day-to-day problems confronted everyone. But Gergen and others made a point of having regular meetings at Blair House, across the street from the White House, to discuss long-term communications planning. The reason the meetings were held at Blair House was to get away from the hustle and bustle of the White House so that the participants could concentrate more closely on what they were doing. Among those usually in attendance were Gergen, Deaver, Ursomarso, Wirthlin, and Staff Secretary Richard G. Darman. In addition, Reagan's old political advisor, Stu Spencer, often flew in from California for the meetings.[32]

Reagan's original communications apparatus was short-lived. The system was thrown into disarray on 30 March 1981, when Press Secretary Brady was shot in the head during an assassination attempt on President Reagan. Although Brady's two deputies, Karna Small and Larry Speakes, were supposedly on an equal footing, Small did not feel comfortable with briefing. As she herself put it: "I did not like to brief and didn't feel that my background had prepared me for it."[33] Brady and others agreed. And so when Brady was shot, Larry Speakes was thrust into the role of principal spokesman for the Reagan administration. But there was also concern at the White House about his ability to fill Brady's shoes. His shaky first briefing in the hectic hours after the assassination attempt prompted Secretary of State Haig to race into the briefing room to declare, "I am in charge here." But in fact, Haig's ensuing out-of-breath and inaccurate remarks ultimately proved to be far more devastating than Speakes's performance.[34]

Ursomarso was with Haig in the Situation Room of the White House when that incident occurred. They had gathered there in the basement of the West Wing with other top government officials, including Defense Secretary Caspar Weinberger, CIA Chief William Casey, National Security Advisor Richard Allen, Attorney General William French Smith, Meese, Deaver, and Gergen, to monitor the crisis. The vice president was out of town. The assembled group was watching Speakes on television. He had just returned from the hospital and was conducting a briefing upstairs in the Press Room. To Haig's dismay, Speakes responded to question after question by saying that he did not know the answer. "The official White House spokesman was being asked who was running the government at a time of national crisis, and he was responding that he did not know," Haig later wrote. "He was being asked if the country was being defended, and he was saying that he did not know."[35] Haig turned to Richard Allen and exclaimed, "We've got to get him off!" With that, he and Allen bolted out of their chairs and began running to the briefing room. Ursomarso saw them, turned to Gergen, and said, "Come on! We've gotta move." Gergen and Ursomarso ran after them, and as they reached the briefing room, Ursomarso got ahead of Haig and stood in front of the door. "I just knew in my mind that something was not as it should be," Ursomarso recalled. "So I stood there and I said to Haig: 'Don't go in there. Don't go into the briefing room.' He had run up there, he was overheated, he was obviously agitated and concerned. So I said, 'Don't go in there.' And he said, 'I have to.' " For a split second they stared at each other in what seemed like an interminable silence. Then Ursomarso weakened. "There I was a staff person standing in the way of a cabinet secretary who wanted to go into the briefing room," he continued with a laugh. "So I figured at this point, 'I'm a staff member. He's a cabinet secretary. I lose.' And I don't think David was very anxious to be the guy who stopped him. Whereupon he went into the briefing room and made the 'I'm in charge here' bit with David and I standing there helpless to give him the hook or anything else."[36]

Although Speakes's performance the day of the shooting was understandable, concern about him continued. According to one top administration official, "Larry was a disaster in those early briefings after Jim was shot."[37] Gergen puts it more mildly, "Frankly, we didn't think that we were getting all that we needed in terms of advocacy out of Speakes at that time."[38] In fact, those around Reagan seriously considered naming a new press secretary. Baker wanted to appoint Gergen to that post, but the convalescing Brady reacted angrily to suggestions that either he or Speakes be replaced.[39] Thus, instead of personnel changes in the Press Office, Gergen was named "assistant to the president for communications." The major change was that now the Press Office, as well as Ursomarso's operation and the speechwriting team, reported to Gergen. Most important, the new arrangement called for Gergen to share the daily briefing responsibilities with Speakes. Speakes typically briefed the White House press corps on Monday, Wednesday, and Friday, and Gergen briefed on Tuesday and Thursday. Responsibility for briefing on Saturday alternated between the two.

The new arrangement provoked problems. For one thing, the lines of authority—ambiguous to begin with—were muddied even further. As Lou Gerig put it: "After the assassination attempt all bets were off on how things were done because you weren't sure who was calling the shots. You didn't know if Gergen was or Speakes was."[40] But there was also overlap between Gergen and Ursomarso. Essentially, both were directors of communication, with different ranks. As the *National Journal* reported at the time, "That's right, there's a communications office within the communications office."[41] In an attempt to deal with that problem, Gergen appointed Peter Roussel to conduct a review of the White House communications apparatus. Roussel, an old friend of Jim Baker's, had previously worked as an aide to White House Chief of Staff Donald Rumsfeld during the Ford administration.

Gergen requested Roussel's review in an effort to do away with "duplication and wasted effort" within the communications apparatus. He was concerned, for instance, that Ursomarso's operation and Lou Gerig's Office of Media Liaison were two autonomous units that reported to different people. He also noted examples of overlap between the Office of Communications and the Press Office. For example, both had been "dealing on an everyday basis with the public affairs officers in the agencies."[42] Gergen was afraid that such a system would lead to confusion and to the danger that the two offices would send conflicting messages. Therefore, he felt that the overall communications apparatus should be trimmed down so that it could work more efficiently under his central guidance. Ursomarso knew Roussel, so when Roussel came by his office Ursomarso told him: "Pete, this is the damndest thing I've ever seen here. I've got four people I'm working for. I've got all this commotion going on. David is trying to fill in as press secretary because Brady's not here. I'm about at wits end. Why don't you make some sense of this thing? If you can make some sense, I'll leave."[43]

After receiving Roussel's review, Gergen rearranged the structure of the communications apparatus. Ursomarso left, and the Office of Communications became an umbrella term for all of Gergen's operation. Lou Gerig also left, and the Office of Media Liaison was renamed the Office of Media Relations. It was taken out from under the jurisdiction of the Press Office and made a separate unit led by Karna Small. In addition, Michael Baroody was put in charge of the Office of Public Affairs, which coordinated the media activities of the departments and agencies. So within Gergen's Office of Communications was the Press Office, the Media Relations Office, the Public Affairs Office, the Speech-writing Office, the Media Advance Office, the Photo Office, the White House news summary, and the White House radio actuality service.[44] Other operational units that existed apart from Gergen's domain included the Political Affairs Office led by Lyn Nofziger, the Office of Public Liaison led by Elizabeth Dole, the Congressional Relations Office led by Max Friedersdorf, and the Intergovernmental Affairs Office (which served as a liaison with governors and mayors throughout the country) led by Rich Williamson.

Although the rearranged communications operation consolidated Gergen's power and did away with some of the duplication and overlap, it did nothing to ameliorate the tension with Speakes. On that front, the feud had only just begun.

THE OFFICE OF COMMUNICATIONS UNDER DAVID GERGEN

I n 1982, David Gergen noted that his job was the first of its kind to bring together, under a single jurisdiction in the White House, so many communications operations.[45] Larry Speakes, for one, was not happy with the new arrangement. As he later put it, "Guerrilla warfare broke out almost at once between Gergen and his staff and me and mine."[46] Speakes labeled those he felt were pro-Gergen as "enemies" in the ensuing turf battles. "We would throw every chunk [we could] in the way of those guys to keep them from being able to do their job," Speakes said.[47] In his memoirs, Speakes noted that nothing "could sink someone in the White House faster than a derogatory nickname." So Speakes started calling Gergen—whose height was six feet, five inches—"the Tall Man." Speakes wrote, "Top White House staffers and the press [soon] began referring to him as 'Tall,' which was a source of ridicule at Gergen's expense that helped give me the upper hand in our rivalry."[48] But Speakes did not stop there. "We used Gergen's height against him in another way," he wrote. "The podium in the briefing room is motorized so that you can adjust its height. Before Gergen would brief, Mark Weinberg of my staff would go out and drop the podium to its lowest height. Then Gergen would go out and tower over it like Ichabod Crane. He never was able to figure out why the podium struck him well below the waist."[49]

One person who witnessed the rivalry between Speakes and Gergen, and who had known Speakes for some time, observed that Speakes had always tended to be "super-sensitive" and "not too secure."[50] The circumstances in the wake of Brady's shooting simply aggravated that tendency. For instance, Speakes had a habit of inviting various people, including a representative from the Media Relations Office, to his morning staff meeting. Speakes felt that Karna Small was part of the enemy camp, and he made some crack to that effect during the staff meeting. Sue Mathis, who was attending the meeting for Small, relayed the remark back to Small, and Speakes found out about it. As Speakes said: "The next morning I had one of my guys at the door of the office, and when Sue Mathis showed up, he said 'Sorry, you can't come to this meeting.' And so Karna got all upset. For a long period of time I would not let anybody in from that office."[51]

Frank Ursomarso recalled a similar incident. Shortly after the shooting, but before he left the Office of Communications, Ursomarso wandered into the briefing room for part of Speakes's daily exchange with the Washington press corps. The briefing room was wired for sound so that reporters could listen to the briefings at their cubicles rather than having to be physically present in the briefing room. There was also a speaker in Ursomarso's office. He could have just listened in to the briefing on that, but there was a lull in his work, and he felt like seeing some of the reporters. So, he walked over from the old EOB to the West Wing of the White House and stood at the back of the room while Speakes briefed. Speakes was furious. He felt that Ursomarso was there to observe and grade him. When Speakes confronted him, Ursomarso said: "I wasn't observing you. I just figured I'd walk over and see what was going on. I'm not trying to give you a hard time or look over your shoulder." According to Ursomarso, Speakes did not believe this. "He felt that we were somehow, someway trying to upstage him."[52] In Speakes's mind, Gergen had been plotting, since the transition, to become press secretary and saw this as his golden opportunity.[53] Gergen denies that, and Ursomarso says that he never detected any unusual rivalry between Brady and Gergen.[54]

Whatever the intentions of the various players, the sharing of briefing responsibilities did not work, and Gergen ultimately relinquished all briefing responsibilities to Speakes. "Larry saw it as a definite threat," Gergen explained. "That was one of the chief reasons it didn't work. And it was hard for me to be spokesman two days a week and to try to do this other stuff three days a week. It just got to be too much. You have to spend all your time doing it. And, it was an odd arrangement. I think we were wise in abandoning it."[55] Gergen added that Speakes's briefings improved as time went by.

Speakes was not the only one who expressed displeasure with Gergen. Conservatives, in particular, complained that Gergen—like Baker and Deaver—was too pragmatic, that he did not "let Reagan be Reagan." They also complained that Gergen was too cozy in his relationship with reporters, and they accused him of being a major source of White House leaks.[56] As one senior White House aide put it, Speakes was the press secretary who spoke on the record, and Gergen was the press secretary who spoke off the record.[57] Such people felt that Gergen was being too accessible to the press in his regular background briefings. As one critic told Dick Kirschten: "This is impolite and off the record, but [Gergen] spent the first several hours of each day being a reporter with special access, and the last six to eight hours of each day being a background briefer."[58]

In some respects, Dave Gergen and Herb Klein were very much alike. Both were professionals who enjoyed a friendly relationship with reporters and worked against an overt politicization of their communications operations. As the political observer Mark Hertsgaard has written:

> Gergen's primary allegiance was not the triumph of the Republican party, or the so-called conservative agenda. His concern, rather, was with the future of the American system. To be sure, he was a conservative, but his basic loyalties went deeper than that. . . . Gergen returned to what he "knew would be a cauldron" in the White House not out of any ideological commitment to Ronald Reagan . . . [but as an] opportunity to work from within to break the string of failed or interrupted presidencies that in his view stretched from Carter back to Kennedy.[59]

Gergen's attitude was also tempered by his experiences in the Nixon White House. In an interview with Hertsgaard, Gergen said: "All of us came out of the Watergate years feeling *very* strongly about the importance of trust in government, of developing relationships in this town that stood on something more than simply power. . . . I knew a lot of people who went to jail, people whose careers crashed, people who were at the top who went to the bottom. . . . The people I saw who went down were either highly partisan or extremely ambitious."[60]

In his capacity as communications director, Gergen worked closely with other members of the White House team. He took part in the president's legislative strategy group headed by Baker and Meese.[61] He also participated in the meetings of the "Friday Group," which met across the street at Blair House for lunch every week. As indicated earlier, the purpose of those meetings was to set long-range communications strategies. As it became obvious that Reagan would recover from his gunshot wound, the group met to discuss how to use the "new capital" that Reagan had earned from the assassination attempt. According to Hertsgaard, the group endorsed Gergen's suggestion that Reagan's first public appearance after the shooting be "a nationally televised speech before a joint session of Congress to give a fresh boost to [Reagan's] economic program. This would focus official Washington's and therefore the news media's attention back on the economy, the issue the apparatus wanted to stress, and away from Central America."[62] The assassination attempt had occurred when Reagan officials were still concerned about Secretary of State Haig's high visibility on Central America.

The plan to build new capital from the assassination attempt proved to be enormously successful. Partly because of that strategy, Reagan was able to push through Congress a sweeping economic program that included the largest budget and tax cuts in American history. In setting the new course, the Reagan team demonstrated a mastery of Congress not witnessed since the heydey of Lyndon Johnson and his Great Society.[63] The strategy that engendered that success was merely an extension of the one that the Reagan communications team had been following since the president's inauguration. As Gergen put it, "For the first time in any presidency, we molded a communications policy around our legislative strategy."[64]

Reagan's early success also relied on the power that the White House was able to wield over the departments. Policy-making powers were given to six cabinet councils. Each cabinet council was chaired by President Reagan, although working sessions were chaired by members of the cabinet. For instance, working sessions of the cabinet council on economic affairs were led by Treasury Secretary Donald Regan. Attendance at such sessions was open to all cabinet members, but Vice President Bush and other top White House personnel were also members of the councils. According to Edwin Meese, the system was designed to ensure that department heads remained loyal to the White House. As he put it in an interview with Dick Kirschten of the *National Journal*: "The difference in this presidency is that Reagan has used his system so that the Cabinet members all feel closer to him than they do to their departments. And he gives them ample opportunity to remember that."[65]

Gergen continued to cater to the needs of local media. The radio actuality service in the White House was retained and was run by Bill Hart. Like President Carter's, it was a passive service. That is, radio stations had to call the White House on a toll-free line to gain access to the actualities. Hart also continued the practice of including a voice-wrap with the clip so that radio stations could broadcast the actuality in its entirety with no additional work. This was especially useful for small radio stations that were not able to prepare their own newscasts. Hart closed the voice-wrap with the words: "From the White House, this is the White House Broadcasting Service." Hart stated, "And that's exactly what it was called."[66] Unlike the actualities of the Carter service, Reagan's featured only clips of the president rather than including statements by cabinet members and other administration officials. Furthermore, there was no real effort to target the morning and evening drive times, as Carter's operation had done.

Local media also continued to be targeted through the Media Relations Office. By the end of Reagan's first three years in office, this office had sponsored more than 150 special briefings for local media and other specialized opinion makers.[67] Like Nixon, Reagan was intent on capturing the heart of the "great Silent Majority" of Americans. In 1982, Reagan told reporters, "I know that what we've been doing doesn't read well in the *Washington Post* or the *New York Times*, but, believe me, it reads well in Peoria."[68] He also made it clear to those present at the briefings why they were there. He told one such group: "You obviously know that you are here because we believe that the main source of strength in this fight [for the administration's economic program] is going to be the people themselves. . . . And you are in a position to help with this."[69]

Besides local media, Gergen made use of private organizations to take administration messages directly to the people. For instance, a privately financed group called the "Coalition for a New Beginning" was used in 1981 to generate public support for Reagan's economic program. The organization engaged in an "education campaign" that utilized direct mail and speaking appearances by prominent citizens throughout the country. The work of the coalition gave administration officials time to concentrate on other duties. As Gergen put it at the time: "You're not going to see Cabinet officers fanning out across the country in the next two or three weeks. Their first responsibility is here in Washington getting their departments organized."[70]

Gergen also tried to offset any damage from network newscasts or documentaries by immediately putting an administration spin on the stories. According to Dick Kirschten, Gergen tried to influence such stories before they were aired. Kirschten has written that Gergen typically called all three major networks about an hour and a half before their final deadline to find out what sort of coverage they would be giving the administration. According to Kirschten's source, there was then "a flurry around here trying to influence what they were doing."[71] When CBS Television aired a documentary entitled *People Like Us* in April 1982, which was critical of the administration's treatment of the nation's poor, Kirschten reported that Gergen was again on the offensive. Before the documentary was aired, Gergen sent Van Gordon Sauter, CBS

News president, a telegram "complaining that 'over the past 48 hours, the Administration has sought repeatedly to ensure that the special scheduled this evening, *People Like Us*, presents a fair, balanced picture to your viewers. So far, our efforts have met with total resistance.' "[72] As soon as the documentary had aired, the White House released fact sheets, sponsored briefings, and even requested television time for a filmed response to take issue with the points made by the CBS broadcast.[73] Similar efforts were made the next year when ABC television broadcast the movie *The Day After*, which graphically depicted the aftermath of an atomic war. Gergen persuaded ABC to give administration officials television time after the movie to defend the administration's nuclear weapons policy. Proadministration arguments were also included in a booklet, "President Reagan on Peace, Arms Reduction and Deterrence," which the White House distributed after the broadcast.[74]

Finally, the Office of Communications under Gergen made an unprecedented effort to communicate to an international as well as domestic audience. "[Reagan's] was the first presidency I had been aware of—or at least in which I had worked—in which it was obvious that a president had to communicate to more than a domestic audience," Gergen said. "We never did that during Ford. In fact, under no other administration that I'm aware of. Carter had a film early on when he was president—a speech to an international audience that was distributed through USIA. But public diplomacy became a very important part of communications in the Reagan presidency. It had not been theretofore."[75]

One way that such public diplomacy was charted was through a weekly luncheon meeting that included Larry Speakes and the public affairs officers from the State Department, the Pentagon, and the U.S. Information Agency. According to Speakes, the group plotted long-range strategies for communicating foreign affairs issues. In doing so, it referred to the latest polling data—for instance, data "from Europe on the president's message on such and such" or data showing "trouble brewing" in Tokyo because of the Japanese view of the administration. The group members also discussed trips abroad by administration officials. For instance, they might say: "[Secretary of State] George Schultz is going to Europe. What's he going to do? What's he going to say over there?"[76]

Gergen says that the administration made a particular effort to reach an international audience in 1981–82 to deflect criticism of the administration's decision to deploy nuclear weapons in Europe.[77] There was a very strong nuclear-freeze movement in Europe at that time, and the administration feared losing its European allies' support for the deployment decision. The administration tried to deflect some of that criticism by presenting to the Soviets an arms proposal that it knew would not be accepted. In the proposal, called the Zero Option, the Reagan administration agreed to stop the deployment but only if the Soviets would dismantle three of their classes of missiles in Europe. The administration launched an extensive public relations campaign in western Europe on behalf of the Zero Option. The president kicked off the campaign with a speech that was transmitted "live" via satellite to Europe and that aired on European prime-time television.[78]

National Security Advisor Robert McFarlane later told Mark Hertsgaard that an all-out effort to counteract the freeze movement was also unleashed in this country. The administration took its message to fourteen major media markets, where surrogates hammered away at the administration line. Every deputy assistant secretary and above was given a quota to fill. Within a sixty-day time span, each had to spend four days in one of the fourteen media markets. In those four days, McFarlane recalled, each surrogate "had to do a *minimum* of [a] meeting with a [newspaper] editorial board, a drive-time talk show, a meeting with a civic club and a speech in a campus setting." He concluded, "By late '82, we ended up with about six hundred appearances by somebody at the DAS [deputy assistant secretary] level or above."[79]

Despite all its efforts, the Reagan administration—like all other recent administrations—was plagued with leaks, internal bickering, and a declining measure of public support. Reagan's public approval rating in 1982 was particularly alarming to the White House. By August it had dropped to 41 percent.[80] The administration responded with an unprecedented attempt to control the flow of government information. On 12 January 1982, the president sent a directive to all administration officials requiring them to get advance clearance from the White House on any press interview that dealt with national security issues.[81] Within two weeks of that directive, twenty-five Defense Department officials took lie-detector tests to prove that they had not leaked confidential information.[82] On 2 April 1982, Reagan signed an executive order that made it easier to classify government documents.[83] In March 1983, he signed an executive order that permitted the use of lie-detector tests on any federal employee with access to classified information.[84] In January 1985, the Pentagon began using random lie-detector tests simply to determine the "trust-worthiness, patriotism and integrity" of its nonintelligence employees.[85] The administration also abolished the public affairs office at the CIA, supported legislation that would make it a criminal offense to reveal classified national security information, and set out to limit the Freedom of Information Act.[86] In short, the administration attempted to impose an unprecedented degree of censorship on government officials. Later, when U.S. military forces invaded the island of Grenada, the administration barred press coverage and then proceeded to release to the television networks its own videotapes of the operation. Those videotapes did not show a single scene of combat footage.[87] As a result of the "liberation" of Grenada, Reagan's public approval ratings increased to their highest level in two years. They continued to grow through the 1984 presidential election.[88]

The administration also guarded access to the president. In early 1982, Deaver instituted a new rule that prohibited questions at photo opportunities.[89] The point was to prevent a verbal gaffe from tarnishing the president's visual image. In short, much of Reagan's success as a communicator was based on the centralized control of information. Steven Weisman, of the *New York Times*, called this the "art of controlled access."[90] The Reagan White House controlled the agenda, kept the offensive, deflected criticism from the president, made sure that the administration spoke with one voice, and molded its communications strategy around its legislative strategy. Through it all, the Office of Communications played a major role.

Gergen, however, was unhappy with the direction that the administration had taken. The way the administration had handled the Grenada invasion particularly bothered him. He had not even been informed of the invasion until it was already under way.[91] "[That] was a major break for me," he said in 1986. "The pressures build up over time to restrict information, to use polygraphs. The resentment builds up against the press. And it becomes harder and harder to maintain the kind of standards that we were committed to when I came in. In that sense I thought I was less effective internally, and I found it more difficult to justify and defend."[92] And so Gergen left the Reagan administration in January 1984. Through the upcoming presidential campaign, Michael Deaver took over as the de facto communications chief.

INTERREGNUM: THE 1984 PRESIDENTIAL ELECTION

As we have seen, the Office of Communications often plays its most important role in election years; 1984 was no exception. When Gergen left the White House, the post of communications director remained vacant for a year. For all practical purposes, Michael Deaver took control of the office during that time, with his aide, Michael A. McManus, Jr., serving as the office's acting director. In some respects, the way the Office of Communications was run in 1984 was similar to the way it had operated in 1976. As in the earlier operation, there was a tightly regimented line-of-the-day meeting, as well as an additional daily meeting that resembled the 1976 Communications Group. Participants in the 1984 counterpart to the Communications Group included Deaver, McManus, Baker, Meese, Speakes, Darman, McFarlane, Craig Fuller, Michael Baroody, and Margaret D. Tutwiler, who served as liaison with the Reagan-Bush Committee.

Gergen had started the line-of-the-day meeting before leaving the White House. Never before in any administration had the line-of-the-day been so well choreographed. In part, the Reagan administration was aided by the advent of new technology. Not only was the line spread to the departments through morning conference calls, but it was also accessible throughout the executive branch by computer. Thus, officials could find out what the line was just by punching a few keys on their office terminals.[93] During the campaign, the line-of-the-day operation was expanded to include not only the administration itself but the entire campaign apparatus. Throughout the United States, the president, members of the administration, campaign workers, and dozens of surrogate speakers were hammering away at the same theme. At the end of the day, aides at the Reagan-Bush Committee prepared a memorandum assessing how well the line had played on the evening newscasts.[94] Access to the president was strictly controlled so that reporters had little choice but to follow the line. As Reagan said in response to a reporter's question that deviated from his line that day: "If I answer that question none of you will say anything about what we're here for today. I'm not going to give you a different lead."[95]

Reagan aides also made sure that stirring visual images were available to bolster the daily theme. Throughout the first term, Deaver proved to be a master at setting the stage for the president. He knew how to pick a backdrop that would symbolize the point the administration was trying to make, and he concentrated on the most minute details—down to what lighting and camera angles would be most flattering to the president. As Treasury Secretary Donald Regan later wrote:

> [Deaver] saw—designed—each Presidential action as a one-minute or two-minute spot on the evening network news, or picture on page one of

the *Washington Post* or the *New York Times*, and conceived every Presidential appearance in terms of camera angles. . . . Every moment of every appearance was scheduled, every word was scripted, every place where Reagan was expected to stand was chalked with toe marks. The President was always prepared for a performance, and this had the inevitable effect of preserving him from confrontation and the genuine interplay of opinion, question, and argument that forms the basis of decision.[96]

The emphasis on visual detail meant that the White House often favored camera crews over reporters. The pattern had been set back when Reagan first accepted the Republican presidential nomination in July 1980. His advance men gave camera crews access to the nominee but locked out reporters. According to Laurence Barrett of *Time* magazine: "We started pounding on the doors, but we didn't get in. They don't give a damn about the print people. They were only interested in getting the cameras up there."[97] Things didn't change much in the White House. As the ABC White House correspondent Sam Donaldson put it: "I would see Jimmy Carter almost every working day of his presidency. With Reagan, cameras always get in. It's reporters they don't want there."[98] This emphasis on the visual was just another way of circumventing reporters and taking administration messages directly to the people.

Deaver put his instinct for the visual to good use during the 1984 presidential election campaign. Richard Cohen, senior political producer of CBS News that year, later discussed Deaver's role with the journalist Martin Schram. "Do you know who was the real executive producer of the television network news?" he asked Schram. "Michael Deaver was the executive producer of the evening news broadcasts—yes he was. Michael Deaver decided what would be on the evening news each night. He laid it out there. I mean, he knew exactly who we were, what we went for. He suckered us."[99] Quite simply, Deaver helped to create a counter-reality through his visuals. The idea was to divert people's attention away from substantive issues by creating a world of myths and symbols that made people feel good about themselves and their country.

As the 1984 campaign approached, Reagan's communications operation took a number of technological strides that helped the administration spread its word to the American people. This was particularly true of the Office of Media Relations, which Merrie Spaeth took over from Karna Small in March 1984. The following September, her office began to phase out the U.S. mail as a way of distributing fact sheets and other materials to editors and opinion leaders throughout the country. "I thought mailings were useless," Spaeth said. "I mean, they were expensive, they took a long time, and you really couldn't guarantee the currency of the mailing list."[100] Therefore, Spaeth began distributing material electronically as part of the ITT Dialcom news services data base. By accessing item 52 on the menu, any subscriber to the service could scroll through all the material made available to the press by the Press Office, the First Lady's office, the vice president's office, and the Office of Management and Budget. Whatever the subscribers wanted, they could print. Through the "White House News Service," as it was called, information was made available instantaneously, and for the first time, local media throughout the country had access to virtually the same information that was available to the White House press corps.[101]

Spaeth also made use of the emerging satellite technology. "It occurred to me that it would be wonderful if we could penetrate the local news package 'live' by having administration officials interviewed 'live' in Washington," Spaeth recalled.[102] What she wanted to do was to update the old telephone/videotape/overnight-mail system of distributing interviews to local television stations, the system that Rich Nelson had begun under Carter. Bill Hart, who continued Nelson's radio actuality service in the Reagan administration, abandoned the videotape service because it was too cumbersome. In 1984, the Washington, D.C., Chamber of Commerce—which was just across the street from the White House—was setting up its own satellite system. Spaeth found out that the chamber had unused satellite time from 11:00 A.M. to 1:00 P.M. "So," she said, "we cut a deal where they gave me free satellite time and I gave them the last interview of whoever it was we were working with, including the president." The routine of the interviews themselves was much the same as it had been under Nelson. "We would do five or six sequential interviews 'live'—one right after the other," Spaeth continued. "And we would put up an easel next to the camera with the call letters of the station and the name of the person and the city where they were. You find after three or four of them you forget whether this is Tulsa or Tuscaloosa."[103]

Spaeth was aided enormously by the chamber of commerce capability. With it, she was able to choose exactly which media markets she wanted to target. If she had instead arranged the interviews with a station group such as Cox, she would have been forced to beam the interviews to a preexisting market. That would have undermined the effectiveness of the system on topical issues when the administration wanted to target specific locales. By using the chamber of commerce facilities, Spaeth could target any combination of locales she chose by creating her own market to match the issue. Again, the whole point of the system was to take the administration's line directly to the people. As Spaeth put it, "The satellite interviews, of course, were a superb way around the White House press corps."[104] Mark Bindrim of the chamber of commerce concurred, "With the satellite, you can bypass the three major TV networks and the AP and UPI wire services."[105]

Reagan's campaign apparatus also made extensive use of satellite capabilities during the 1984 campaign, and the Office of Media Relations played an important role at the Republican National Convention in Dallas. There, Spaeth set up satellite interviews with local television stations around the country. She left one member of her staff in Washington. "The rest of us moved [to Dallas] lock, stock, and barrel," she said. "The weekend before the convention as all the journalists were arriving, we were roving through the convention center getting names and phone numbers [of representatives from local television stations]. We put a lock on the cabinet secretaries' time and anybody else we could get who was noteworthy from 5:00 to 7:00 in the evenings. Then what we would do each morning is get on the phone with the stations, and our goal was to have one important person per group of stations live each night. So if you were the Jefferson Pilot group, you would have Secretary Dole or Secretary Bell or Bill Clark at some point during your broadcast for a live interview. They would have to share that interview with other stations in the group, but at least one of them could be live and they could say, 'Secretary Clark visited our Jefferson Pilot booth just a few minutes ago.' It was an unbelievable madhouse, but by and large we pretty much met our goal."[106]

During the convention, the Reagan team also took advantage of broadcast capabilities provided by the Republican National Committee. Previously, independent television stations that wanted to cover convention proceedings had had to subscribe to the network pool. That was a very expensive proposition. Because of that expense, the three major networks had a virtual monopoly on live coverage of the convention. Republican television consultants such as Bill Carruthers and Mark Goode wanted to transmit convention coverage that was not filtered by the networks. In other words, they wanted coverage with their own "spin" on it. By 1984, they knew such coverage could be picked up not only by independent television stations and smaller networks (such as the Spanish International Network) but also by the burgeoning number of cable channels throughout the country. With the exception of CNN, cable had little news-gathering ability of its own. And so they created the Republican Television Network. As Bill Carruthers recalls, they decided: "Look, it's our hall. We're paying for it. We'll put our cameras in there and we'll provide full-blown, multi-camera coverage of the convention—for nothing. Free." Then, he continues, they could tell television stations: "You bring your anchor guy in, we'll let you do interviews with your anchor guy, we'll provide you a camera for that, we'll provide locations for you in the hall, etc., etc."[107]

Coverage by the Republican Television Network was actually more complete than that of the other major networks. Mark Goode pointed out that in 1984 they brought in ten mobile camera units and covered the convention as fully as possible. That included gavel-to-gavel coverage of everything that took place on the podium, speeches by delegates on the floor, and important floor demonstrations. By contrast, the network pool covered the convention with only three or four cameras and did not provide gavel-to-gavel coverage. In addition to the television service, the Republicans provided an audio feed of the convention free of charge to any radio station that wanted to plug into it. Several thousand radio stations did just that. "All of the major services plugged into us," Goode said. "AP and UPI and everybody that feeds all those independent [radio] stations. Mutual took their feed from us [as well as others]." He also noted the high number of television stations that took advantage of the service. "Every major station group in the country plugged in at the convention, meaning people like Westinghouse, Metromedia, and the Tribune group. A number of major independents took the feed. PBS took the feed. The Spanish International Network. There were several hundred stations on that."[108] The Republicans even offered the feed to the four major networks, but only CNN took any of it. The other networks were less hesitant in 1988.

All told, somewhere around a thousand television stations broadcast the Republican feed, according to Goode. "We felt we were very well served by it," Goode continued. "Our interest was in providing the greatest exposure possible for our candidates and our party platform. We said to the stations, 'If you want to customize, localize your convention in any way you choose, that's fine. Do whatever you want with it. We're putting no strings on this. It's yours. All you have to do is come and plug in.' "[109] Goode said that an example of how a station might localize the convention was if the mayor of Kansas City was one of the convention speakers. Surely, Kansas City affiliates would want to cover that, but in all likelihood the networks would cut away from that because the mayor of Kansas City was not of particular national interest.

Before the advent of the Republican Television Network, Kansas City affiliates would have been out of luck. With it, they could switch away from their own network's coverage and pick up that of the Republican Television Network.

Goode contends that since the feed from the Republican Television Network contained absolutely no commentary and featured no reporters, it was "totally objective."[110] Bill Carruthers is less restrained in his comments about the service: "It was very successful because we were obviously shooting the convention the way *we* wanted to shoot it. And you didn't have the network naysaying newscasters and reporters running around the floor trying to put everything down."[111] Quite simply, the Republicans knew that in the end, it was the visual image that Americans would respond to and remember.

Back at the White House, Merrie Spaeth spearheaded a drive to install a television studio at the White House so that members of the administration would not be dependent on facilities like those of the chamber of commerce for the production and transmission of satellite interviews. Larry Speakes thought it was a great idea.[112] Others were less enthusiastic. "The White House was terrified that it would be accused of managing the news," Spaeth said. "I never understood why they were so terrified, because that's what we tried to do every day. But they were terrified of it and they felt it would create a tremendous outcry." They were afraid not only of charges of media manipulation, she continued, but also about "what it would look like in terms of spending taxpayer money."[113] Despite Spaeth's offer to fund the project with private funds, the White House remained skittish, and the television studio never got off the ground. Even the Secret Service seemed to stand in the way of Spaeth's plan. One day she organized a demonstration of how such a system would work by setting up a temporary studio in the Media Relations Office in the Old Executive Office Building next to the White House. To transmit the demonstration, Spaeth had to hang a small microwave dish out of the fifth floor of the building. Even though she had permission for her task, Secret Service agents did not take kindly to the sight of the unusual object protruding from the EOB. "Every time we would hang the dish out, some secret service guy would see it, draw his revolver, race over to the EOB, tear up five flights of stairs, and flatten us against the wall," Spaeth recalled with a laugh.[114]

Finally, Spaeth supplemented the passive radio actualities that were provided by the Press Office. To gain access to those, radio stations had to take the initiative and call a toll-free telephone number at the White House. "I didn't want to wait for them to call the service, I wanted to call them," Spaeth explains. "Aggressiveness characterized everything that we did," she continues. So her office called radio stations and offered the actualities directly. Likewise, the office called local newspapers and offered them statements for use in their stories. The Press Office actuality line "only hit radio stations," she adds. "I was after everything. And, of course, if you call a weekly newspaper—you know, they get a call from the White House, you can really get ink." For example, the White House took the initiative with things like disaster statements in the wake of an earthquake or hurricane. "Instead of just putting them out," she concludes, "we would call every media outlet in the state that it affected and give them a statement or an actuality because it dramatically increased the press we got."[115]

Under Deaver's direction, the stagecraft, the attention to local media, and the administration's adherence to a carefully orchestrated line paid off. In short, the Office of Communications provided the imagery and the messages that reinforced Reagan's "Morning in America" campaign theme. In the November election, Reagan won forty-nine states, thus becoming the first president since Dwight Eisenhower to win back-to-back landslides.

THE OFFICE OF COMMUNICATIONS UNDER PATRICK BUCHANAN

David Gergen once argued that criticism should be deflected from the president by having other administration officials act as "lightning rods." He said: "My theory on that is that you only have one four-star general in battle, but you've got a lot of lieutenants who can give blood. And if the going is getting hot and heavy, it is far better to have your lieutenants take the wounds than your general."[116] Patrick Buchanan—who joined the Reagan administration as director of communications in February 1985—would serve just such a role.

Buchanan's arrival was the result of a major shake-up of White House personnel in the wake of Reagan's landslide reelection. Chief of Staff James Baker and Treasury Secretary Donald Regan exchanged posts, and Michael Deaver left the administration to set up a private consulting firm. Regan apparently chose Buchanan in an effort to protect himself from right-wing criticism. Indeed, Buchanan was a conservative's conservative. As a speechwriter and editor of the "Daily News Summary" for Richard Nixon, Buchanan had drafted Vice President Spiro Agnew's tirade against the media in November 1969. Later, when Watergate engulfed the White House, Buchanan wrote a strategy memo to Nixon. In that July 1973 memo, Buchanan urged that the Watergate issue be changed "from a question of whether the President 'knew' of the cover-up . . . to a question of whom do you wish to govern this nation— the President or the men who would destroy him." He continued: "Our adversaries do not simply wish to show Nixon's involvement, they wish to castrate the President, to strangle the New Majority in its crib, to reverse the democratic verdict at the polls in November. . . . If we have to drift into demagoguery, so be it."[117]

After leaving the White House in October 1974, Buchanan confirmed his reputation as a conservative ideologue through syndicated columns and lively participation on the television show "The McLaughlin Group." Buchanan had a keen intellect and a feisty desire to engage opponents in debate. His abilities were obvious at an early age. He had grown up in a conservative Irish Catholic household whose two heroes were General Douglas MacArthur and the anti-communist crusader Senator Joseph McCarthy (Rep.-Wis.). The young Pat could talk before he could walk, and he is said to have memorized the Rosary while still in his crib.[118]

Michael Deaver was afraid that Buchanan was too much of an ideologue, and he argued against hiring Buchanan. As the reporters Jane Mayer and Doyle McManus have written: "Deaver warned that [Buchanan] was too strident and would jeopardize the administration's successful blend of hard-line policy and smooth salesmanship."[119] Regan was not persuaded by Deaver's argument. One of Buchanan's new underlings, the Reagan speechwriter Peggy Noonan, was also suspicious of her new boss because of his reputation. "He is bad, he is just a bad, bad man, and you watch out," an acquaintance had ominously warned her.[120] But Noonan later claimed that she had "never seen such a gap between public persona and private personality." She wrote: "He is neither bombastic nor especially combative. He tends to speak softly." And, she concluded triumphantly, he loves poetry. "Once, in one of the first speeches I ever wrote with him in charge, I used the phrase 'show an affirming flame,' and he underlined it and asked me later, 'That's Auden, isn't it?' I was delighted. Yes, Auden's 'September 1, 1939.' "[121]

In fact, Buchanan made a particular effort in his first three months on the job to keep a low profile. In stark contrast to Gergen, he sheltered himself from reporters and refused to grant any interviews.[122] Still, the tactic proved to be unsuccessful. Reporters were wary of Buchanan and he received extensive

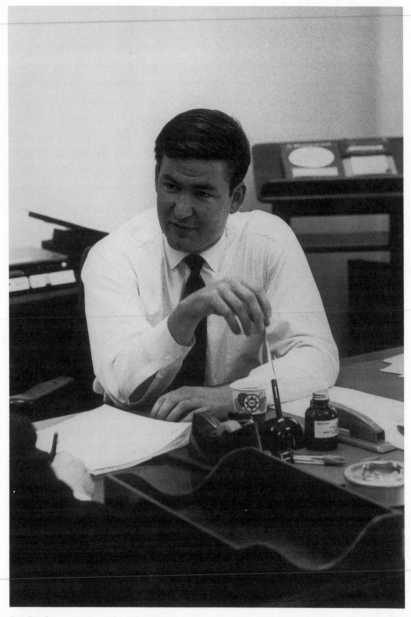

Pat Buchanan returned to the White House in 1985 as President Reagan's director of communications. Buchanan had previously served in the White House during the Nixon administration as a speechwriter. (Courtesy Nixon Presidential Materials Project)

(often unfavorable) coverage in the media. Such coverage was most pronounced in April 1985, when the White House announced that President Reagan would lay a wreath at a military cemetery at Bitburg, Germany, during a ten-day trip to that country. There was immediate outcry over the fact that nearly fifty members of Adolf Hitler's elite SS corps were buried in the cemetery. Buchanan became a focus of the controversy because he had engaged in a televised debate in 1982 in which he had advocated terminating the Justice Department's Office of Special Investigations (OSI), which was responsible for investigating Nazi war criminals in the United States. At that time he had questioned the "singularity" of the Holocaust and had called the OSI's activities a "fruitless exercise" and "not a proper use of [government] resources."[123]

Media accounts speculated that Buchanan had encouraged Reagan not to cancel his visit to the Bitburg cemetery.[124] When Reagan announced that he would expand his itinerary during the trip to visit the Bergen-Belsen concentration camp, NBC News reported that Buchanan had been observed at a White House meeting writing the phrase "succumbing to the pressure of Jews" over and over on his notepad.[125] With that, Buchanan broke his vow of silence. The NBC account proved to be exaggerated (Buchanan apparently wrote the phrase just once as a notation of what someone else had said), and numerous Jewish spokesmen came to Buchanan's defense. But once Buchanan was out of his corner, he never returned to it. In the months ahead Buchanan proved to be vocal, partisan, and combative.

Despite the difference between the two men, Buchanan's responsibilities were much the same as Gergen's had been. There were, however, two notable differences. Buchanan did not have jurisdiction over the Press Office, as Gergen had, and he won a battle with Reagan's political advisor Edward J. Rollins to take control of the Office of Public Liaison, which maintained links with special-interest groups. As Rollins put it, "I saw the office as a 'political realignment' tool, but the way Don [Regan] has things compartmentalized, it is seen as a 'getting the word out' function and therefore falls to Pat."[126] In addition to Public Liaison, Buchanan also had jurisdiction over Public Affairs, Speechwriting, and Media Relations.

From the start of his tenure, Buchanan had a great deal of power. On 11 April 1985, the *New York Times* reported that Buchanan was "one of the most powerful policy-making figures in the Reagan administration."[127] Like Gergen before him, Buchanan was a member of the Legislative Strategy Group. The core group consisted of Chief of Staff Regan, Buchanan, Rollins, and Max Friedersdorf and M. B. Oglesby, of the Legislative Affairs Office.[128] The old Friday Group that used to meet weekly at Blair House to plot long-range strategy was also revamped and continued to meet—usually on Saturday mornings in the West Wing of the White House. Members of this "public diplomacy group," as it was now called, included Buchanan, Speakes, Cabinet Secretary Alfred H. Kingon, Staff Secretary David L. Chew, and representatives from the Advance Office, the Legislative Affairs Office, the National Security Council, and the Office of Management and Budget. The group was responsible for planning the forthcoming week's communications agenda.[129]

Buchanan was a staunch advocate of the conservative agenda. Apparently, he was willing to use his control over the communications apparatus to influence policy in that direction. For instance, Robert McFarlane, the normally unflappable national security affairs advisor, in an April 1985 staff meeting exploded at Buchanan over his refusal to follow the advice of the national security advisors in drafting speeches for Reagan's upcoming European trip. McFarlane reportedly told Buchanan in no uncertain terms that speechwriters were "not supposed to make policy."[130]

Buchanan appears to have been particularly eager to promote a conservative approach to foreign policy. As John Judis wrote in the *New Republic*, Buchanan "waged a lonely but often extremely visible struggle within the White House for the right's foreign policy agenda."[131] In so doing, Buchanan increasingly alienated Donald Regan. In March 1985—without clearance from Regan—Buchanan published an essay on the op-ed page of the *Washington Post* urging Congress to vote for aid to the contra rebels in Nicaragua. In the essay, Buchanan wrote, "With the vote on *contra* aide, the Democratic Party will reveal whether it stands with Ronald Reagan and the resistance—or Daniel Ortega and the communists."[132] At a meeting of the "public diplomacy group" on 3 March 1986, Buchanan urged that the theme for the upcoming week should be the danger that Nicaragua would become, as he put it, "a privileged sanctuary for terrorists and subversives just two days' driving time from Harlingen, Texas."[133] According to a 1987 report by the General Accounting Office, Buchanan also encouraged the preparation of propaganda by a unit within the State Department. Such activities violated Section 501 of the Appropriations Act, which provided funds for the State Department.[134]

The activities by the State Department's Office for Public Diplomacy for Latin America and the Caribbean (S/LPD) were similar to the letters-to-the-

editor operation that Buchanan had participated in during the Nixon administration. The explicit goal of the S/LPD was "to gain sufficient bipartisan
support in Congress to permit approval of increased assistance, economic and
military, to Central America and to preclude crippling restrictions on actions in
support of U.S. policy objectives in the region."[135] In pursuit of that goal, the
S/LPD helped to write op-ed articles supporting the administration's Central
America policy without any indication to the newspaper or its readers that the
articles were government-sponsored. A memo dated 13 March 1985, from
Otto J. Reich, head of the S/LPD, to President Reagan and Patrick Buchanan
read: "Attached is a copy of an op-ed piece that ran two days ago in *The Wall
Street Journal*. Professor [John] Guilmartin [of Rice University] has been a
consultant to our office and collaborated in the writing of this piece. It is
devastating in its analysis of the Nicaraguan arms build-up. Officially, this
office had no role in its preparation." The memorandum continued: "Two op-
ed pieces, one for *The Washington Post* and one for *The New York Times*, are
being prepared for the signatures of [Nicaraguan] opposition leaders Alphonso
Rubello, Adolpho Callero and Arturo Cruz. These two op-ed pieces are being
prepared by one of our consultants and will serve as a reply to the outrageous
op-ed piece by Daniel Ortega in today's *New York Times*."[136]

The General Accounting Office concluded that the S/LPD had "engaged in
prohibited, covert propaganda activities designed to influence the media and
public to support the Administration's Latin American policies." The office
added, "The use of appropriated funds for these activities constitutes a viola-
tion of a restriction on the [use of federal funds by the State Department] for
publicity or propaganda purposes not authorized by Congress."[137] Reich later
said that the GAO report was "vastly exaggerated."[138]

By December 1986, Donald Regan felt that Buchanan was going too far. In
the midst of the breaking Iran-Contra scandal, Buchanan published an op-ed
piece in the *Washington Post* (again without Regan's approval).[139] He hailed
Lieutenant Colonel Oliver North as a hero and bitterly attacked Republicans
for not supporting Reagan during the scandal.

Of all the lurid features in the bizarre tapestry of "Contragate," perhaps
the most revealing is the behavior of the Republican Party establishment,
which owes all it has and all it is to Ronald Wilson Reagan. With a few
exceptions . . . the whole damn pack has headed for the tall grass.
What a classic portrait in ingratitude!

. . . Do these Republicans truly think the investigative engines of a hostile Congress and the artillery of an Adversary Press are all being wheeled again into position—simply "to get at the truth"? Do they seriously believe these pious declamations from the Democratic left that "we must not have another failed presidency"? Do they not recognize that the target here is not Donald Regan but Ronald Reagan—that what liberalism and the left have in mind is the second ruination of a Republican presidency within a generation?[140]

Peggy Noonan has suggested that Pat Buchanan was really a "dead duck" from the day he walked into the White House because he had so many enemies.[141] Two years later, in February 1987, Buchanan finally resigned as director of communications. By then, Chief of Staff Regan was also under fire because of the Iran-Contra scandal. Nancy Reagan was lobbying her husband to get Regan out of the administration, as were other Reagan advisors such as Michael Deaver and Stu Spencer.[142] With Buchanan's departure, Regan took the opportunity to try to co-opt the opposition. He suggested that Spencer be named the new director of communications. "That was a move strictly designed on the old thesis that you keep your enemies close to you," Spencer explained, "because I had finally made the decision in my mind, as others had prior, that it was in the President's best interests that Don Regan leave. And he knew that. In fact, when he told the Reagans [about the idea] they laughed and said, 'He's not going to come back and be Director of Communications.' "[143] Regan has admitted his motives: "If [Spencer] was going to sharpen the knives, I thought, then he might as well come right into the kitchen. But, there were also sound managerial reasons for wanting Spencer. He knew the Reagans and their public relations requirements better than anybody, and as I had reason to know, he was a gifted handler of the press."[144]

Spencer turned down the offer, as the Reagans had predicted. Nancy Reagan then pushed for her choice: John O. Koehler. Koehler had worked at the U.S. Information Agency and came with the recommendation of the USIA chief and Reagan family friend Charles Wick.[145] That sealed the decision. But only a week after Koehler was named, "NBC Nightly News" broke a story that the new communications director, who was born and raised in Germany, had been a member of the Hitler Youth when he was a boy.[146] That revelation was enough to force his resignation.

Don Regan's fortunes were also falling. He tendered his resignation—at the president's request—shortly after Koehler's departure. The Iran-Contra affair had severely damaged the administration's image, and the president turned to former Senate Majority Leader Howard Baker of Tennessee to restore order as his new chief of staff. At the time, Baker was in Florida for a family vacation, where he was planning his own bid for the presidency in 1988. The president called him there and asked him to come to the White House to discuss the possibility of becoming his chief of staff. Baker knew that if he agreed to join the White House, he would have to cancel his plans to run for the presidency. Nonetheless he acceded to the president's request for a meeting. Baker also knew what bad press the president was receiving because of the Iran-Contra affair. As soon as his phone conversation with the president ended, Baker called his longtime Senate press secretary, Thomas C. Griscom, told him about the president's offer, and asked him if he would come along to the White House as director of communications if Baker became chief of staff. Griscom was hesitant. He had just been named president of the Washington subsidiary of the New York advertising firm Ogilvy and Mather. Despite the hesitation, Griscom agreed.[147] When Baker met with Reagan, he said that one of his conditions for accepting the job was that Griscom become communications director.[148] The president agreed, and Griscom assumed the new post in April 1987.

THE OFFICE OF COMMUNICATIONS UNDER TOM GRISCOM

The precise jurisdiction of the Office of Communications changed with almost every new communications director in the Reagan administration. There was also a correlation between the tenure of chiefs of staff and communications directors, a dynamic that influenced the operating styles of the office.

Larry Speakes had left the Press Office by the time Griscom became communications director. The new press secretary was Marlin Fitzwater. Griscom put the Press Office back within the Office of Communications, and he brought the Office of Political and Intergovernmental Affairs under his jurisdiction as well. Also under the communications office were the speechwriting, media relations, scheduling, and advance offices. Griscom moved the Office of Public Liaison out of the communications office, although he says that if he had it to do over again, he would leave public liaison where it was.[149]

One of the first things that Griscom did in his new post was to try and take control of the communications agenda and steer the media away from their obsession with the Iran-Contra affair. He felt that Pat Buchanan had used the communications director post primarily as a conservative advocacy position and had not sufficiently concentrated on long-range planning and the coordination of messages and actions from the administration. Reviewing the past two years, Griscom felt that the president's actions and the visual images of those actions had not always supported the messages that the administration was trying to transmit. "To me, communications is much broader than just words," Griscom said. "It is the presentation of the words, it's the image, it's visuals. All that goes into shaping a message. So we decided that we needed to go back and recapture what Mike Deaver had done in the first four years, and that was to worry about the atmospherics and how the atmospherics and the words come together to present one package." Buchanan hadn't totally ignored such things, Griscom added, but he felt that Buchanan had paid attention to them only on a piecemeal basis. "I did not find a sense that there was any coordinated effort," he said. "What we were trying to do was to put the coordination back in place."[150]

To that end, Griscom put together a Planning Group, which met twice a week in his office at the White House. The group included about a dozen people, ranging from the press secretary to representatives of the cabinet and National Security Council. The pollster Richard Wirthlin joined the group once a week to offer advice based on his most recent survey research data. The goal was to plan thematic messages for the administration and to reassert a long-range communications agenda. In particular, Griscom wanted to divert attention away from the Iran-Contra affair. The communications operation was structured, he said, "to figure out how to get Ronald Reagan repositioned and get other issues out front."[151] As part of that effort, Griscom tried to move news about Iran-Contra away from the White House. He later pointed out that the White House was worried "about who was going to be seen on T.V. around this country every night talking about Iran-Contra." He added, "If we could figure out how to get the T.V. story up on Capitol Hill, which is part of what we did, we were satisfied we had done a good day's work."[152] He and his planning group then tried to associate the president with other issues. For instance, they came up with the idea of having President Reagan spearhead an "Economic Bill of Rights." Their goal was for Reagan to recapture the domestic agenda by concentrating on themes that had worked for him in the past. Thus, they had the president make rhetorical calls for such things as a balanced budget and a line-item veto.[153] At the same time, the Office of Public Affairs started distributing a monthly economic bulletin to media around the country. It included camera-ready articles touting the economic growth experienced during the Reagan administration. One, entitled "Setting Records for Jobs and Noninflationary Growth," began: "Continued growth led the economy to its 70th month of expansion in September, the longest period of peacetime prosperity in the nation's history."[154] Accompanying the text were camera-ready graphics illustrating the points made in the articles. Griscom noted that the texts of the president's weekly radio addresses were also printed in a camera-ready format and sent to newspapers.[155] Such mailings were part of an effort to provide more outlets for the president's message.

Griscom also made Reagan much more visible to the media while being careful not to make him more accessible to questions from the media. "If you sit there and you're trying to deal with the Iran-Contra problem, then part of the responsibility as communications director is to figure out how to work out of that problem, how you get the president positioned right, how you get the focus on other issues," Griscom explained. "You know going in that you don't sit back and offer him up in an environment where if he gets asked a question, he can't answer it. It just reinforces the feeling that he must be hiding something when, in effect, the lawyers say he can't talk about that."[156]

Griscom even went so far as to shield Marlin Fitzwater from certain information about Iran-Contra so that he would have deniability when briefing the White House press corps. Griscom took part in White House strategy sessions every morning and every evening during the time that Congress was holding hearings on Iran-Contra. Fitzwater had access to all of those. However, as Griscom pointed out, "There were times when Marlin knew he did not want to be in those meetings so that he could acknowledge that he didn't know."[157]

Griscom also worked closely with the speechwriters. By now the strategies were well-worn. Each speech had several sound-bites built in. In so doing, the White House basically determined what excerpts from the speech appeared on the evening newscasts. The speeches also contained a clear enough message that the White House basically controlled the media's lead on the story.[158] Griscom even used focus groups to fashion the themes that Reagan presented to the American people. For instance, focus groups were used to plan the president's State of the Union address, his speech to Congress about the summit meeting with Soviet leader Mikhail Gorbachev, and the administration's response to the Iran-Contra affair. The focus groups consisted of about twenty people. Each group was designed to represent the demographic characteristics of the country at large. The participants were given handouts and were asked to read, rate, and react to the various thematic messages. They were then led through a discussion session that raised questions about the statements.[159] The groups helped the administration to fashion messages that were appealing and believable. The White House not only was constructing a spectacle but also was consulting members of the audience on what they wanted to see.[160]

Griscom stated that an important part of his job was "to help set, influence, determine public opinion."[161] You do that, he said, by controlling and managing the agenda. The White House was not always successful at that. The way it handled the president's nomination of Robert Bork to the U.S. Supreme Court is a prime case in point. Yet overall, Griscom's tenure was very successful. The Iran-Contra scandal faded, and Reagan's popularity increased dramatically. In fact, Reagan left office with the highest popularity rating of any recent president.[162] Confident that they had achieved their goal of restoring order to the administration, Baker and Griscom left the White House in June 1988. Kenneth Duberstein replaced Baker as chief of staff, and Mari Maseng replaced Griscom as communications director for the remainder of Reagan's lame-duck presidency.

The 1988 presidential election showed that candidates of both parties had adopted the strategies that Reagan's communications advisors had perfected: control the agenda, control access, control the sound-bites, and control the visual image. As usual, fact sheets were distributed, satellite interviews were arranged, and surrogate speakers—including super-surrogate Ronald Reagan—were fanned out across the nation. It was a campaign of symbols: flags and Willie Horton and Michael Dukakis looking silly driving a tank. The Republican Television Network again covered the Republican convention, and the Democrats created a counterpart for their own convention. After the votes were cast and George Bush was sworn in, the campaign continued—without the brass bands and the hoopla, of course. But it continued, sponsored in part by the White House Office of Communications.

CHAPTER EIGHT

THE BUSH YEARS

POSTSCRIPT

I t is striking how little things change as administrations come and
go. By January 1989, when George Herbert Walker Bush became
president, the White House Office of Communications was fully entrenched as
an accepted and expected part of the new administration. Following in the
wake of Ronald Reagan, however, Bush was anxious to avoid charges of
manipulating the media. Therefore, he took pains to distance himself from the
overt stagecraft of the Reagan years. After several years of a fairly high profile,
the Office of Communications and its new director, David F. Demarest, Jr.,
shrank into relative anonymity. It soon became clear that one of the messages
Bush wanted to convey was that his was not a symbolic presidency. That meant
pushing the "Deaveresque" aspects of the office into the background, providing a great deal of access to the press, and easing up on control of the
administration line. It even meant that Bush tried to distance himself from
Reagan as well. A telling sign was that when Bush took office, all photographs
of Reagan were removed from the West Wing of the White House. Although
the walls were adorned with pictures of Bush in the company of heads of state,
members of the press, his wife, and even former Presidents Ford and Carter,
there were no pictures of Bush with Reagan.[1] The symbolic presidency had not
disappeared, but some of its imagery had.

Communications Director Demarest—a protégé of former Republican National Committee Chairman Bill Brock—had also served as director of communications in the 1988 Bush campaign. In large part, Bush's campaign

apparatus was a mirror image of the one employed by Nixon in 1968. Roger Ailes was a media consultant in both campaigns, and Bush followed the Nixon practice of having both a traveling press spokesman and a director of communications during the general election campaign. As communications director, Demarest was responsible for coordinating the overall communications strategy of the campaign. His major duties included the surrogate speakers operation and the line-of-the-day program. Every day during the campaign, Demarest attended a senior staff meeting. "We would go over what the themes were of the day, the speeches, and the messages that we were trying to get out," Demarest said. "Then I would go back to my staff and say, 'OK, this is what is up for tomorrow.' And we would put together the line-of-the-day by about three or four o'clock that afternoon, clear it with everybody so that everybody was on board, and then distribute it to all [Republican] Hill members, and to the RNC and their computer network. We also had another twenty or thirty 'level one' surrogates—the John Towers of the world—that we would get it to, as well as our own senior staff." Saying this, Demarest sat back in his chair and laughed: late afternoons were "fax central," he noted.[2] Demarest was also in charge of "spin control" after the presidential debates. Stu Spencer, who was back for yet another campaign, was impressed with Demarest. "He was *very* good in the campaign," Spencer stated.[3]

When Bush was elected president, he chose Demarest to be "Director of Public Affairs" during the transition period. Demarest's job was to coordinate the public image of the transition. His goal was to set the tone for the Bush administration by giving the American people a sample of things to come. As he put it, the transition was meant to serve as a kind of "preview to the movie."[4] The theme that he wanted to stress in that preview was "the politics of inclusion." And so Bush met with a wide spectrum of individuals at the White House, including Michael Dukakis and Jesse Jackson. Then the visitors—whether they were friendly Republicans, Democrats like Dukakis or Jackson, or representatives of an environmental group—were paraded in front of cameras to talk about Bush's receptive ear. The goal was to move away from the sharp partisanship of the campaign, to show that Bush was willing to listen to divergent views, and to make the American people feel more comfortable about their president-elect.[5] Demarest was still an image maker, but his transition title was aimed at deflecting attention from that imagery.

As president, Bush has enjoyed enormous popularity. He has done so, however, with a remarkably thin domestic agenda. After the largely issueless

1988 presidential campaign, some observers noted that a largely issueless administration seemed to be taking shape. Even former Communications Director David Gergen—a longtime supporter of Bush—was dismayed by the new administration's inability to formulate an agenda and by its early handling of the ill-fated nomination of John Tower to become secretary of defense. Gergen went public with his criticism in a March 1989 essay in the *Washington Post*. Having successfully urged Ronald Reagan to make the most of his first one hundred days in office, and having always stressed the utmost importance of long-term planning, Gergen was particularly disturbed by Bush's failure to pursue a substantive, long-term agenda. Bush was too reactive, he complained.

> For years, Bush has shied away from what he has called "the vision thing," but he needs to overcome his misgivings and adopt some larger view of what he wants to achieve as president. Surely, he wants to do more than manage problems as they come his way, and surely the country needs more, too. . . .
>
> Once the White House knows where it wants to go, it can more easily formulate a successful public strategy. For the moment, it is being nibbled and nicked to death by small stories because the administration is generating so few big stories to dominate the news.
>
> . . . . [T]he administration can still pull itself back from the cliff—but it had better hurry.[6]

The administration was pulled back from the edge of the cliff as much by external events as anything else. The coming months saw the crumbling of communism in eastern Europe, the fall of the Berlin Wall, and the end of the cold war. With no immediate crises facing the administration, Bush found himself riding a wave of unprecedented popularity. But still, the administration was not formulating an agenda. That worried some insiders. For instance, former Communications Director Frank Ursomarso said in June 1990 that the Bush administration was on the brink of a potential crisis because of its continuing failure to set an agenda. He was particularly distressed by the administration's handling of the budget crisis and its indecision about whether or not to ask for a tax increase. It was essential, he explained, for the administration to "figure out what they're doing, because they don't have a strategy and it's obvious they don't have a strategy, and they're just hoping the thing's going to come together and it isn't."[7] Ursomarso's observations were prophetic. Within four months, the administration faced its worst crisis yet when its federal budget compromise failed in the House of Representatives. In the coming days the administration fumbled badly by sending conflicting messages, appearing indecisive, and demonstrating no control of the agenda.

The Bush administration was pulled back from the cliff yet again by events in the Persian Gulf. The president became a man with a mission: overcoming the evil of Saddam Hussein. Bush's popularity shot back up just as quickly as it had plummeted during the budget crisis. Now he was a wartime president. Moreover, he was a wartime president who presided over what initially appeared to be a remarkably swift and successful defeat of a villainous opponent. Bush had found the most potent symbol of all. Pundits, who just six months earlier had forecast his political doom, now claimed that the president was all but invincible.

The war with Iraq also served as a catalyst for increased control of information flow. Secretary of Defense Dick Cheney helped to achieve the type of control over war coverage that presidents in the past wished they had had over White House coverage. The Department of Defense allowed reporters to travel to the war zone, but coverage was strictly limited. Only small, closely supervised, Pentagon-approved pools of correspondents could cover the actual fighting. Pool reporters were constantly accompanied by Defense Department public affairs officers, who controlled where they could go and who they could interview. All copy was then subject to censorship by the military. The Pentagon was especially concerned about what visual images would be seen by the American people. By keeping television crews away from the fighting and releasing its own visually hypnotic films of high-tech bombing raids ("military Nintendo," as the *Nation* put it),[8] the Pentagon sanitized the war. Indeed, much of the coverage of the war consisted of official Allied briefings for reporters. Notably lacking were stories about the number of Iraqis killed by U.S. bombing. Official briefers simply refused to discuss such figures. The result was what Pentagon Spokesman Pete Williams called "the best war coverage we've ever had."[9] As the war correspondent William Boot wrote, "The Pentagon evidently saw control of the news media as an essential element in its psywar strategy—keeping the American public united behind the war until the will of the Iraqi army was broken."[10]

Persian Gulf coverage was a classic example of government and the media collaborating to manipulate popular passions and shape our nation's political discourse. In a less overt and coercive way, that is what the Office of Communications tries to do on a day-to-day basis. By selecting symbols, constructing meaning, and offering a variety of threats and reassurances, the office helps to create a particular perspective of the political landscape for public consumption. Through it all, the media are often willing partners. The reason is obvious: many of the office's functions are beneficial not only to the president but to the media as well. Providing access, staging photo opportunities, and distributing information are services that the media have come to rely on. As we have seen, it was largely the media's expectation that such functions continue that kept the Office of Communications alive after Watergate, and it was the mutually beneficial aspects of the office that helped to ensure its institutionalization.[11]

However, efforts to manipulate popular passions may have serious implications for democratic theory. In his book *The Rhetorical Presidency*, Jeffrey Tulis points out the profound effect that the mass media have had on the character of constitutional rule: "Television news not only carries the messages of governing officials to the people; it also selects issues to present to the government for action of some sort. 'Real' expressions of mass opinion, which in the past were sporadically expressed in protest and petition, are replaced by the news's continual sophisticated analyses that serve as a surrogate public."[12] The problem is compounded, however, by the fact that the analyses of the "surrogate public" are often shaped more by the Office of Communications, and other institutions like it, than by the people themselves. In that light, Tulis's observations are even more troubling. Constitutional government, he concludes, "has become a kind of government by assembly without a genuine assembling of the people. In this fictive assembly, television speaks to the president in metaphors expressive of the 'opinions' of a fictive people, and the president responds to the demands and moods created by the media with rhetoric designed to manipulate popular passions rather than to engage citizens in political debate."[13]

Manipulating the media and emphasizing style—often at the expense of substance—are now thought to be essential parts of modern presidential power. As Richard Nixon wrote in his memoirs: "[Modern presidents] must try to master the art of manipulating the media not only to win in politics but in order to further the programs and causes they believe in; at the same time they must avoid at all costs the charge of trying to manipulate the media. In the modern presidency, concern for image must rank with concern for substance."[14]

The Office of Communications, then, is a vehicle for orchestrating a distinctly modern form of presidential power—power over executive branch communications by coordinating news flow and controlling information policy, power over the establishment media by providing a mechanism for co-opting and/or circumventing the media, and power over other policymakers by mobilizing public support for presidential policy initiatives. The danger is that the power the Office of Communications helps to create will lead to a less deliberative process in government and provide us with a citizenry that is inundated with the symbolic spectacle of politics but ill-equipped to judge its leaders or the merits of their policies.

APPENDIX

The following organization charts illustrate how the structure and jurisdiction of the Office of Communications have changed over time. The charts are preceded by a list of those who have headed the office. For the sake of convenience, these people are all listed as "Directors of the White House Office of Communications," although their precise titles have changed some over time. For instance, the official title of David F. Demarest, Jr., is "Assistant to the President for Communications."

The structure of the Office of Communications has often changed within single administrations. For instance, there are three charts for the Nixon administration, showing the office in 1969, 1970, and 1972. In all three, the director of communications reported directly to the White House chief of staff. It should be noted that by 1970, the White House had actively circumvented the authority of Communications Director Klein. Thus, Deputy Director Magruder (acting on instructions from Chief of Staff Haldeman) was primarily responsible for running the office in 1970. Likewise, Deputy Director Clawson (acting on instructions from Charles Colson) was primarily responsible for running the office in 1972. Dotted lines indicate de facto lines of power.

Throughout the Nixon administration, the Office of Communications and the Press Office remained two separate entities. That changed during the first part of the Ford administration, when the Office of Communications fell under the jurisdiction of the Press Office (see 1975 chart). The two became separate entities again during the 1976 presidential campaign (see 1976 chart).

At the outset of the Carter administration, there was no Office of Communications per se. Some of its functions were carried out by Deputy Press Secretary Wurfel and the Office of Media Liaison, which fell under his jurisdiction (see 1977 chart). By 1978, a separate Office of Communications had been resurrected, but the Office of Media Liaison also continued to exist under the jurisdiction of the Press Office.

Since the Carter administration, the Office of Communications has always been either separate from or superior to the Press Office. It is separate from the Press Office in the 1981, 1985, 1988, and 1989 charts. The Press Office falls under the jurisdiction of the Office of Communications in the 1982 and 1987 charts. As one can see, various other staff units (such as the Speechwriting Office and the Public Affairs Office) sometimes fall under the jurisdiction of the Office of Communications.

DIRECTORS OF THE WHITE HOUSE
OFFICE OF COMMUNICATIONS, 1969–1990

RICHARD NIXON

Herbert G. Klein (January 1969–June 1973)
  [Jeb Stuart Magruder, deputy director, 1970–1971]
  [Ken W. Clawson, deputy director, 1971–1973]

Ken W. Clawson (January 1974–August 1974)

GERALD FORD

*Paul Miltich and James Holland (August 1974–November 1974)
*Gerald L. Warren (November 1974–June 1975)
*Margita White (June 1975–June 1976)
David R. Gergen (July 1976–January 1977)

JIMMY CARTER

**[none] (January 1977–June 1978)
  Gerald Rafshoon (July 1978–August 1979)
  [none] (September 1979–January 1981)

RONALD REAGAN

Frank A. Ursomarso (February 1981–June 1981)
David R. Gergen (June 1981–January 1984)
Michael A. McManus, Jr. (Acting Dir.) (January 1984–January 1985)
Patrick Buchanan (February 1985–February 1987)
John O. Koehler (February 1987–March 1987)
Thomas C. Griscom (April 1987–June 1988)
Mari Maseng (July 1988–January 1989)

GEORGE BUSH

David F. Demarest, Jr. (January 1989–)

---

*Communications office under the jurisdiction of the Press Office.

**The functions of the Office of Communications were performed by deputy press secretaries and the Office of Media Liaison.

1969

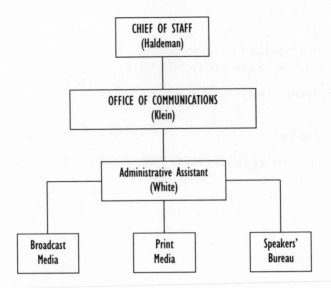

1970

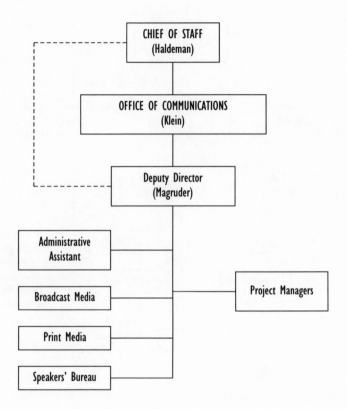

1972

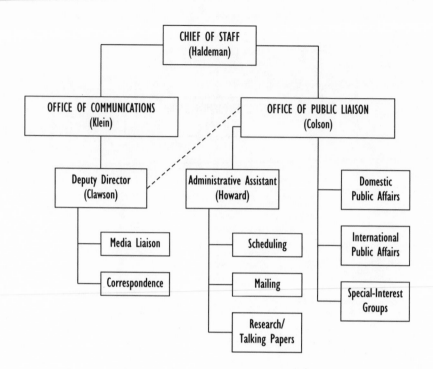

1975

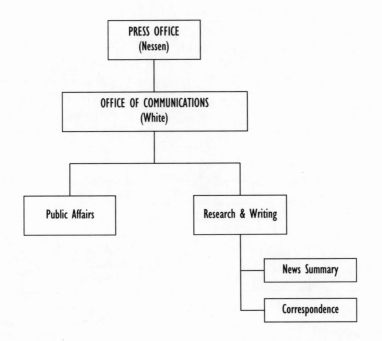

AUGUST 1976

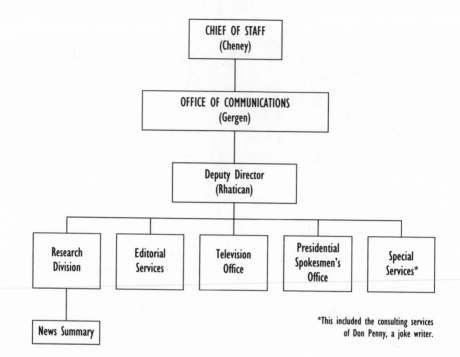

CHIEF OF STAFF
(Cheney)

OFFICE OF COMMUNICATIONS
(Gergen)

Deputy Director
(Rhatican)

Research Division

Editorial Services

Television Office

Presidential Spokesmen's Office

Special Services*

News Summary

*This included the consulting services
of Don Penny, a joke writer.

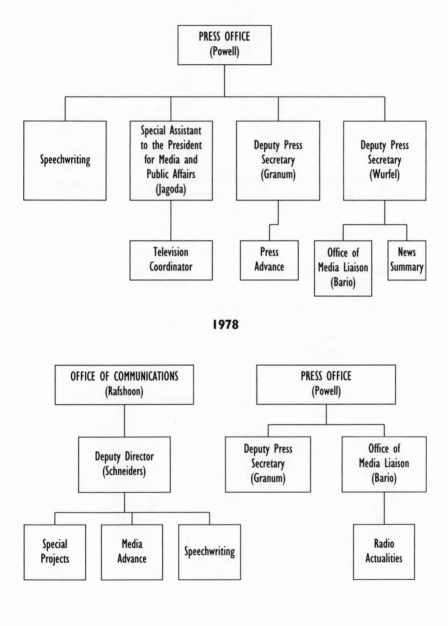

1977

PRESS OFFICE
(Powell)

- Speechwriting
- Special Assistant to the President for Media and Public Affairs (Jagoda)
  - Television Coordinator
- Deputy Press Secretary (Granum)
  - Press Advance
- Deputy Press Secretary (Wurfel)
  - Office of Media Liaison (Bario)
  - News Summary

1978

OFFICE OF COMMUNICATIONS
(Rafshoon)

- Deputy Director (Schneiders)
  - Special Projects
  - Media Advance
  - Speechwriting

PRESS OFFICE
(Powell)

- Deputy Press Secretary (Granum)
- Office of Media Liaison (Bario)
  - Radio Actualities

FEBRUARY 1981

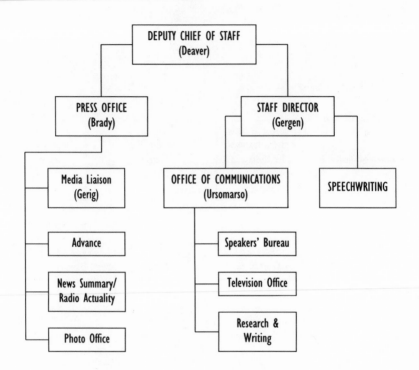

1982

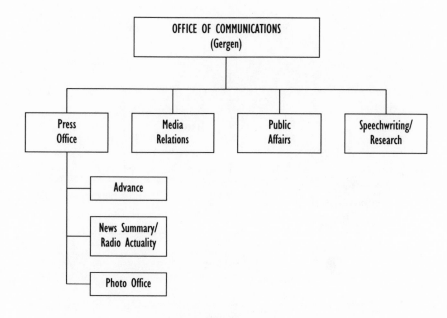

1985

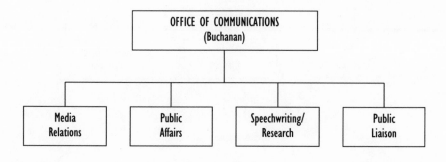

1987

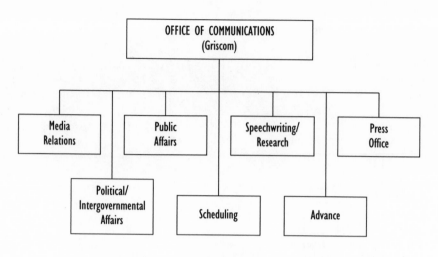

JULY 1988

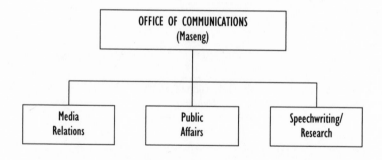

1989

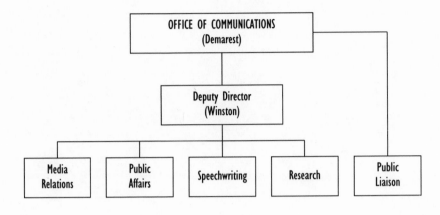

NOTES

ABBREVIATIONS

CCF	Charles Colson Files
DGF	David Gergen Files
GRF	Gerald Rafshoon Files
GRFL	Gerald R. Ford Library
HKF	Herbert Klein Files
HRHF	H. R. Haldeman Files
JCL	Jimmy Carter Library
JPF	Jody Powell Files
LBJL	Lyndon B. Johnson Library
MRDP	Michael Raoul-Duval Papers
NPMP	Nixon Presidential Materials Project
POF	President's Office Files
RGF	Rex Granum Files
RNP	Ronald Nessen Papers
WHCF	White House Central Files
W&WF	Gerald Warren and Margita White Files

CHAPTER ONE

1. Cheney interview, 10 March 1989.
2. Paletz and Entman, *Media Power Politics*, 16.
3. Cheney interview, 10 March 1989.
4. Entman, "Imperial Media," 89.
5. Cheney interview, 10 March 1989.
6. McGinniss, *Selling of the President*.
7. Colson interview, 11 July 1989.
8. Ursomarso interview, 26 June 1990.
9. Kernell, *Going Public*.
10. Ibid., 23.
11. Ibid., 35.
12. Rose, *Postmodern President*, chapter 7.
13. Tulis, *Rhetorical Presidency*, 95.
14. For example, see Tulis, "Two Constitutional Presidencies," 59; and Lowi, *Personal President*.
15. Cornwell, *Presidential Leadership of Public Opinion*, 17.
16. Kernell, *Going Public*, 63–66.
17. See, for instance, Moe, "Politicized Presidency"; and Crenson and Rourke, "By Way of Conclusion."

18. For discussions of this use of the Bureau of the Budget, see Maass, "In Accord with the Program of the President"; Neustadt, "Presidency and Legislation"; and Neustadt, "Approaches to Staffing the Presidency."

19. Earlier, Hagerty had been press secretary to New York Governor Thomas E. Dewey. In that post, Hagerty witnessed Dewey's creation of a Public Information Council in 1946. The council consisted of departmental public information officers who used it to coordinate news flow and plan public relations. No doubt Hagerty had that model in mind when he began similar meetings in the White House. For a discussion of Dewey's system, see Rubin, *Public Relations and the Empire State*, chapter 5.

20. Memo from Robert Humphreys to Leonard W. Hall, 7 December 1954, in Lavine, *Smoke-Filled Rooms*, 105.

21. Lavine, *Smoke-Filled Rooms*, chapters 1 and 2; see also Kelley, *Professional Public Relations and Political Power*, 1, 149–51.

22. Cornwell, *Presidential Leadership of Public Opinion*, 230–31.

23. Christian interview, 14 November 1989.

24. Much has been written about the Committee on Public Information. For a thorough bibliography, see Vaughn, *Holding Fast the Inner Lines*, 361–83. Important works on the subject include Creel, *How We Advertised America*; Mock and Larson, *Words That Won the War*; and

Cornwell, "Wilson, Creel, and the Presidency," 189.

25. Vaughn, *Holding Fast the Inner Lines*, 194.

26. Ibid., 205.

27. Mock and Larson, *Words That Won the War*, 92–112.

28. Vaughn, *Holding Fast the Inner Lines*, chapters 3–5.

29. Cornwell, "Wilson, Creel, and the Presidency," 191.

30. Mock and Larson, *Words That Won the War*, 113.

31. Ibid., 125.

32. Cornwell, "Wilson, Creel, and the Presidency," 190.

33. Cornwell, *Presidential Leadership of Public Opinion*, 49.

34. Creel, *How We Advertised America*, 401.

35. Cornwell, *Presidential Leadership of Public Opinion*, 57.

36. Winkler, *Politics of Propaganda*, 21. For a discussion of *ad hoc* attempts to coordinate news flow among the myriad agencies and bureaus of the New Deal, see McCamy, *Government Publicity*, 190–95.

37. Dorris, "Five Executive Assistants President's 'Eyes and Ears,' " section 4, 7.

38. For a history of the office, see Winkler, *Politics of Propaganda*, 21.

39. Cornwell, *Presidential Leadership of Public Opinion*, 227.

40. Quoted in Kernell, *Going Public*, 70.

41. Ibid., 72–73.

42. Quoted in Grossman and Kumar, *Portraying the President*, 89.

43. Christian interview, 14 November 1989.

44. Christian, "Another Perspective," 121.

45. Quoted in Berman, "Johnson and the White House Staff," 191.

46. Christian interview, 14 November 1989.

47. Turner, *Lyndon Johnson's Dual War*, 158–60.

48. Quoted in Chapman, "Inter-Agency Harmony Is Kintner's Job," A6.

49. Berman, "Johnson and the White House Staff," 195.

50. Letter, Moyers to Kintner, 8 April 1966, "Staff Aides FG 11-8-1/ Kintner," Box 20, WHCF, LBJL.

51. Christian interview, 14 November 1989. Christian added that Kintner's power is sometimes exaggerated by historians because he was such a prolific memo writer. Martha Joynt Kumar has also made this observation. See Kumar, "Presidential Libraries," 212. For a different perspective, see Berman, "Johnson and the White House Staff," 195–99.

52. To date, the Office of Communications has been the focus of almost no scholarly attention. The only such works that treat the office at all appear to be (chronologically): Grossman and Kumar, *Portraying the President*, 25–26, 89–92, and passim; Wiedenkeller, *Präsident und Medien*, 84–87, 174–76, and passim; my own master's thesis (1985) and doctoral dissertation (1988) at Johns Hopkins University, Baltimore, Maryland; Patterson, *Ring of Power*, 177–90; and Kernell, "Evo-

lution of the White House Staff," 211–17.

   The obscurity of the Office of Communications stands in stark contrast to the White House Press Office and various other aspects of presidential-press relations, which have received thorough treatments. Examples of works in this area include (chronologically): Pollard, *Presidents and the Press*; Cornwell, *Presidential Leadership of Public Opinion*; Sigal, *Reporters and Officials*; Nimmo, *Political Communication and Public Opinion in America*; Graber, *Mass Media and American Politics*; Grossman and Kumar, *Portraying the President*; Paletz and Entman, *Media Power Politics*; Rubin, *Press, Party, and Presidency*; Seymour-Ure, *American President*; Edwards, *Public Presidency*; Kernell, *Going Public*; Bennett, *News*; Press and Verburg, *American Politicians and Journalists*.

   Neglect of the Office of Communications is surprising given its primary role in planning and executing the strategies of the modern public presidency. That neglect is even more surprising given the recent spate of scholarly work dealing with various aspects of the public presidency. (For instance: Edwards, *Public Presidency*; Kernell, *Going Public*; Lowi, *Personal President*; Tulis, *Rhetorical Presidency*.)

53. Haldeman interview, 17 July 1989. Haldeman's mention of "tapes" refers to the tape-recorded conversations of President Nixon and his advisors.

CHAPTER TWO

1. Quoted in Culbert, "Johnson and the Media," 223; see also Turner, *Lyndon Johnson's Dual War*, 231.
2. Culbert, "Johnson and the Media," 224.
3. Quoted in Turner, *Lyndon Johnson's Dual War*, 232.
4. White, *Making of the President*, 102.
5. For example, see Frankel, "Why the Gap between L.B.J. and the Nation," 7.
6. Remarks in Chicago before the National Association of Broadcasters, 1 April 1968, in *Public Papers of the Presidents: Lyndon B. Johnson (1968–69)*, 482–83.
7. Johnson, "Agenda for the Future," 45.
8. For example, see McGinniss, *Selling of the President*.
9. Quoted in Ambrose, *Nixon*, 138.
10. Quoted in Nixon, *Memoirs*, 303.
11. Ibid., 304.
12. Ibid., 291.
13. Klein, *Making It Perfectly Clear*, 57.
14. Ibid., 21.
15. Ibid., 11.
16. White interview, 17 June 1988; Ziegler interview, 4 November 1988.
17. Ehrlichman interview, 28 April 1989.
18. For an account of this, see McGinniss, *Selling of the President*. Cf. Klein, *Making It Perfectly Clear*, 19–20.
19. Ehrlichman, *Witness to Power*, 47–48.
20. Klein, *Making It Perfectly Clear*, 324; Haldeman, *Ends of Power*, 74.
21. Ehrlichman, *Witness to Power*, 47.
22. Goldman, "President's Palace Guard," 28; Rather and Gates, *Palace Guard*, 123.
23. Quoted in Porter, *Assault on the Media*, 30–31.
24. Ehrlichman interview, 28 April 1989.
25. Klein, *Making It Perfectly Clear*, 32–33.
26. Finch interview, 12 July 1989.
27. White interview, 17 June 1988.
28. Klein, *Making It Perfectly Clear*, 18.
29. Ibid., 32–33.
30. Nixon interview by Frost, 1977. Ronald Ziegler repeated that assertion to me in 1988 (Ziegler interview, 4 November 1988).
31. Brauer, *Presidential Transitions*, 126.
32. Nixon, *Memoirs*, 355.
33. Ibid., 338–39.
34. Brauer, *Presidential Transitions*, 136–40.
35. Ibid., 133.
36. Haldeman, *Ends of Power*, 55.
37. Colson oral history interview, 15 June 1988, 36; Colson oral history interview, 21 September 1988, 33.
38. Haldeman, *Ends of Power*, 57.
39. Nixon, *Memoirs*, 337.
40. Haldeman, *Ends of Power*, 56.
41. Goldman, "President's Palace Guard," 24.
42. Haldeman, *Ends of Power*, 53.
43. Ehrlichman, *Witness to Power*, 48.
44. Finch interview, 12 July 1989.
45. Safire, *Before the Fall*, 113.
46. Ibid., 113–14.
47. Haldeman interview, 17 July 1989.
48. Ehrlichman interview, 28 April 1989.

49. Brauer, *Presidential Transitions*, 135.
50. Colson interview, 11 July 1989.
51. Finch interview, 12 July 1989.
52. Magruder, *An American Life*, 93.
53. Haldeman, *Ends of Power*, 74.
54. Haldeman interview, 17 July 1989.
55. Klein, *Making It Perfectly Clear*, 38.
56. Haldeman interview, 17 July 1989. John Ehrlichman also confirms that. "Q: Do you think that Klein was upset at not being named press secretary? A: Oh, I know he was" (Ehrlichman interview, 28 April 1989).
57. Ziegler interview, 4 November 1988. According to Klein, "Haldeman had rented apartments and rooms in the small but old and comfortable Wyndham Hotel in Manhattan for some of us who were senior in the campaign" (Klein, *Making It Perfectly Clear*, 14).
58. Klein, *Making It Perfectly Clear*, 38; Bonafede, "Herbert Klein," 393. According to Ziegler: "It soon became clear that the president needs not a press spokesman but a press secretary. There's a lot more to being press secretary than press spokesman. So it quickly became clear, and I guess they felt, 'Well, he can do it despite his young age.' And so they gave me the chance and, as you know, I served in that position longer than anyone else that had it" (Ziegler interview, 4 November 1988).
59. Finch interview, 12 July 1989.
60. Haldeman interview, 17 July 1989.
61. Ehrlichman interview, 28 April 1989.

62. Ziegler interview, 4 November 1988.
63. Haldeman interview, 17 July 1989.
64. Klein, *Making It Perfectly Clear*, 42.
65. Gold, *PR as in President*, 50.
66. Klein, *Making It Perfectly Clear*, 42.
67. Semple, "Nixon Reported Wooing Democrat," A1.
68. Quoted in ibid., A35.
69. Ibid.
70. Ibid.

CHAPTER THREE

1. For example, see Osborne, *Nixon Watch*, 34–35.
2. Bonafede, "Herbert Klein," 393.
3. Apple, "Nixon's Soft Voice," A35.
4. Semple, "Nixon's Inner Circle Meets," 62.
5. Bonafede, "Herbert Klein," 392.
6. Quoted in Semple, "Nixon's Inner Circle Meets," 63.
7. "Superchief of Information," 30.
8. Klein, *Making It Perfectly Clear*, 188.
9. Rather and Gates, *Palace Guard*, 153; Klein, *Making It Perfectly Clear*, 188, 204.
10. Klein, *Making It Perfectly Clear*, 188. Use of such language was also noted in Semple, "Nixon's Inner Circle Meets," 64.
11. For example, see Bonafede, "Herbert Klein," 393; and Rather and Gates, *Palace Guard*, 152.
12. Semple, "Nixon's Inner Circle Meets," 64.
13. Haldeman interview, 17 July 1989.

14. Klein, *Making It Perfectly Clear*, 183.
15. Spear, *Presidents and the Press*, 103.
16. White interview, 17 June 1988.
17. "Press Covers Government," 25.
18. Spears, *Presidents and the Press*, 103 (notes omitted).
19. Klein, *Making It Perfectly Clear*, 184; White interview, 17 June 1988.
20. White interview, 17 June 1988.
21. Klein, *Making It Perfectly Clear*, 185.
22. Witcover, "Two Hats of Herbert Klein," 27.
23. Spear, *Presidents and the Press*, 104.
24. Memo, Haldeman to Klein, 17 February 1969, "H. R. Haldeman I (1 of 3)," Box 1, HKF, NPMP.
25. Klein, *Making It Perfectly Clear*, 185.
26. Spear, *Presidents and the Press*, 105.
27. Magruder, *American Life*, 94.
28. In a memo to H. R. Haldeman and John Ehrlichman dated 7 February 1969, Klein said that he had tested Labor Secretary George Schultz and Interior Secretary Walter Hickel for television appearances. "Of the two," Klein wrote, "Schultz will need a little more rehearsal, which we are doing" (Memo, Klein to Haldeman and Ehrlichman, 7 February 1969, "H. R. Haldeman I [1 of 3]," Box 1, HKF, NPMP).
29. Klein, *Making It Perfectly Clear*, 203.
30. Ibid., 185, 204; Porter, *Assault on the Media*, 211.
31. Quoted in "White House Media Services," 2137.
32. Memo, Haldeman to Klein, 20 March 1969, "Memos/Herb Klein (March 1969)," Box 49, HRHF, NPMP.
33. Memo, Haldeman to Klein, 27 March 1969, "Memos/Herb Klein (March 1969)," Box 49, HRHF, NPMP.
34. Memo, Klein to Haldeman, 29 March 1969, "H. R. Haldeman I (1 of 3)," Box 1, HKF, NPMP.
35. Memo, Haldeman to Klein, 27 May 1970, "H. R. Haldeman II (1 of 5)," Box 1, HKF, NPMP.
36. Klein, *Making It Perfectly Clear*, 325.
37. Memos, Klein to Haldeman, 20 March 1969, and Haldeman to Klein, 24 March 1969, "H. R. Haldeman I (1 of 3)," Box 1, HKF, NPMP.
38. Memo, Haldeman to Klein, 2 March 1970, "H. R. Haldeman I (3 of 3)," Box 1, HKF, NPMP.
39. Memo, Haldeman to Klein and Ziegler, 9 March 1970, "H. R. Haldeman I (3 of 3)," Box 1, HKF, NPMP.
40. Klein, *Making It Perfectly Clear*, 21–22.
41. Spear, *Presidents and the Press*, 106.
42. Witcover, "Two Hats of Herbert Klein," 27.
43. Magruder, *American Life*, 93.
44. Bonafede, "Campaign '72 Report," 1657.
45. Memo, Wright to Green, 18 November 1969, "Memos/Herb Klein (December 1969)," Box 55, HRHF, NPMP.

46. Memo, Klein to Haldeman, 24 January 1970, "H. R. Haldeman I (2 of 3)," Box 1, HKF, NPMP.

47. Memo, Costello to Klein, 28 February 1971, "Klein (February 1971)," Box 73, HRHF, NPMP.
Speakers from some departments were more successful at generating media attention than others. For instance, 21 speakers from the State Department visited 18 cities in 17 states in January 1971. They generated 17 radio interviews, 61 television interviews, and 7 magazine and newspaper interviews. During the same time frame, 26 speakers from the Transportation Department visited 21 cities in 13 states. Although they generated 16 magazine and newspaper interviews, they attracted only 4 radio and 6 television interviews.

48. For an excellent description of Nixon's congressional liaison operation, see Bonafede and Glass, "Nixon Deals Cautiously with Hostile Congress," 1353–66.

49. Memo, Haldeman to Klein, 9 February 1969, "H. R. Haldeman I (1 of 3)," Box 1, HKF, NPMP.

50. Bonafede and Glass, "Nixon Deals Cautiously with Hostile Congress" 1357.

51. Klein, *Making It Perfectly Clear*, 120.

52. Colson interview, 11 July 1989.

53. Memo, Klein to Haldeman, 11 July 1969, "H. R. Haldeman I (1 of 3)," Box 1, HKF, NPMP.

54. Haldeman's handwritten notes on Memo, Klein to Haldeman, 11 July 1969, "H. R. Haldeman I (1 of 3)," Box 1, HKF, NPMP.

55. Information concerning the publishing and distribution of these publications is based on a series of internal White House memoranda generated by Landauer's request for information. Most useful is "Memorandum to the Files" from Paul Costello, dated 14 September 1970, in which lengthy answers to Landauer's written questions are provided. A copy of the short answers provided to Landauer appears in "Memorandum to the Files" from Costello dated 16 October 1970. Attached to that memo is a complete listing of the booklets published by the Government Printing Office, including their quantity, the cost, and who footed the bill. See also Letter, Landauer to Costello, 11 September 1970, and Memo, Magruder to Haldeman, 22 October 1970. All of this material is located in "H. R. Haldeman II (4 of 5)," Box 1, HKF, NPMP. An article concerning the distribution of the booklets was published in the *Wall Street Journal*, 9 February 1971, 16.

56. Based on an eight-page log of White House mailings obtained from the Republican National Committee in 1973 by Scott M. Cutlip. See also Cutlip, "Nixon's Office of Executive Communication," 13.

57. Klein, *Making It Perfectly Clear*, 189.

58. Memo, Klein to Haldeman and Ehrlichman, 7 February 1969, "H. R. Haldeman I (1 of 3)," Box 1, HKF, NPMP.

59. Ibid.

60. Memo, President to Ehrlichman, 5 February 1969, in Oudes, *From: The President*, 16.

61. Magruder, *American Life*, 95.

62. Memo, Klein to Haldeman, 7 July 1969, "H. R. Haldeman I (2 of 3)," Box 1, HKF, NPMP.

63. Memo, President to Haldeman, 22 September 1969, in Oudes, *From: The President*, 46.

64. Memo, Klein to Haldeman, 29 September 1969, "H. R. Haldeman I (2 of 3)," Box 1, HKF, NPMP.

65. Klein, *Making It Perfectly Clear*, 186.

66. Safire, *Before the Fall*, 341.

67. Quoted in Keogh, *President Nixon and the Press*, 39.

68. Safire, *Before the Fall*, 341–65.

69. Ibid., 343.

70. Wicker, *One of Us*, 89.

71. Nixon, *Six Crises*, 107–8.

72. Ibid., 118–19.

73. "President Kennedy—Press Conferences—Televised," attached to Memo, Ziegler to Haldeman, 10 February 1970, "Press and Media No. 2 (part 2)," Box 141, HRHF, NPMP.

74. "President Johnson—Press Conferences," ibid. Times for his televised press conferences in 1964 were not provided in the memo but are located in *Public Papers of the Presidents: Lyndon B. Johnson (1963–64)*.

75. Porter, *Assault on the Media*, 37.

76. Memo, Haldeman to Kissinger and Buchanan, 14 January 1970, in Oudes, *From: The President*, 88.

77. Figures for Truman through Nixon are provided in Table 5.4, "Presidential News Conferences, 1949–1984," in King and Ragsdale, *Elusive Executive*, 268. Of course, not all of these exchanges were televised. Figures for Franklin Roosevelt are from Grossman and Kumar, *Portraying the President*, 245.

78. The number of prime-time appearances on national television by presidents during their first nineteen months in office rose from four under Kennedy, to seven under Johnson, to fourteen under Nixon (Minow, Martin, and Mitchell, *Presidential Television*, 171). At the middle of Nixon's first term, CBS President Frank Stanton commented that Nixon had "appeared on network prime-time television as many times as Presidents Eisenhower, Kennedy, and Johnson combined" (quoted in Spear, *Presidents and the Press*, 86).

79. H. R. Haldeman notes, Meeting between the President and Haldeman, 3 November 1969, "Haldeman Notes, July–December 1969 (October–December 1969—Part 2)," Box 40, HRHF, NPMP.

80. "PR Points to Be Made," attached to Memo, Higby to Klein, 16 September 1970, quoted in full in Klein, *Making It Perfectly Clear*, 125–28.

81. Ambrose, *Nixon*, 33.

82. Smith, *Power Game*, 393.

83. Quoted in Klein, *Making It Perfectly Clear*, 127.

84. Quoted in ibid., 126.

85. Bigart, "Kennedy's Advisers Think Nixon 'Goofed,' " 2.

86. Quoted in Klein, *Making It Perfectly Clear*, 126–27.

87. Ambrose, *Nixon*, 18. Nixon refers to such audits in Nixon, *In the Arena*, 35.

88. Ambrose, *Nixon*, 29.

89. Eisenhower, *Pat Nixon*, 379. See also Nixon, *In the Arena*, 37–38.

90. Safire, *Before the Fall*, 152.

91. Allin interview by Cutlip, 23 November 1973.

92. According to Allin, the News Summary Office monitored the Associated Press and United Press International news wires and received about forty daily newspapers and twenty-five magazines (counting quarterlies and monthlies). In addition, the office monitored the three network news shows, PBS Television's "Washington Week in Review," the syndicated "Agronsky and Company," the CBS Morning News, NBC's "Today," and the CBS radio program "Spectrum" (Cutlip interview with Allin, 23 November 1973; see also Sheldon, "How Nixon Gets News"). For a complete list of the newspapers reviewed regularly by the news summary as of 1973, see "Newspapers on President's Source List," 4.

93. Allin interview by Cutlip, 23 November 1973.

94. Robert Pierpoint, transcript of the CBS morning radio program "Firstline Report," 10 July 1970, attached to Memo, Buchanan to Haldeman, 21 July 1970, "H. R. Haldeman II (2 of 5)," Box 1, HKF, NPMP.

95. Allin interview by Cutlip, 23 November 1973.

96. Ibid.

97. Quoted in "Nixon Sees the News Media through 'Faulty Lens,' " 1.

98. "Daily News Summary," 20 September 1969, page 3, "News Summaries—September 1969," Box 30, POF, NPMP.

99. Memo, Haldeman to Klein, 27 March 1969, "H. R. Haldeman I (1 of 3)," Box 1, HKF, NPMP.

100. Memo, Haldeman to Klein, 26 May 1969, "H. R. Haldeman I (1 of 3)," Box 1, HKF, NPMP.

101. Memo, Haldeman to Klein, 3 June 1969, "H. R. Haldeman I (1 of 3)," Box 1, HKF, NPMP.

102. Memo, Klein to Haldeman, 3 June 1969, "H. R. Haldeman I (1 of 3)," Box 1, HKF, NPMP.

103. A copy of the list was attached to a memo from Haldeman to Klein, 11 June 1969, "H. R. Haldeman I (1 of 3)," Box 1, HKF, NPMP.

104. Quoted in Ehrlichman, *Witness to Power*, 274.

105. Memo, Alexander Butterfield to H. R. Haldeman, 19 May 1969, reprinted in Safire, *Before the Fall*, 345–46.

106. Ehrlichman, *Witness to Power*, 275.

107. Note, Higby to Klein, 7 August 1970, "H. R. Haldeman II (3 of 5)," Box 1, HKF, NPMP.

108. Safire, *Before the Fall*, 345.

109. Ziegler interview, 4 November 1988.

110. Ambrose, *Nixon*, 303–4.

111. Porter, *Assault on the Media*, 40.

112. "Daily News Summary," no date, page 2, "News Summaries (October 1969)," Box 31, POF, NPMP.

113. Broder, "Breaking of the President," quoted in Safire, *Before the Fall*, 171.

114. "Daily News Summary," no date, page 2, "News Summaries (October 1969)," Box 31, POF, NPMP.

115. Safire, *Before the Fall*, 172.

116. Quoted in ibid., 175.

117. Ibid., 177.

118. Ibid., 352. Complete transcripts of Nixon's speech and the "instant analysis" of all three networks can be found in Keogh, *President Nixon and the Press*, 160–90.

119. Klein, *Making It Perfectly Clear*, 169–70.

120. Porter, *Assault on the Media*, 45.

121. Klein, *Making It Perfectly Clear*, 168; cf. Porter, *Assault on the Media*, 44.

122. Ziegler interview, 4 November 1988.

123. Quoted in Porter, *Assault on the Media*, 43.

124. Safire, *Before the Fall*, 352.

125. Memo, Klein to Haldeman, 12 November 1969, "H. R. Haldeman I (2 of 3)," Box 1, HKF, NPMP.

126. Klein, *Making It Perfectly Clear*, 170–71.

127. Text of Agnew speech, 13 November 1969, in Keogh, *President Nixon and the Press*, 192–95.

128. Porter, *Assault on the Media*, 43.

129. Klein, *Making It Perfectly Clear*, 172.

130. Ibid.

131. Ziegler interview, 4 November 1988.

132. Memo, Klein to Haldeman, 14 November 1969, "H. R. Haldeman I (2 of 3)," Box 1, HKF, NPMP.

133. Porter, *Assault on the Media*, 48. Many of these letters were generated by the White House itself. See Ambrose, *Nixon*, 311.

134. Safire, *Before the Fall*, 353.

135. Memo, President to Haldeman, 24 November 1969, in Oudes, *From: The President*, 71.

136. Memo, President to Haldeman, 1 December 1969, in ibid., 76.

137. Grossman and Kumar, *Portraying the President*, 111; Goode interview, 28 November 1989.

138. Memo, President to Haldeman, 1 December 1969, in Oudes, *From: The President*, 77.

139. Carruthers interview, 10 October 1989; Goode interview, 28 November 1989.

140. Goode interview, 28 November 1989.

141. Memo, President to Haldeman, 1 October 1969, in Oudes, *From: The President*, 53.

142. Ehrlichman interview, 28 April 1989.

143. White interview, 17 June 1988.

144. Ibid.

145. Haldeman interview, 17 July 1989.

146. Mollenhoff interview, 7 April 1989.

147. Klein, *Making It Perfectly Clear*, 107–8.

148. Ibid., 108.

149. Memo, President to Haldeman, 22 September 1969, in Oudes, *From: The President*, 44–46.

150. Memo, Cole to Haldeman, 23 September 1969, "H. R. Haldeman I (2 of 3)," Box 1, HKF, NPMP.

151. Handwritten Note, Haldeman to Klein, 24 September 1969, "H. R. Haldeman I (2 of 3)," Box 1, HKF, NPMP.

152. Lukas, *Nightmare*, 7–8.

153. Nixon, *Six Crises*, 82, 83.

154. Magruder, *American Life*, 77–78.

155. Ibid., 55–56.

156. Ibid., 79–80 (the two memos are quoted therein).

157. Ibid., 84.

158. Memo, Magruder to Haldeman, 17 October 1969, in U.S. Congress, Senate, *Final Report*, 267–68 (Exhibit 10). The complete text of the memo is also found in Porter, *Assault on the Media*, 244–49.

159. Memo, Butterfield to the President, 7 October 1969, in Oudes, *From: The President*, 54.

160. Memo, Butterfield to the President, 17 October 1969, in ibid., 61–63. This includes a copy of a "Media Monitoring Report."

161. Memo, Butterfield to Magruder, 23 December 1969, "Memos/Magruder (December 1969)," Box 55, HRHF, NPMP.

162. Memo, Butterfield to Magruder, 24 December 1969, "Memos/Magruder (December 1969)," Box 55, HRHF, NPMP.

163. Memo, Haldeman to Magruder, 16 January 1970, "Memos/Magruder (January 1970)," Box 56, HRHF, NPMP.

164. Memo, Haldeman to Magruder, 17 January 1970, "Memos/Magruder (January 1970)," Box 56, HRHF, NPMP.

165. "Special TV Report: Senator Muskie on the Nationally-Televised CBS Merv Griffin Show (11:30 P.M.–1:00 A.M., Tuesday, September 30 [1969])," "News Summaries (October 1969)," Box 31, POF, NPMP.

166. Magruder, *American Life*, 90.

167. For a full discussion of the dynamics of "exit" and "loyalty" in an organizational setting, see Hirschman, *Exit, Voice, and Loyalty*.

168. Ehrlichman, *Witness to Power*, 167.

169. Mollenhoff, *Game Plan for Disaster*, 34.

170. Haldeman interview, 17 July 1989.

171. Ehrlichman interview, 28 April 1989.

172. Haldeman interview, 17 July 1989.

173. Ehrlichman interview, 28 April 1989.

174. Ziegler interview, 4 November 1988.

175. Mollenhoff interview, 7 April 1989.

176. Colson interview, 11 July 1989.

177. Haldeman interview, 17 July 1989.

178. Magruder, *American Life*, 90.

179. Ibid., 93.

180. Klein, *Making It Perfectly Clear*, 199.

181. Memo, President to Haldeman, 10 October 1969, in Oudes, *From: The President*, 59.

182. "Tentative Plan: Carswell Nomination," 25 March 1970, "EX FG 51/A (1/1/70–3/31/70)," Box 4, WHCF—FG 51, NPMP. Similar plans were put into effect during the ill-fated nomination of Clement Haynsworth to the Supreme Court the previous fall. For a full account of the lobbying and public relations tactics used by the administration on behalf of Haynsworth, see Maltese, "Selling of Clement Haynsworth," 338.

183. Memo, Magruder to Haldeman, 5 February 1970, quoted in Magruder, *American Life*, 106.

184. Klein, *Making It Perfectly Clear*, 110.

185. Ibid., 185.
186. Magruder, *American Life*, 117–18.
187. Ibid., 95.
188. Memo, Haldeman to Magruder, 8 December 1969, "Memos/Magruder (December 1969)," Box 55, HRHF, NPMP.
189. Memo, Magruder to Haldeman, 4 December 1969, "Memos/Magruder (December 1969)," Box 55, HRHF, NPMP.
190. Magruder, *American Life*, 95.
191. U.S. Congress, Senate, *Final Report*, 151.
192. Talking Paper, Haldeman to Magruder, [May 1970], Exhibit 18 in ibid., 292.
193. Memo, Magruder to Haldeman, 6 May 1970, Exhibit 18 in ibid., 293.
194. U.S. Congress, Senate, *Final Report*, 151.
195. Magruder, *American Life*, 95.
196. Memo, Baukol to Colson, 26 April 1971, Exhibit 19 in U.S. Congress, Senate, *Final Report*, 298.
197. Magruder, *American Life*, 96.
198. Colson oral history interview, 21 September 1988, 38.
199. U.S. Congress, Senate, *Final Report*, 154.
200. Memo, Higby to Klein, 1 December 1970, Exhibit 29 in ibid., 322.
201. Klein, *Making It Perfectly Clear*, 118.
202. U.S. Congress, Senate, *Final Report*, 155.
203. Ibid., 154–57.

CHAPTER FOUR

1. Mollenhoff interview, 7 April 1989; White interview, 17 June 1988.
2. Safire, *Before the Fall*, 486.
3. Quoted in Hersh, "Colson Says He Thought He and Colleagues Were 'Above the Law,' " A29.
4. Grossman and Kumar, *Portraying the President*, 90–91.
5. Magruder, *American Life*, 96.
6. Spear, *Presidents and the Press*, 108.
7. Klein, *Making It Perfectly Clear*, 129; Magruder, *American Life*, 103–5.
8. Memo, Magruder to Haldeman, 14 September 1970, "H. R. Haldeman II (3 of 5)," Box 1, HKF, NPMP.
9. Memo, Klein to Haldeman, 17 November 1970, "H. R. Haldeman II (4 of 5)," Box 1, HKF, NPMP.
10. Memo, Snyder to Klein, 13 November 1970, "H. R. Haldeman II (4 of 5)," Box 1, HKF, NPMP. A complete list of all appearances is attached to the memo.
11. Memo, Klein to Finch, Haldeman, and Rumsfeld, 21 September 1970, "H. R. Haldeman II (3 of 5)," Box 1, HKF, NPMP.
12. Memo, Snyder to Klein, 18 September 1970, "H. R. Haldeman II (3 of 5)," Box 1, HKF, NPMP.
13. Magruder, *American Life*, 123.
14. Memo, Magruder to Haldeman, [September 1970], quoted in ibid., 123.
15. Colson interview, 11 July 1989.
16. Magruder, *American Life*, 126–27.
17. Safire, *Before the Fall*, 327–31.
18. Magruder, *American Life*, 128–29.
19. Quoted in Safire, *Before the Fall*, 331.
20. Statement by Jim Keogh, quoted in Magruder, *American Life*, 129.
21. Safire, *Before the Fall*, 330.

22. Magruder, *American Life*, 129.

23. Safire, *Before the Fall*, 336.

24. "Campaign Report," 2425.

25. Quoted in Robert Strout, "New Nixon Technique Selects Columnists for Briefing," *Christian Science Monitor*, 13 November 1970, in "H. R. Haldeman II (4 of 5)," Box 1, HKF, NPMP. The columnists were Richard Wilson, a columnist for Cowles Publications; Clark Mollenhoff, a former Nixon aide who was then bureau chief of the *Des Moines Register and Tribune*; Willard Edwards of the *Chicago Tribune* Press Service; William S. White of the *United Features* syndicate; Nick Thimesch of the *Newsday* syndicate; Roscue and Geoffrey Drummond of the *Los Angeles Times* syndicate; Stewart Alsop of *Newsweek*; and James J. Kilpatrick of the *Washington Star* syndicate.

26. Memo, Odle to Haldeman and Klein, 16 November 1970, "H. R. Haldeman II (4 of 5)," Box 1, HKF, NPMP.

27. Letter, Finch to the "Editor," 9 November 1970, quoted in "For the Record . . . Mr. Finch Views the Election Results," *Washington Post*, 12 November 1970, in "H. R. Haldeman II (4 of 5)," Box 1, HKF, NPMP.

28. David S. Broder, " 'A Famous Victory'—Whatever It Was," *Washington Post*, 12 November 1970, in "H. R. Haldeman II (4 of 5)," Box 1, HKF, NPMP.

29. Lydon, "Rough Ex-Nixon Aide," A24.

30. Colson oral history interview, 15 June 1988, 46.

31. Safire, *Before the Fall*, 486.

32. Colson oral history interview, 15 June 1988, 20.

33. Ibid., 47.

34. Ibid., 17; Colson exit interview, 12 January 1973, 12.

35. Colson oral history interview, 15 June 1988, 17. Later in the same interview, Colson modifies his statement just a bit: "Nixon would call in [Henry] Kissinger without Haldeman. Ehrlichman [too], but John Ehrlichman was pretty careful about keeping Bob Haldeman informed. I wasn't" (ibid., 18).

36. Ibid., 18.

37. Haldeman, *Ends of Power*, 59.

38. Ziegler interview, 4 November 1988.

39. Colson interview, 11 July 1989.

40. Colson oral history interview, 15 June 1988, 20.

41. White, *Breach of Faith*, 143–44.

42. "Nixon Hatchet Man," 1; Colson, *Born Again*, chapter 5.

43. Magruder, *American Life*, 64.

44. Klein, *Making It Perfectly Clear*, 278.

45. Lukas, *Nightmare*, 11.

46. Colson oral history interview, 15 June 1988, 39–40.

47. Memo, Colson to Haldeman, 25 September 1970, quoted in Spear, *Presidents and the Press*, 142.

48. Colson oral history interview, 15 June 1988, 40.

49. Memo, Klein to Colson, [October 1970], quoted in Magruder, *American Life*, 135.

50. Colson interview, 11 July 1989.

51. Rhatican interview, 31 January 1990.

52. Klein, *Making It Perfectly Clear*, 282; Magruder, *American Life*, 135.

53. Magruder, *American Life*, 136.
54. Colson interview, 11 July 1989.
55. Ibid.
56. Klein, *Making It Perfectly Clear*, 287.
57. Bonafede, "Nixon Personnel Staff Works to Restructure Federal Policies," 2441–42.
58. Colson interview, 11 July 1989.
59. Malek interview, 25 October 1988.
60. Magruder, *American Life*, 138.
61. Malek interview, 25 October 1988.
62. Shumway interview, 30 January 1990.
63. Magruder, *American Life*, 143.
64. Memo, Klein to the President, 3 March 1971, "Communications Reorganization (Part I)," Box 119, HRHF, NPMP.
65. Ibid.
66. Memo, Colson to Huntsman, 11 June 1971, "Communications Reorganization (Part I)," Box 119, HRHF, NPMP.
67. White interview, 17 June 1988.
68. Memo, Malek to Higby, 26 March 1971, "Communications Reorganization (Part II)," Box 119, HRHF, NPMP. See also Memo, Haldeman to Klein and Colson, 26 March 1971, "Communications Reorganization (Part II)," Box 119, HRHF, NPMP; and Memo, Malek to Haldeman, 31 March 1971, "Communications Reorganization (Part I)," Box 119, HRHF, NPMP.
69. Klein, *Making It Perfectly Clear*, 287.
70. Shumway interview, 30 January 1990.
71. Rhatican interview, 31 January 1990.
72. Colson interview, 11 July 1989.
73. Ibid. Clawson confirms that he was the de facto director of the Office of Communications since joining it as deputy director in February 1972 and that he worked closely with Colson in Nixon's reelection campaign (Clawson interview by Cutlip, 16 October 1973).
74. Shumway interview, 30 January 1990.
75. Shumway interview by Cutlip, 25 October 1973; Shumway interview, 30 January 1990.
76. Memo, Colson to Huntsman, 11 June 1971, "Communications Reorganization (Part I)," Box 119, HRHF, NPMP.
77. Memo, Klein to the President, 24 June 1971, "H. R. Haldeman III (1 of 2)," Box 2, HKF, NPMP.
78. Colson interview, 11 July 1989.
79. Buchanan interview by Cutlip, 27 November 1973.
80. Memo, Klein to the President, 24 June 1971, "H. R. Haldeman III (1 of 2)," Box 2, HKF, NPMP.
81. Memo, Klein to Colson, 13 September 1971, "Herb Klein," Box 9, CCF, NPMP.
82. Memo, Klein to Colson, 5 November 1971, "Herb Klein," Box 9, CCF, NPMP.
83. Memo, Colson to Klein, 8 November 1971, "Herb Klein," Box 9, CCF, NPMP.
84. Ehrlichman interview, 28 April 1989.
85. Haldeman interview, 17 July 1989.
86. Klein, *Making It Perfectly Clear*, 292–93.
87. Transcript of a conversation between the president and H. R.

Haldeman, 23 June 1972, quoted in ibid., 293–94.

88. Haldeman interview, 17 July 1989.
89. Ehrlichman interview, 28 April 1989.
90. Colson interview, 11 July 1989.
91. David Gergen, quoted in Smith, *Power Game*, 405–6.
92. Ibid., 406.
93. Colson interview, 11 July 1989; Colson exit interview, 12 January 1973, 8.
94. Colson interview, 11 July 1989.
95. Colson exit interview, 12 January 1973.
96. Carruthers interview, 10 October 1989; Goode interview, 28 November 1989.
97. Weaver, "G.O.P. Carefully Created Fresh Show for Viewers," A46; Semple, "Vote for Brinkley a Welcome Script Change," A46.
98. White, *Making of the President— 1972*, 326.
99. Gergen interview, 10 March 1989.
100. Spear, *Presidents and the Press*, 181.
101. David Gergen, quoted in Smith, *Power Game*, 405.
102. Carruthers interview, 10 October 1989.
103. Colson interview, 11 July 1989.
104. Klein, *Making It Perfectly Clear*, 379.
105. Ibid., 380–81.
106. Ziegler interview, 4 November 1988.
107. Klein, *Making It Perfectly Clear*, 381.
108. Ibid., 382.
109. Eisenhower, *Pat Nixon*, 362.
110. Klein, *Making It Perfectly Clear*, 382.

111. Ibid., 392.
112. Memo, Klein to the President, 23 April 1973, "Klein," Box 110, HRHF, NPMP.
113. Klein, *Making It Perfectly Clear*, 393–94.
114. *Congressional Record*, 27 June 1973, H5537–42.
115. Sidey, "So Long to Old Herb Klein," 24.
116. Klein exit interview, 13 July 1973, 31.
117. Klein, *Making It Perfectly Clear*, 395.
118. Ephron, "Ken Clawson Is No Joke," 60; Apple, "A Nixon Spear-Carrier," A45; Deposition of Ken W. Clawson, Washington, D.C., 2 May 1973, taken on behalf of the plaintiff in *Public Citizen, Inc.* v. *Ken W. Clawson*, Civil Action No. 759–73, United States District Court for the District of Columbia, 5–6 (hereafter cited as Clawson deposition).
119. Quoted in Ephron, "Ken Clawson Is No Joke," 61.
120. Quoted in ibid.
121. Ibid.
122. Clawson interview by Cutlip, 16 October 1973.
123. Evans and Novak, "Departure of Herb Klein," 23. Clawson himself confirmed that in an interview with Scott M. Cutlip (Clawson interview by Cutlip, 16 October 1973).
124. Memo, Colson to Malek, 9 November 1972, "Fred Malek/Dan Kingsley," Box 10, CCF, NPMP.
125. Spear, *Presidents and the Press*, 212.
126. Clawson deposition, 2 May 1973, 24.

127. Ibid., 20.
128. "The Battle of the Budget, 1973," in ibid., Exhibit 1.
129. Causey, "PR Men Gird for 'Battle of Budget,'" D9.
130. Section 1913 of Title 18, United States Code; Section 608(a) of the Treasury, Postal Service, and General Government Appropriation Act, 1973, P.L. 92–351. See "Complaint for Declaratory and Injunctive Relief," *Public Citizen, Inc.* v. *Ken W. Clawson*, Civil Action No. 759–73, United States District Court for the District of Columbia. See also Causey, "U.S. Speech-Writing Kit Is Recalled," B17.
131. "Complaint for Declaratory and Injunctive Relief," *Public Citizen, Inc.* v. *Ken W. Clawson*, 1.
132. Causey, "U.S. Speech-Writing Kit Is Recalled," B17.
133. Quoted in Ephron, "Ken Clawson Is No Joke," 58.
134. Ibid.
135. Bonafede, "Communications Office Is Reduced," 1181.
136. Colson interview, 11 July 1989.
137. Klein, *Making It Perfectly Clear*, 205.
138. Speakes interview, 8 April 1989.
139. Bernstein and Woodward, *All the President's Men*, 137–41.
140. Lukas, *Nightmare*, 163.
141. Bonafede, "Staff, Style Changes Slow in Coming," 1062. Ziegler insists otherwise—both then and now—but virtually everyone else associated with the Office of Communications (including Ken Clawson) says that the two operations remained separate and that Clawson reported to Haldeman's successor, Alexander Haig (Clawson interview by Cutlip, 16 October 1973; Ziegler interview, 4 November 1988). Larry Speakes, who worked under Clawson in the Office of Communications, concurs. He says that the Office of Communications remained "entirely separate" from the Press Office and that "Clawson really struggled to keep it that way" (Speakes interview, 8 April 1989). See also Ephron, "Ken Clawson Is No Joke," 61.
142. Clawson, "A Loyalist's Memoir," D3.
143. Quoted in Ephron, "Ken Clawson Is No Joke," 62.
144. Speakes interview, 8 April 1989.
145. Ibid.
146. Ibid.; Speakes, *Speaking Out*, 40.
147. Bonafede, "More Musical Chairs," 1123.
148. Spear, *Presidents and the Press*, 214.
149. Ford interview, 7 April 1989.
150. Speakes interview, 8 April 1989.
151. Ephron, "Ken Clawson Is No Joke," 64; see also Woodward and Bernstein, *Final Days*, 159.
152. Speakes interview, 8 April 1989.
153. *Public Papers of the Presidents: Richard Nixon*, 901, 905.
154. Ibid., 956.
155. Spear, *Presidents and the Press*, 213.
156. Shabecoff, "Nixon Foes Held Source of Leaks"; Burby, "Impeachment Report," 990.
157. Clawson, "A Loyalist's Memoir," D3; Speakes, *Speaking Out*, 45.

158. Clawson, "A Loyalist's Memoir," D3.
159. Speakes, *Speaking Out*, 45.
160. Spear, *Presidents and the Press*, 222.
161. For example, see Drew, *Washington Journal*, 57–58.
162. Spear, *Presidents and the Press*, 222.
163. Quoted in ibid., 222–23.
164. Organization Chart of the White House Staff, "Haldeman, Executive Reorganization (Part 1)," Box 124, HRHF, NPMP.
165. Witcover, "Two Hats of Herbert Klein," 27.
166. Memo, Haldeman to Klein, 4 February 1970, "H. R. Haldeman I (3 of 3)," Box 1, HKF, NPMP.
167. Seidman, *Politics, Position, and Power*, 111.
168. Safire, *Before the Fall*, 247.
169. Nathan, *Plot That Failed*, 45.
170. Ibid., 47.
171. Iglehart, "Major HEW Legislation Tailored by White House 'Working Groups,'" 486.
172. Seidman, *Politics, Position, and Power*, 115.
173. Magruder, *American Life*, 102.
174. Memo, Haldeman to Klein, 19 April 1970, "H. R. Haldeman I (3 of 3)," Box 1, HKF, NPMP.
175. "Daily News Summary," 1 December 1969, page 2, with President's margin notes, "News Summaries—December 1969," Box 31, POF, NPMP.
176. Bonafede, "Nixon Orders 500 Jobs," 912.
177. Hess, *Government/Press Connection*, 12 (notes omitted).
178. U.S. Congress, Senate, *Watergate and Related Activities*, Exhibit 44, 1683.
179. Spear, *Presidents and the Press*, 213.
180. Magruder, *American Life*, 102–3.
181. Ibid., 103.
182. Ehrlichman, *Witness to Power*, 255.
183. Draft memo, President to Haldeman, 8 March 1971, in Oudes, *From: The President*, 227.
184. Ehrlichman, *Witness to Power*, 255.
185. Ibid.
186. Colson interview, 11 July 1989.
187. Haldeman interview, 17 July 1989.
188. Shumway interview, 30 January 1990.
189. Wise, *Politics of Lying*, 406–7; Shumway interview, 30 January 1990.
190. Ambrose, *Nixon*, 456.
191. Safire, *Before the Fall*, 496; Shumway interview, 30 January 1990.
192. Klein, *Making It Perfectly Clear*, 286–87; Safire, *Before the Fall*, 493.
193. Ambrose, *Nixon*, 456.
194. In a memo to Colson, Klein later cited the Burns incident as an example of how Colson undermined Klein's "credibility" and "good name" (Memo, Klein to Colson, 5 November 1971, page 2, "Herb Klein," Box 9, CCF, NPMP).
195. Shumway interview, 30 January 1990.

CHAPTER FIVE

1. TerHorst interview, 18 July 1989.
2. Ford, *Time to Heal*, 41.

3. Memo, Helm to terHorst, 13 August 1974, "Publicity—Newsleaks, 8/9/74–10/8/74," Box 143, WHCF—PR/16, GRFL.
4. Ford, *Time to Heal*, 132.
5. TerHorst, "President Ford and the Media," 209–11.
6. Ford interview, 7 April 1989.
7. TerHorst interview, 18 July 1989.
8. Ford interview, 7 April 1989.
9. TerHorst interview, 18 July 1989.
10. Ibid.
11. Ibid.
12. Letter, terHorst to Johnson, 29 August 1974, "Publicity—Newsleaks, 8/9/74–10/8/74," Box 143, WHCF—PR/16, GRFL.
13. Nessen, *It Sure Looks Different*, 14.
14. Talking Paper, "Subject: Paul Miltich," 24 October 1974, "Paul Miltich (1)," Box 137, RNP, GRFL.
15. Talking Paper, "Subject: Jerry Warren," 17 October 1974, "Gerald Warren (10/74–1/75)," Box 139, RNP, GRFL.
16. Nessen, *It Sure Looks Different*, 31.
17. Klein, *Making It Perfectly Clear*, 184.
18. Spear, *Presidents and the Press*, 235.
19. Warren interview, 11 October 1989.
20. Speakes, *Speaking Out*, 40.
21. "White House's Warren," 73.
22. Ford interview, 7 April 1989.
23. Warren interview, 11 October 1989.
24. Ibid.
25. Talking Paper, "Subject: Jerry Warren," 17 October 1974, "Gerald Warren (10/74–1/75)," Box 139, RNP, GRFL.
26. Memo, Miltich to Nessen, 25 October 1974, "Paul Miltich (1)," Box 137, RNP, GRFL.
27. Talking Paper, "Subject: Jerry Warren," 17 October 1974, "Gerald Warren (10/74–1/75)," Box 139, RNP, GRFL.
28. Ibid.; Talking Paper, "Subject: Paul Miltich," 24 October 1974, "Paul Miltich (1)," Box 137, RNP, GRFL.
29. Memo, Nessen to Jones, 28 October 1974, "Gerald Warren (10/74–1/75)," Box 139, RNP, GRFL.
30. Memo, Nessen to Cheney, 16 January 1975, "Dick Cheney, 1975 (1)," Box 127, RNP, GRFL.
31. Memo, Nessen to Miltich, 15 February 1975, "Paul Miltich (2)," Box 137, RNP, GRFL.
32. Warren interview, 11 October 1989.
33. Speakes interview, 8 April 1989.
34. White interview, 17 June 1988.
35. Warren interview, 11 October 1989.
36. Memo, Warren to Nessen, 18 December 1974, "Gerald Warren (10/74–1/75)," Box 139, RNP, GRFL.
37. White interview, 17 June 1988.
38. Memo, Nessen to Rumsfeld, 25 July 1975, "Rumsfeld (7/75–11/75)," Box 133, RNP, GRFL.
39. Memo, Buchanan to terHorst, 17 August 1974, page 4, "Press Office—Philosophy," Box 24, RNP, GRFL.
40. Nessen, *It Sure Looks Different*, chapter 25 and passim.
41. Ibid., 164–65, 167, 170, and chapter 13 passim.

42. King and Ragsdale, *Elusive Executive*, Table 6.2, 302.

43. "Rx for Ailing White House Press Operation," 39.

44. Extensive notes from the meetings are found in "Press Office Improvement Meeting—6/28/75 (1-3)," Box 23, RNP, GRFL.

45. Memo, Baroody and Warren to Rumsfeld, 7 May 1975, "Mailing Operations (1)," Box 1, W&WF, GRFL.

46. Bonafede, "Communications Office Role Is Reduced," 1181.

47. Memo, White to Cheney, 21 November 1975, "Mailing Operations (1)," Box 11, W&WF, GRFL.

48. Memo, White to Nessen, 3 March 1975, "President, 1975 (1)," Box 131, RNP, GRFL; Memo, White to the President, 23 April 1975, "PR 16 (4/17-5/6/75)," Box 143, WHCF—PR/16, GRFL.

49. Memo, Nessen to Connor, 12 March 1975, "PR 16 (3/11-3/25/75)," Box 143, WHCF—PR/16, GRFL.

50. Memo, White to Nessen, 3 March 1975, "President, 1975 (1)," Box 131, RNP, GRFL.

51. Memo, White to Nessen, 4 June 1975, "American Newspaper Publishers Association (2), June 11, 1975," Box 1, W&WF, GRFL.

52. Rollan D. Melton, "A Reno Newsman's Big Day at the White House," *Nevada State Journal*, 12 June 1975, in "American Newspaper Publishers Association, June 11, 1975 (1)," Box 1, W&WF, GRFL.

53. Memo, White to Nessen, 22 May 1975, "Margita White (5/75)," Box 141, RNP, GRFL; Memo, Jones to Rustand, 19 June 1975, "PR 16 (6/11-6/25/75)," WHCF, GRFL.

54. Ford interview, 7 April 1989.

55. "Functions of the Office of Communications," [July 1975], page 2, "Rumsfeld (7/75-11/75) (1)," Box 133, RNP, GRFL.

56. For example, Memo, White to Public Affairs Officers, 15 July 1975, "Mailings, July 1975 (2)," Box 11, W&WF, GRFL.

57. Memo, Warren to the Cabinet, 6 June 1975, "Gerald Warren, Cabinet (1)," Box 140, RNP, GRFL.

58. Bonafede, "Communications Office Role Is Reduced," 1181.

59. "Functions of the Office of Communications," [July 1975], page 2, "Rumsfeld (7/75-11/75) (1)," Box 133, RNP, GRFL.

60. Memo, White to Cavanaugh, 3 May 1976, "Margita White, Cabinet, Op-Ed (1)," Box 143, RNP, GRFL.

61. "Press Improvement Meeting," Notes of afternoon session (2:20 P.M.), 18 October 1975, "Press Improvement Meeting, 10/18/75 (2)," Box 23, RNP, GRFL.

62. Memo, Guthrie to Rumsfeld, 11 October 1974, "PR 16-3 (Presidential News Analysis, 8/9/74-5/15/75," Box 160, WHCF—PR/16-3, GRFL.

63. William H. McNitt, Finding Aid for the James B. Shuman Files, page 3, GRFL.

64. Letter, Witt (Director of Public Relations, Republican Governors Association) to Warren, 27 January

1975, "Gerald Warren, 10/74–1/75," Box 139, RNP, GRFL.

65. Memo, Warren to Nessen, 29 January 1975, with handwritten notes from Nessen to Warren, "Gerald Warren, 10/74–1/75," Box 139, RNP, GRFL.

66. "Press Aides Meet at White House," *First Monday* (March 1975), in "Gerald Warren, 3/75," Box 139, RNP, GRFL.

67. Memo, White to Nessen, 28 October 1975, "Margita White, 10/20/75–10/31/75," Box 142, RNP, GRFL.

68. Lang, "Margita White," 1.

69. White interview, 17 June 1988.

70. Bonafede, "Communications Office Role Is Reduced," 1181.

71. Bonafede article in "Margita White, 8/8/75–8/25/75," Box 141, RNP, GRFL.

72. "Press Plan: The President's Tax/Budget Reduction Program," 17 October 1975, "Press Improvement Meeting, 10/18/75," Box 23, RNP, GRFL.

73. "Tax/Budget Cut Spokesmen: Appearances and Media Events," [October/November 1975], "Press Improvement Meeting, 10/18/75 (2)," Box 23, RNP, GRFL.

74. Cheney interview, 10 March 1989.

75. King and Ragsdale, *Elusive Executive*, Table 6.2, 303.

76. Nessen, *It Sure Looks Different*, 196.

77. "Press Office Improvement Meeting," notes of afternoon session (2:20 P.M.), 18 October 1975, page 5, "Press Improvement Meeting, 10/18/75 (2)," Box 23, RNP, GRFL.

78. White interview, 17 June 1988.

79. Memo, White to Nessen, 26 November 1975, page 1, "Advocate Program, Organization and Scheduling (1)," Box 1, DGF, GRFL.

80. Ibid., 2.

81. Ibid., 6.

82. White interview, 17 June 1988.

83. Cheney interview, 10 March 1989.

84. Witcover, *Marathon*, 410.

85. Nessen, *It Sure Looks Different*, 206.

86. Ford, *Time to Heal*, 375.

87. Cheney interview, 10 March 1989.

88. Rumsfeld interview, 7 April 1989.

89. Nessen, *It Sure Looks Different*, 149.

90. Raoul-Duval interview, 3 December 1987.

91. Cheney interview, 10 March 1989.

92. Gergen interview, 10 March 1989.

93. Memo, "Notes on a Revised Communications Effort," Cavanaugh, Duval, and Gergen to Cheney, 23 April 1976, "Communications Flow," Box 14, MRDP, GRFL.

94. Ibid.

95. Memo, "Some Additional Thoughts by Duval on the Revised Communications Effort," Duval to Cheney, undated [circa 23 April 1976], "Communications Flow," Box 14, MRDP, GRFL.

96. Gergen interview, 10 March 1989.

97. Rhatican interview, 31 January 1990.

98. Ford interview, 7 April 1989.

99. Duval, Notes of a meeting between Duval and Cheney, 24 April 1976, 10:00 A.M., "Communications Flow," Box 14, MRDP, GRFL.

100. Duval, Notes of a meeting among

Dick Cheney, John Marsh, William Seidman, James Cannon, Jerry Jones, David Gergen, Foster Channock, [Doug?] Smith, John Carlson, William Hyland, James Cavanaugh, Vallis, Mike Duval, and James Conner, 9 May 1976, 11:00 A.M., "Richard Cheney—Meeting Notes," Box 14, MRDP, GRFL.

101. Duval, Notes of a meeting between Cheney and Duval, on or about 10 July 1976, "Richard Cheney—Meeting Notes," Box 14, MRDP, GRFL.

102. Gergen interview, 10 March 1989.

103. Carruthers interview, 10 October 1989.

104. Cheney interview, 10 March 1989.

105. Carruthers interview, 10 October 1989.

106. Memo, Jones and Gergen to the President, 30 July 1976, "David Gergen (3)," Box 135, RNP, GRFL.

107. Cheney interview, 10 March 1989.

108. Rhatican interview, 31 January 1990.

109. Ibid.

110. Ibid.

111. Gold, *PR as in President*, 4–5.

112. Rumsfeld interview, 7 April 1989.

113. Cheney interview, 10 March 1989.

114. Rumsfeld interview, 7 April 1989.

115. Cheney interview, 10 March 1989.

116. Raoul-Duval interview, 3 December 1987.

117. A discussion of the plan, plus excerpts from it, appears in Schram, *Running for President*, 279–301; the original strategy plan can be found in "Campaign Plan—Final Copy 3 of 4," Box 13, MRDP, GRFL.

118. Strategy Plan, page 74, "Campaign Plan—Final Copy 3 of 4," Box 13, MRDP, GRFL.

119. Nessen, *It Sure Looks Different*, 247.

120. Cheney interview, 10 March 1989.

121. Ibid.

122. Carruthers interview, 10 October 1989.

123. Cheney interview, 10 March 1989.

124. Strategy Plan, page 59, "Campaign Plan—Final Copy 3 of 4," Box 13, MRDP, GRFL.

125. Gold, *PR as in President*, 63, 111.

126. Spencer interview, 8 April 1989.

127. Transcript of "Press Office Advance Meeting," 6 August 1976, 4:15 P.M., page 8, "Press Office Improvement Session, Press Advance (2)," Box 24, RNP, GRFL.

128. Ibid., 22.

129. Memo, Muhlberg to Gergen, 3 September 1976, "Office of Communications—Administration," Box 6, DGF, GRFL.

130. Rhatican interview, 31 January 1990.

131. Ibid.

132. Transcript of "Communications, Advocates, News Summary, and Research Staff Meeting," Situation Room, 7 August 1976, 9:45 A.M., pages 3–4, "Press Improvement Session, 8/6–7/76, Communications, etc.," Box 24, RNP, GRFL.

133. "Advocates Program," undated, "Advocates—General," Box 32, RNP, GRFL.

134. Ibid.; Spencer interview, 8 April 1989.

135. "Advocates Program," undated, "Advocates—General," Box 32, RNP, GRFL.

136. Memo, Connor to Cabinet Members, 2 September 1976, "Advocate Program—Organization and Scheduling (2)," Box 1, DGF, GRFL.
137. Memo, Greener to Rhatican, 1 September 1976, "Advocate Program—Organization and Scheduling (2)," Box 1, DGF, GRFL.
138. Draft of memo from Rhatican to Cabinet Schedulers (written by Greener), "Advocates Program—Organization and Scheduling (2)," Box 1, DGF, GRFL.
139. Memo, Connor to Cabinet Members, 2 September 1976, "Advocate Program—Organization and Scheduling (2)," Box 1, DGF, GRFL.
140. Greener interview, 1 November 1989.
141. Rhatican interview, 31 January 1990.
142. Greener interview, 1 November 1989.
143. Rhatican interview, 31 January 1990.
144. Ibid.
145. Nessen, *It Sure Looks Different*, 253.
146. Rhatican interview, 31 January 1990.
147. Nessen, *It Sure Looks Different*, 253.
148. Ibid., 263; transcripts of the practice sessions are found in "Debate Working Papers," Box 26, MRDP, GRFL.
149. Spencer interview, 8 April 1989.
150. Gergen interview, 10 March 1989; Cheney interview, 10 March 1989; Spencer interview, 8 April 1989;

Greener interview, 1 November 1989.
151. Cheney interview, 10 March 1989.

CHAPTER SIX

1. Bario interview, 25 October 1988.
2. Schneiders interview, 31 October 1988.
3. Ibid.
4. Wurfel interview, 1 February 1990.
5. Fallows, "Passionless Presidency," 39.
6. Clark, "Power Vacuum," 296.
7. Rozell, *Carter Presidency*, 216.
8. Clark, "Power Vacuum," 296.
9. Wurfel interview, 1 February 1990.
10. Ibid.
11. Memo, Wurfel to Powell, 27 June 1977, "Memos: Wurfel, 6/2/77–8/29/77," Box 48, JPF, JCL.
12. Wurfel interview, 1 February 1990.
13. Carter, *Keeping Faith*, 87–88.
14. Fallows, "Passionless Presidency," 34.
15. Memo, Wurfel to Rafshoon, 30 May 1978, "Office of Media Liaison," Box 4, GRF, JCL.
16. Ibid.
17. Bario interview, 25 October 1988. Agendas for all of these conferences are available in the Jody Powell Files at the Jimmy Carter Library.
18. A twenty-page list, "Mailings from the Office of Media Liaison of the White House Press Office," dated 30 May 1979, can be found in "Memos: Media Liaison, 1/22/79–5/30/79," Box 44, JPF, JCL.
19. "Specialized Mailings to the Black Media," [February 1978],

"Memos: Media Liaison, 1/11/78–6/27/78," Box 44, JPF, JCL.

20. Memo, Bario to Wurfel and Powell, 28 February 1978, "Memos: Media Liaison, 1/11/78–2/27/79," Box 44, JPF, JCL.

21. Memo, Powell to Senior Staff, 21 November 1978, with handwritten note by Powell, "Memos: Media Liaison, 7/18/78–12/4/78," Box 44, JPF, JCL.

22. Memo, Wurfel to Powell, 26 February 1979, "Memos: Wurfel, 1/8/79–8/20/79," Box 49, JPF, JCL.

23. Memo, Wurfel to Rafshoon, "Functions of Office of Media Liaison," 30 May 1978, "Office of Media Liaison," Box 4, GRF, JCL.

24. Spencer interview, 8 April 1989.

25. Hart interview, 7 November 1989; Maynes interview, 27 December 1989; Nelson interview, 19 October 1989; O'Leary interview, 12 January 1990; Reigner interview, 18 January 1990; Rosenker interview, 16 January 1990.

26. Memo, Woods to Nessen, 8 December 1975, "Randall Woods, 12/8/75–3/5/76," Box 145, RNP, GRFL.

27. Ibid.

28. Report No. B-178648, 21 September 1973, General Accounting Office, Washington, D.C.

29. Memo, Woods to Nessen, 8 December 1975, "Randall Woods, 12/8/75–3/5/76," Box 145, RNP, GRFL.

30. TerHorst interview, 18 July 1989.

31. Letter, Maier to Powell, 5 October 1977, "Memos: Wurfel, 10/3/77–10/31/77," Box 48, JPF, JCL.

32. Letter, Powell to Maier, 25 October 1977, "Memos: Wurfel, 10/3/77–10/31/77," Box 48, JPF, JCL.

33. Wurfel interview, 1 February 1990.

34. Bario interview, 25 October 1988.

35. Memo, Wurfel to Powell, 2 November 1977, "Memos: Wurfel: 10/3/77–10/31/77," Box 48, JPF, JCL.

36. Memo, Wurfel to McCullough, 7 June 1978, "Walt Wurfel," Box 35, GRF, JCL.

37. Memo, Wurfel to Schneiders, 21 June 1978, "Memos: Wurfel, 6/1/78–7/29/78," Box 49, JPF, JCL.

38. Memo, Wurfel to Hugh Carter and Beaman, 11 July 1978, "Walt Wurfel," Box 35, GRF, JCL.

39. Bario interview, 25 October 1988.

40. Nelson interview, 19 October 1989.

41. Memo, Nelson to Wurfel and Bario, 15 November 1978, "Memos: Walt Wurfel, 8/1/78–12/19/78," Box 49, JPF, JCL.

42. The following transcript of a radio actuality transmission from 4 June 1979 illustrates the different parts of a prepackaged White House actuality:

[BILLBOARD]

NELSON: This is the White House Press Office with three news actualities for Monday evening, June 4th, 1979. Cut one—6o seconds with voice wrap and 30 seconds without—E.P.A. Administrator Douglas Costle, commenting on increased supplies of unleaded gasoline. . . .

[CALIBRATION TONE]

[COUNTDOWN]

[VOICE WRAP]

NELSON: The Carter Administration Monday took steps which White House Officials say will increase supplies of unleaded gasoline over the summer. Environmental Protection Agency Administrator Douglas Costle told reporters at the White House that the ban on MMT, a gasoline additive, will be lifted temporarily.

[CUT]

COSTLE: MMT is an octane-boosting additive that allows you, in effect, to get more unleaded out of a barrel of crude oil than you might otherwise get. It was banned by the 1977 Clean Air Act Amendments but the Administrator of E.P.A. was given authority to waive the ban in extraordinary circumstances. I'm going to suspend, until October First, the ban on the use of MMT.

[VOICE WRAP]

NELSON: Over a period of time, MMT use contributes to smog in urban areas, but Costle said environmentally safe substitutes for MMT will be available to refiners after the ban is reinstated. In Washington, this is Rich Nelson of the White House Press Office.

The transcript of the radio actuality transmission is an attachment to

"Answers to Senator Schmitt's Questions," found in "Media Liaison Office, 1/19/79–7/27/79," Box 19, RGF, JCL.

43. Nelson interview, 19 October 1989.
44. Ibid.
45. Memo, Wurfel to Powell, "Reaction to Radio Actuality Service," 12 December 1978, "Memos: Wurfel, 8/1/78–12/19/78," Box 49, JPF, JCL.
46. Answers to Questions Submitted for the Record by Senators Ted Stevens and Harrison Schmitt on the White House Radio Tape Service, "Memos: Media Liaison, 6/4/79–7/29/79," Box 44, JPF, JCL.
47. Bario interview, 25 October 1988.
48. Nelson interview, 19 October 1989.
49. Memo, Klein to Haldeman, 14 September 1970, "H. R. Haldeman II (3 of 5)," Box 1, HKF, NPMP.
50. "A Plan for Putting the GOP on TV News," [September 1970], "H. R. Haldeman II (3 of 5)," Box 1, HKF, NPMP.
51. Memo, Klein to Haldeman, 14 September 1970, "H. R. Haldeman II (3 of 5)," Box 1, HKF, NPMP.
52. Memo, Colson to Haldeman, 17 November 1970, in Oudes, *From: The President*, 172.
53. Nelson interview, 19 October 1989.
54. Memo, Wurfel to Rafshoon and Schneiders, 16 June 1978, "Walt Wurfel," Box 35, GRF, JCL; Nelson interview, 19 October 1989.
55. Memo, Wurfel to Rafshoon and Schneiders, 16 June 1978, "Walt Wurfel," Box 35, GRF, JCL.
56. Answers to Questions Submitted for the Record by Senators Ted Stevens and Harrison Schmitt on the

White House Radio Tape Service, "Memos: Media Liaison, 6/4/79–7/29/79," Box 44, JPF, JCL.

57. Fallows, "Passionless Presidency," 39.

58. Quoted in Bonafede, "Carter's Recent Staff Shakeup," 953.

59. Bonafede, "Carter Sounds Retreat," 1852.

60. Bonafede, "Carter's Recent Staff Shakeup," 955; Bonafede, "Carter Sounds Retreat," 1853–55. See also Bonafede, "White House Wheels Are Turning," 389.

61. "Jordan's New Role," 1356.

62. Bonafede, "Carter's Recent Staff Shakeup," 954–55; Bonafede, "Tough Job of Normalizing Relations with Capitol Hill," 54.

63. Bonafede, "Has the Rafshoon Touch Left Its Mark," 589.

64. Schram, *Running for President*, 57ff.

65. Rafshoon interview, 17 June 1988.

66. Bonafede, "Rafshoon to the Rescue," 1096.

67. Bonafede, "If the Rafshoon Fits, Wear It," 1331.

68. Rafshoon exit interview, 12 September 1979, 3.

69. Rafshoon interview, 17 June 1988; Rafshoon exit interview, 12 September 1979, 3.

70. "Greg Schneiders," 592. For more background on Schneiders, see Stroud, *How Jimmy Won*, chapter 22.

71. Schneiders interview, 31 October 1988.

72. Fallows, "Passionless Presidency," 39.

73. Rafshoon interview, 17 June 1988.

74. "Assistant to President for Communications," undated [circa May 1978], "Office Procedures: Memos (1)," Box 29, GRF, JCL.

75. Schneiders interview, 31 October 1988.

76. Rafshoon exit interview, 12 September 1979, 7; Schneiders interview, 31 October 1988.

77. Bonafede, "Has the Rafshoon Touch Left Its Mark," 592.

78. Memo, Schneiders to Rafshoon, 14 December 1978, "Memos from Schneiders, December 1978," Box 28, GRF, JCL. For a time, Coleman worked separately from the speechwriting unit.

79. Memo, Rafshoon to the Senior Staff, 31 July 1978, "Memos from Rafshoon, July 1978," Box 28, GRF, JCL.

80. Memo, Rafshoon to the President, 19 July 1978, page 2, "Memos from Rafshoon, July 1978," Box 28, GRF, JCL.

81. Ibid., 4.

82. Memo, Rafshoon to the President, "Thematics at the Press Conference," 20 July 1978, "Memos from Rafshoon, July 1978," Box 28, GRF, JCL.

83. Memo, Rafshoon to the President, 1 September 1978, "Memos from Rafshoon, September 1978," Box 28, GRF, JCL.

84. Memo, Rafshoon to Eizenstat, 10 August 1978, "Memos from Rafshoon, August 1978," Box 28, GRF, JCL.

85. Memo, Rafshoon to Senior Staff and Heads of Departments and Agencies, 10 August 1978, "Memos from Rafshoon, August 1978," Box 28, GRF, JCL.

86. Schneiders interview, 31 October 1988.
87. Rafshoon interview, 17 June 1988.
88. Rafshoon exit interview, 12 September 1979, 10.
89. "Energy, Economy, Efficiency" issue of "The White House News and Views," undated, "Newsletter," Box 56, GRF, JCL.
90. Schneiders interview, 31 October 1988.
91. Rafshoon exit interview, 12 September 1979, 10.
92. Schneiders interview, 31 October 1988.
93. Bonafede, "Has the Rafshoon Touch Left Its Mark," 591.
94. Wurfel interview, 1 February 1990.
95. Schneiders interview, 31 October 1988.
96. Bonafede, "It's a Whole New Ball Game," 1518; Bonafede, "Camp David Cure," 1607; "Foreign Policy Triumphs," 30.
97. Bario interview, 25 October 1988.
98. Carter interview by MacNeil, 18 January 1989.
99. King and Ragsdale, *Elusive Executive*, Table 6.2, 304.
100. Powell, *Other Side of the Story*, 111.
101. Quoted in Rozell, *Carter Presidency*, 207.
102. Wurfel interview, 1 February 1990.
103. Carter interview by Nelson, 6 January 1990.
104. Powell, *Other Side of the Story*, 173.
105. Jordan, *Crisis*, 359–60.
106. Rafshoon exit interview, 12 September 1979, 18.
107. Schneiders interview, 31 October 1988.
108. Rafshoon exit interview, 12 September 1979, 17–18.
109. Memo, Rafshoon to the President, undated [summer 1979], "Memos from Rafshoon, June–August 1979," Box 29, GRF, JCL. Emphasis in original.
110. Rozell, *Carter Presidency*, 211.
111. Schneiders interview, 31 October 1988.
112. Quoted in Hertsgaard, *On Bended Knee*, 299.
113. Carter interview by MacNeil, 18 January 1989.
114. Rafshoon interview, 17 June 1988.
115. Schneiders interview, 31 October 1988.
116. Nixon, *Memoirs*, 354.
117. Bario interview, 25 October 1988.
118. Schneiders interview, 31 October 1988.
119. Rafshoon interview, 17 June 1988.
120. Quoted in Wiedenkeller, *Prasident und Medien*, 109.
121. Schneiders interview, 31 October 1988.
122. Rafshoon exit interview, 12 September 1979, 6.
123. Memo from Rafshoon, "SALT—Office of Communications Plan," 12 October 1978, "SALT—3," Box 6, GRF, JCL.
124. Memo, Rafshoon to the President, "Development of Public Support for SALT II," 6 December 1978, pages 3, 5, "Memos from Rafshoon, December 1978," Box 28, GRF, JCL. Emphasis in original.
125. Ibid., 7–8.
126. Schneiders interview, 31 October 1988.
127. "SALT Task Force," undated, "SALT—2," Box 6, GRF, JCL.

128. Memo, Rafshoon to the President, "Development of Public Support for SALT II," 6 December 1978, page 8, "Memos from Rafshoon, December 1978," Box 28, GRF, JCL.

129. Schneiders interview, 31 October 1988.

130. "State Conferences on SALT," undated, "SALT—2," Box 6, GRF, JCL.

131. Memo, Raymond to Rafshoon and Schneiders, 6 February 1979, "SALT—2," Box 6, GRF, JCL.

132. Memo, Rafshoon to Moore, Wexler, Watson, and Kraft, 21 March 1979, "Memos: Rafshoon, 1/4/79–8/3/79," Box 46, JPF, JCL.

133. Memo, Rafshoon to the Senior Staff, "Operation Response," 27 March 1979, "Memos: Rafshoon, 1/4/79–8/3/79," Box 46, JPF, JCL.

134. Ibid.

135. Smith, "Rafshoon Gathers List of Carter Advocates."

136. Carter, *Keeping Faith*, 239–40.

137. Ibid., 262.

138. Ibid., 265.

139. Bonafede, "Campaigning by TV," 1704–5.

140. Quoted in Jordan, *Crisis*, 296.

141. Schneiders interview, 31 October 1988.

142. Rafshoon interview, 17 June 1988.

143. Bonafede, "Catering to Political Reporters," 563.

144. Ranney, "Carter Administration," 34.

145. Memo, Purks to Shields, 3 April 1980, "Memos: Media Liaison, 4/3/80–7/31/80," Box 45, JPF, JCL.

146. Memo, Bario to Wexler, "Surrogate Media for Steal Trips," 29 September 1980, "Memos: Media Liaison, 8/1/80–11/18/80," Box 45, JPF, JCL.

147. Rafshoon interview, 17 June 1988.

148. Memo, Jordan to Cheney, 21 July 1979, quoted in Riddlesperger and King, "Jimmy Carter and the Administrative Presidency," 21.

CHAPTER SEVEN

1. The Reagan administration's entire legislative agenda for 1981 consisted of only four major issues: budget reform, tax reform, the AWACs sale, and the farm bill. See Wayne, "Congressional Liaison," 56.

2. Schieffer and Gates, *Acting President*, 80.

3. Von Damm, *At Reagan's Side*, 143.

4. For a full account of this, see Schieffer and Gates, *Acting President*, 77–86.

5. Ursomarso interview, 26 June 1990; von Damm, *At Reagan's Side*, 157.

6. Dickenson, *Thumps Up*, 419.

7. Quoted in Kirschten, "Communicator President," 66.

8. Dickenson, *Thumbs Up*, 425.

9. Gergen interview, 10 March 1989.

10. Dickenson, *Thumbs Up*, 28–30.

11. Ibid., 32, 426.

12. Ibid., 34.

13. Gergen interview, 10 March 1989.

14. Ibid.

15. Carruthers interview, 10 October 1989.

16. Kirschten, "Life in the White House Fish Bowl," 183.
17. Gergen interview, 10 March 1989.
18. Ursomarso interview, 26 June 1990.
19. Gerig interview, 26 June 1990.
20. Ibid.
21. Hart interview, 7 November 1989.
22. Dickenson, *Thumbs Up*, 40; Hart interview, 7 November 1989.
23. Bonafede, "Selling of the Executive Branch," 1155; Ursomarso interview, 26 June 1990.
24. Ursomarso interview, 26 June 1990.
25. Ibid.
26. Hertsgaard, *On Bended Knee*, 22.
27. Ursomarso interview, 26 June 1990.
28. Ibid.
29. Ibid.
30. Quoted in Smith, *Power Game*, 350–51.
31. Ursomarso interview, 26 June 1990.
32. Ibid.
33. Quoted in Dickenson, *Thumbs Up*, 435.
34. See ibid., 236; Deaver, *Behind the Scenes*, 30–31.
35. Haig, *Caveat*, 159; see also Dickenson, *Thumbs Up*, 236; Deaver, *Behind the Scenes*, 30; and Speakes, *Speaking Out*, 7.
36. Ursomarso interview, 26 June 1990.
37. Quoted in Dickenson, *Thumbs Up*, 236.
38. Gergen interview, 10 March 1989.
39. Dickenson, *Thumbs Up*, 237.
40. Gerig interview, 26 June 1990.
41. "All the President's Men and Women," 1648.
42. Quoted in Kirschten, "In Reagan's White House," 1330.
43. Ursomarso interview, 26 June 1990.
44. Wiedenkeller, *Prasident und Medien*, figure 10, 175.
45. "A Talk with Dave Gergen," 41.
46. Speakes, *Speaking Out*, 244.
47. Speakes interview, 8 April 1989.
48. Speakes, *Speaking Out*, 71.
49. Ibid., 244.
50. Author's interview.
51. Speakes interview, 8 April 1989.
52. Ursomarso interview, 26 June 1990.
53. Speakes interview, 8 April 1989.
54. Gergen interview, 10 March 1989; Ursomarso interview, 26 June 1990.
55. Gergen interview, 10 March 1989.
56. Hertsgaard, *On Bended Knee*, 15–16, 18–19; Speakes, *Speaking Out*, 141.
57. Kirschten, "Communications Reshuffling," 153.
58. Quoted in ibid., 157.
59. Hertsgaard, *On Bended Knee*, 16–17.
60. Quoted in ibid., 16.
61. Kirschten, "In Reagan's White House," 1329.
62. Hertsgaard, *On Bended Knee*, 117.
63. Reagan's sway with Congress was particularly impressive considering that the Republicans held only a slender majority in the Senate (53–47) and remained heavily outnumbered in the House (191–244). Johnson, on the other hand, was the head of a majority party with substantial majorities in both chambers. During the 89th Congress, Democrats outnumbered Republi-

cans 295-140 in the House and 68-32 in the Senate.

64. Quoted in Hertsgaard, *On Bended Knee*, 22-23.

65. Quoted in Kirschten, "Decision Making in the White House," 588; see also Kirschten, "White House Office," 678.

66. Hart interview, 7 November 1989.

67. Hertsgaard, *On Bended Knee*, 37.

68. Quoted in Spear, *Presidents and the Press*, 262.

69. Quoted in Bonafede, "Washington Press," 716.

70. Quoted in "They'll Take All the Help They Can Get," 387.

71. Kirschten, "Communications Reshuffling," 154.

72. Kirschten, "Safety Net Semantics," 776.

73. Ibid.

74. Kirschten, "The Day After *The Day After*," 2484.

75. Gergen interview, 10 March 1989.

76. Speakes interview, 8 April 1989.

77. Gergen interview, 10 March 1989.

78. Hertsgaard, *On Bended Knee*, 273.

79. Quoted in ibid., 281.

80. King and Ragsdale, *Elusive Executive*, Table 6.2, 306.

81. Fritz, "Reagan's Honeymoon with the Press Is Over," 37.

82. Bonafede, "Presidential Placebo," 294.

83. Abrams, "New Effort to Control Information," 25.

84. Hertsgaard, *On Bended Knee*, 41.

85. Smith, *Power Game*, 438.

86. Bonafede, "Presidential Placebo," 294; Abrams, "New Effort to Control Information," 22, 25.

87. Hertsgaard, *On Bended Knee*, 212. A full discussion of media cover-age of the Grenada invasion can be found in chapter 10 of Hertsgaard.

88. King and Ragsdale, *Elusive Executive*, Table 6.2, 306-7.

89. Smith, *Power Game*, 434.

90. Weisman, "President and the Press," 34ff.

91. Hertsgaard, *On Bended Knee*, 215.

92. Quoted in ibid., 236.

93. Ibid., 36.

94. Weisman, "President and the Press," 72.

95. Quoted in ibid.

96. Regan, *For the Record*, 248.

97. Quoted in Spear, *Presidents and the Press*, 266.

98. Quoted in Smith, *Power Game*, 435.

99. Quoted in Schram, *Great American Video Game*, 33.

100. Spaeth interview, 25 January 1990.

101. For more information about the service, see "In 1984: White House Enters Computer Age," 71.

102. Spaeth interview, 25 January 1990.

103. Ibid.

104. Ibid.

105. Quoted in Kirschten, "Buchanan Switches Strategy," 1220.

106. Spaeth interview, 25 January 1990.

107. Carruthers interview, 10 October 1989.

108. Goode interview, 28 November 1989.

109. Ibid.

110. Ibid.

111. Carruthers interview, 10 October 1989.

112. Speakes interview, 8 April 1989.

113. Spaeth interview, 25 January 1990.

114. Ibid.

115. Ibid.

116. Quoted in Hertsgaard, *On Bended Knee*, 32.

117. Memo from Buchanan to the President, July 1973, quoted in Judis, "White House Vigilante," 20.

118. Judis, "White House Vigilante," 18.

119. Mayer and McManus, *Landslide*, 43.

120. Noonan, *What I Saw at the Revolution*, 207.

121. Ibid., 210–11.

122. Kirschten, "Same Reagan, New Team," 1079.

123. Kirschten, "Buchanan Switches Strategy," 1218.

124. For example, see Warner, "Ideologue-in-Residence," 26.

125. Kirschten, "Buchanan Switches Strategy," 1218.

126. Quoted in Kirschten, "Pragmatism of the First Reagan Term," 918.

127. Weintraub, "Buchanan Assumes a Powerful Position," A1.

128. Kirschten, "Second-Term Legislative Strategy," 697; see also Kirschten, "Damage Control Team," 132.

129. Kirschten, "For Reagan Communication Team It's Strictly One Week at a Time," 594.

130. Kirschten, "Deaver's Departure in May," 974.

131. Judis, "White House Vigilante," 21.

132. Quoted in ibid.

133. Quoted in Kirschten, "For Reagan Communication Team It's Strictly One Week at a Time," 596.

134. Pub. L. No. 98–411, 30 August 1984, 98 Stat. 1545. See also Letter from the Comptroller General of the United States to The Honorable Jack Brooks, Chairman, Committee on Government Operations, House of Representatives, 30 September 1987, made available from the General Accounting Office (document number SP-285), page 3.

135. Ibid., 5.

136. Quoted in ibid., 2–3.

137. Ibid., 7–8.

138. Pichirallo, "Ex-Head of State Department Office," A16.

139. Judis, "White House Vigilante," 18.

140. Buchanan, "No One Gave the Order," A15.

141. Noonan, *What I Saw at the Revolution*, 211.

142. Regan, *For the Record*, 56–57.

143. Spencer interview, 8 April 1989.

144. Regan, *For the Record*, 89.

145. Ibid., 88.

146. Ibid., 96.

147. Griscom interview, 5 December 1988.

148. Kirschten, "President's Counselor," 1334.

149. Griscom interview, 5 December 1988.

150. Ibid.

151. Griscom comments in transcript from symposium, "The Presidency, the Press, and the People," 6 January 1990, 41.

152. Ibid., 30.

153. Griscom interview, 5 December 1988.

154. *White House Economic Bulletin*, 7 October 1988, copy in possession of the author.

155. Griscom interview, 5 December 1988.

156. Ibid.

157. Griscom comments in transcript from symposium, "The Presidency,

the Press, and the People," 6 January 1990, 41.

158. Ibid., 103.

159. Griscom interview, 2 May 1990.

160. For a more general treatment of the construction of political spectacle, see Edelman, *Constructing the Political Spectacle*.

161. Griscom interview, 5 December 1988.

162. Roberts, "Reagan's Rating Is Best Since 1940's," A1.

CHAPTER EIGHT

1. Boyd and Molotsky, "Briefing," A12.

2. Demarest interview, 9 March 1989.

3. Spencer interview, 8 April 1989.

4. Demarest speech, 13 December 1988, "8–1."

5. Demarest interview, 9 March 1989; Demarest speech, 13 December 1988.

6. Gergen, "Bush's Start," C1.

7. Ursomarso interview, 26 June 1990.

8. "Full-Court Press," 145.

9. Quoted in Boot, "The Pool," 24.

10. Boot, "Press Stands Alone," 23.

11. For a discussion of the factors leading to the institutionalization of staff functions, see Covington, Pica, and Seligman, "Institutionalization of the Presidency," 14–15.

12. Tulis, *Rhetorical Presidency*, 187.

13. Ibid., 188.

14. Nixon, *Memoirs*, 354.

BIBLIOGRAPHY

MANUSCRIPT COLLECTIONS

The Jimmy Carter Library, Atlanta, Georgia
  Granum, Rex. Files.
  Powell, Jody. Files.
  Rafshoon, Gerald. Files.

The Gerald R. Ford Library, Ann Arbor, Michigan
  Cheney, Richard. Files.
  Collins, Helen. Files.
  Connor, James. Papers.
  Gergen, David R. Files.
  Haig, Alexander. Files.
  Nessen, Ronald H. Files.
  —. Papers.
  President's Daily Diary.
  Raoul-Duval, Michael. Files.
  —. Papers.
  Warren, Gerald L., and Margita E. White. Files.
  White House Central Files.

The Lyndon B. Johnson Library, Austin, Texas
  White House Central Files.

The Nixon Presidential Materials Project, Alexandria, Virginia
  Buchanan, Patrick. Files.
  Colson, Charles. Files.
  Dent, Harry. Files.
  Ehrlichman, John. Files.
  Haldeman, H. R. Files.
  Klein, Herbert. Files.
  President's Office Files.

Scali, John. Files.
White House Central Files.
Young, David R. Files.

INTERVIEWS

Conducted by the Author

Ayers, H. Brandt. Anniston, Alabama. 2 December 1988.
Bario, Patricia. Washington, D.C. 25 October 1988.
Brand, George. By Telephone. 14 July 1989.
Carruthers, William. By Telephone. 10 October 1989.
Cheney, Dick. Washington, D.C. 10 March 1989.
Christian, George. By Telephone. 14 November 1989.
Colson, Charles. Atlanta, Georgia. 11 July 1989.
Demarest, David F., Jr. Washington, D.C. 9 March 1989.
Duval, Michael [see "Michael Raoul-Duval"].
Ehrlichman, John. By Telephone. 28 April 1989.
Finch, Robert. By Telephone. 12 July 1989.
Ford, Gerald R. Hempstead, New York. 7 April 1989.
Gergen, David. Washington, D.C. 10 March 1989.
Gerig, Lou. By Telephone. 26 June 1990.
Goode, Mark. By Telephone. 28 November 1989.
Greener, Bill, III. By Telephone. 1 November 1989.
Griggs, Henry. By Telephone. 22 January 1990.
Griscom, Thomas. Chattanooga, Tennessee. 5 December 1988.
—. By Telephone. 2 May 1990.
Haldeman, H. R. By Telephone. 17 July 1989.
Hart, Bill. By Telephone. 7 November 1989.
Malek, Fred. Washington, D.C. 25 October 1988.
Maynes, Robert. By Telephone. 27 December 1989.
Mollenhoff, Clark. Hempstead, New York. 7 April 1989.
Nelson, Richard C. By Telephone. 19 October 1989.
O'Leary, John. By Telephone. 12 January 1990.
Rafshoon, Gerald. Washington, D.C. 17 June 1988.
Raoul-Duval, Michael. New York, New York. 3 December 1987.
Reigner, Kenneth. By Telephone. 18 January 1990.
Rhatican, William. By Telephone. 31 January 1990.
Rosenker, Mark. By Telephone. 16 January 1990.
Rumsfeld, Donald. Hempstead, New York. 7 April 1989.
Schneiders, Greg. Washington, D.C. 31 October 1988.
Shumway, DeVan. By Telephone. 30 January 1990.

Spaeth, Merrie. By Telephone. 25 January 1990.

Speakes, Larry. Hempstead, New York. 8 April 1989.

Spencer, Stu. Hempstead, New York. 8 April 1989.

Taylor, Kristin. Washington, D.C. 9 March 1989.

terHorst, Jerald F. By Telephone. 18 July 1989.

Ursomarso, Frank. By Telephone. 26 June 1990.

Warren, Gerald L. By Telephone. 11 October 1989.

White, Margita. Washington, D.C. 17 June 1988.

Wilmot, Bruce. By Telephone. 26 October 1989.

Wurfel, Walt. By Telephone. 1 February 1990.

Ziegler, Ronald. Alexandria, Virginia. 4 November 1988.

Conducted by Scott M. Cutlip

Allin, Lyndon ("Mort"). Washington, D.C. 23 November 1973.

Buchanan, Patrick J. Washington, D.C. 27 November 1973.

Clawson, Ken W. Washington, D.C. 16 October 1973.

Costello, Paul. Washington, D.C. 26 November 1973.

Creel, George. Washington, D.C. 2 April 1970.

Friedheim, Jerry F. Washington, D.C. 23 October 1973.

Klein, Herbert G. Washington, D.C. 1 April 1970.

Lisagor, Peter. Washington, D.C. 5 December 1973.

Martin, Paul. Washington, D.C. 19 October 1973.

Mears, Walter. Washington, D.C. 4 December 1973.

O'Connor, Jackie. Washington, D.C. 19 October 1973.

Roberts, Charles. Washington, D.C. 19 November 1973.

Rousek, Robert. Washington, D.C. 19 October 1973.

Shumway, DeVan. Washington, D.C. 25 October 1973.

Sidey, Hugh. Washington, D.C. 5 December 1973.

Small, William. Washington, D.C. 28 November 1973.

Strout, Richard. Washington, D.C. 29 November 1973.

Warren, Gerald L. Washington, D.C. 5 December 1973.

White, Margita. Washington, D.C. 27 November 1973.

Winston, Sanford. Washington, D.C. 2 April 1970.

Other Interviews

Carter, Jimmy. Interview by Robert MacNeil. Telecast on the "MacNeil/Lehrer Newshour," PBS Television, 18 January 1989.

——. Interview by Jack Nelson. Telecast on "Jimmy Carter: Speaking Out," PBS Television, 6 January 1990.

Colson, Charles W. Exit Interview conducted by John R. Nesbitt and Susan Yowell in Room 182 of the Old Executive Office Building. 12 January 1973. Transcript in the Nixon Presidential Materials Project, Alexandria, Virginia.

—. Oral History Interview conducted by Frederick J. Graboske at Mr. Colson's office in Reston, Virginia. 15 June 1988. Transcript in the Nixon Presidential Materials Project, Alexandria, Virginia.

—. Oral History Interview conducted by Frederick J. Graboske and Paul A. Schmidt at Mr. Colson's office in Reston, Virginia. 21 September 1988. Transcript in the Nixon Presidential Materials Project, Alexandria, Virginia.

Klein, Herbert G. Exit Interview conducted by John R. Nesbitt and Terry W. Good in Room 160 of the Old Executive Office Building. 13 July 1973. Transcript in the Nixon Presidential Materials Project, Alexandria, Virginia.

Nixon, Richard. Interview conducted by David Frost. Telecast on syndicated television stations, 1977.

Rafshoon, Gerald. Exit Interview conducted by David Alsobrook in Room 175 of the Old Executive Office Building. 12 September 1979. Transcript in the Jimmy Carter Library, Atlanta, Georgia.

Warren, Gerald L. Exit Interview conducted by Terry W. Good in Room 352 of the Old Executive Office Building. 24 October 1974. Transcript in the Nixon Presidential Materials Project, Alexandria, Virginia.

PUBLISHED SOURCES

Abrams, Floyd. "The New Effort to Control Information." *New York Times Magazine*, 25 September 1983, 22–28, 72–73.

"All the President's Men and Women." *National Journal*, 28 February 1981, 368.

"All the President's Men and Women." *National Journal*, 12 September 1981, 1648.

Ambrose, Stephen E. *Nixon: The Triumph of a Politician (1962–1972)*. New York: Simon and Schuster, 1989.

Apple, R. W., Jr. "A Nixon Spear-Carrier, and Proud of It." *New York Times*, 24 February 1974, A45.

—. "Nixon's Soft Voice: Herbert George Klein." *New York Times*, 26 November 1968, A35.

Baus, Herbert M., and William B. Ross. *Politics Battle Plan*. New York: Macmillan, 1968.

Bennett, W. Lance. *News: The Politics of Illusion*. 2d ed. New York: Longman, 1988.

Berman, Larry. "Johnson and the White House Staff." In Robert A. Divine, ed., *The Johnson Years—Volume I*. Lawrence: University Press of Kansas, 1987.

Bernstein, Carl, and Bob Woodward. *All the President's Men*. New York: Simon and Schuster, 1974.

Bigart, Homer. "Kennedy's Advisers Think Nixon 'Goofed.' " *Milwaukee Journal*, 13 November 1960, 2.

Bonafede, Dom. "Campaigning by TV—It's Expensive, But Does It Make Any Difference?" *National Journal*, 11 October 1980, 1702–6.

—. "Campaign '72 Report: Far Ahead in the Polls, Nixon Campaign Team Waits to See Size of Their Mandate." *National Journal*, 28 October 1972, 1655–62.

—. "The Camp David Cure." *National Journal*, 7 October 1978, 1607.

—. "Carter Sounds Retreat from 'Cabinet Government.'" *National Journal*, 18 November 1978, 1852–57.

—. "Carter's Recent Staff Shakeup May Be More of a Shakedown." *National Journal*, 17 June 1978, 952–57.

—. "Catering to Political Reporters—A Must for Presidential Candidates." *National Journal*, 5 April 1980, 563.

—. "Communications Office Role Is Reduced." *National Journal*, 16 August 1975, 1181.

—. "A Glimmer of Hope Burns in the Heart of the PFC." *National Journal*, 2 October 1976, 1374–80.

—. "Has the Rafshoon Touch Left Its Mark on the White House?" *National Journal*, 14 April 1979, 588–93.

—. "Herbert Klein: Commissar of Credibility." *Nation*, 6 April 1970, 392–96.

—. "If the Rafshoon Fits, Wear It." *National Journal*, 19 August 1978, 1331.

—. "It's a Whole New Ball Game." *National Journal*, 23 September 1978, 1518.

—. "More Musical Chairs." *National Journal*, 7 August 1976, 1123.

—. "Nixon Orders 500 Jobs, $10 Million Cut from Public Relations Budgets." *National Journal*, 2 May 1970, 912–13.

—. "Nixon Personnel Staff Works to Restructure Federal Policies." *National Journal*, 12 November 1971, 2440–48.

—. "Presidential Placebo." *National Journal*, 13 February 1982, 294.

—. "Rafshoon to the Rescue." *National Journal*, 8 July 1978, 1096.

—. "The Selling of the Executive Branch—Public Information or Promotion?" *National Journal*, 27 June 1981, 1153–57.

—. "The Selling of the Government—Flackery and Public Service." *National Journal*, 23 July 1977, 1140–45.

—. "Staff, Style Changes Slow in Coming Despite President's Post-Watergate Reforms." *National Journal*, 21 July 1973, 1057–62.

—. "The Tough Job of Normalizing Relations with Capitol Hill." *National Journal*, 13 January 1979, 54–57.

—. "The Washington Press—An Interpreter or a Participant in Policy Making?" *National Journal*, 24 April 1982, 716–21.

—. "White House Wheels Are Turning for the 1980 Presidential Race." *National Journal*, 10 March 1979, 389–93.

Bonafede, Dom, Jonathan Cottin, and Andrew J. Glass. "Nixon Buoyed by Big Early Lead, Plans Elaborate Campaign under White House Mantle." *National Journal*, 2 September 1972, 1381–93.

Bonafede, Dom, and Andrew J. Glass. "Nixon Deals Cautiously with Hostile Congress." *National Journal*, 27 June 1970, 1353–66.

Boot, William. "The Pool." *Columbia Journalism Review*, May/June 1991, 24–26.

—. "The Press Stands Alone." *Columbia Journalism Review*, March/April 1991, 23–24.

Boyd, Gerald, and Irvin Molotsky. "Briefing: The Face on the Wall." *New York Times*, 7 February 1989, A12.

Brauer, Carl M. *Presidential Transitions: Eisenhower through Reagan*. New York: Oxford University Press, 1986.

Buchanan, Patrick J. "No One Gave the Order to Abandon Reagan's Ship." *Washington Post*, 8 December 1986, A15.

Burby, John F. "Impeachment Report." *National Journal*, 6 July 1974, 989–90.

"Campaign Report: Washington Tensions Increase as Both Parties Claim Election Gains." *National Journal*, 7 November 1970, 2425.

Carter, Jimmy. *Keeping Faith: Memoirs of a President*. New York: Bantam Books, 1982.

Causey, Mike. "PR Men Gird for 'Battle of the Budget.'" *Washington Post*, 4 April 1973, D9.

—. "U.S. Speech-Writing Kit Is Recalled." *Washington Post*, 23 May 1973, B17.

Chapman, William. "Inter-Agency Harmony Is Kintner's Job." *Washington Post*, 2 April 1966, A6.

Christian, George. "Another Perspective." In Kenneth W. Thompson, ed., *The Johnson Presidency*. Lanham, Md.: University Press of America, 1986.

Clark, Timothy B. "The Power Vacuum outside the Oval Office." *National Journal*, 24 February 1979, 296–300.

Clawson, Ken. "A Loyalist's Memoir." *Washington Post*, 9 August 1979, D1, D3.

Colson, Charles W. *Born Again*. Old Tappan, N.J.: Chosen Books, 1976.

Cornwell, Elmer E., Jr. *Presidential Leadership of Public Opinion*. Bloomington: Indiana University Press, 1965.

—. "Wilson, Creel, and the Presidency." *Public Opinion Quarterly* 23 (Summer 1959): 189–202.

Covington, Cary R., Joseph Pica, and Lester Seligman. "Institutionalization of the Presidency." Paper prepared for delivery at the 1983 Annual Meeting of the American Political Science Association.

Creel, George. *How We Advertised America*. New York: Harper and Brothers, 1920.

Crenson, Matthew A., and Francis E. Rourke. "By Way of Conclusion: American Bureaucracy since World War II." In Louis Galambos, ed., *The New American State*. Baltimore: Johns Hopkins University Press, 1987.

Culbert, David. "Johnson and the Media." In Robert A. Divine, ed., *The Johnson Years—Volume I*. Lawrence: University Press of Kansas, 1987.

Cutlip, Scott M. "Nixon's Office of Executive Communication." Paper prepared for delivery at the American Academy of Advertising, Knoxville, Tennessee, 22 April 1975.

Davis, Eric L. "Congressional Liaison: The People and the Institutions." In Anthony King, ed., *Both Ends of the Avenue*. Washington, D.C.: American Enterprise Institute, 1983.

Deakin, James. *Straight Stuff: The Reporters, the White House, and the Truth*. New York: William Morrow and Company, 1984.

Deaver, Michael, with Mickey Herskowitz. *Behind the Scenes*. New York: William Morrow and Company, 1987.

Demarest, David F., Jr. Plenary Speech to a conference of the American Society of Public Administrators, Washington, D.C., Marriott Hotel, 13 December 1988. Federal News Service transcript, "8–1."

Dickenson, Mollie. *Thumbs Up: The Life and Courageous Comeback of White House Press Secretary Jim Brady*. New York: William Morrow and Company, 1987.

Dorris, Henry M. "Five Executive Assistants President's 'Eyes and Ears.' " *New York Times*, 9 March 1941, Section 4, 7.

Drew, Elizabeth. *Washington Journal*. New York: Random House, 1975.

Edelman, Murray. *Constructing the Political Spectacle*. Chicago: University of Chicago Press, 1988.

Edwards, George C., III. *The Public Presidency: The Pursuit of Popular Support*. New York: St. Martin's Press, 1983.

Ehrlichman, John. *Witness to Power*. New York: Simon and Schuster, 1982.

Eisenhower, Julie Nixon. *Pat Nixon: The Untold Story*. New York: Simon and Schuster, 1986.

Entman, Robert M. "The Imperial Media." In Arnold J. Meltsner, ed., *Politics and the Oval Office*. San Francisco: Institute for Contemporary Studies, 1981.

Ephron, Nora. "Ken Clawson Is No Joke." *New York*, 3 June 1974, 58–67.

Epstein, Edward Jay. *Agency of Fear*. New York: G. P. Putnam's Sons, 1977.

—. "Peddling a Drug Scare." *Columbia Journalism Review*, November/December 1977, 51.

Evans, Rowland, and Robert Novak. "The Departure of Herb Klein." *Seminar Quarterly*, September 1973, 23.

Fallows, James. "The Passionless Presidency." *Atlantic*, May 1979, 33–48.

Ford, Gerald R. *A Time to Heal*. New York: Harper and Row, 1979.

"Foreign Policy Triumphs Helped Carter Presidency Weather Domestic Reverses." *CQ Weekly Report*, 6 January 1979, 30–32.

Frankel, Max. "Why the Gap between L.B.J. and the Nation: Failure to Communicate?" *New York Times Magazine*, 7 January 1968, 7.

Fritz, Sarah. "Reagan's Honeymoon with the Press Is Over." *Washington Journalism Review*, April 1982, 37–40.

"Full-Court Press." *Nation*, 11 February 1991, 145.

Gergen, David. "Bush's Start: A Presidency 'On the Edge of a Cliff.' " *Washington Post*, 5 March 1989, C1.

Gold, Vic. *PR as in President*. New York: Doubleday, 1977.

Goldman, Peter. "The President's Palace Guard." *Newsweek*, 19 March 1973, 24–28.

Graber, Doris A. *Mass Media and American Politics*. Washington, D.C.: CQ Press, 1980.

Greenstein, Fred I. "Change and Continuity in the Modern Presidency." In Anthony King, ed., *The New American Political System*. Washington, D.C.: American Enterprise Institute, 1978.

"Greg Schneiders: A Carter Insider Again." *National Journal*, 14 April 1979, 592.

Griscom, Thomas C. Questions and answers from transcript of symposium, "The Presidency, the Press, and the People," University of California at San Diego, 6 January 1990.

Grossman, Michael Baruch, and Martha Joynt Kumar. *Portraying the President*. Baltimore: Johns Hopkins University Press, 1981.

Haig, Alexander M., Jr. *Caveat*. New York: Macmillan, 1984.

Haldeman, H. R., with Joseph DiMona. *The Ends of Power*. New York: Times Books, 1978.

Hartmann, Robert T. *Palace Politics: An Inside Account of the Ford Years*. New York: McGraw-Hill, 1980.

Hersh, Seymour M. "Colson Says He Thought He and Colleagues Were 'Above the Law.'" *New York Times*, 7 July 1974, A29.

Hertsgaard, Mark. *On Bended Knee: The Press and the Reagan Presidency*. New York: Farrar Straus Giroux, 1988.

Hess, Stephen. *The Government/Press Connection*. Washington, D.C.: Brookings, 1984.

——. *Organizing the Presidency*. Washington, D.C.: Brookings, 1976.

Hirschman, Albert O. *Exit, Voice, and Loyalty*. Boston: Harvard University Press, 1970.

Iglehart, John. "Major HEW Legislation Tailored by White House 'Working Groups.'" *National Journal*, 7 March 1970, 486–87.

"In 1984: White House Enters Computer Age." *Broadcasting*, 19 November 1984, 71.

Johnson, Lyndon B. "Agenda for the Future: A Presidential Perspective." In *Britannica Book of the Year: 1969*. Chicago: Encyclopedia Britannica, 1969.

Jordan, Hamilton. *Crisis: The Last Year of the Carter Presidency*. New York: G. P. Putnam's Sons, 1982.

"Jordan's New Role Signals an End to 'Cabinet Government.'" *National Journal*, 18 August 1979, 1356.

Judis, John B. "White House Vigilante." *New Republic*, 26 January 1987, 17–22.

Kelley, Stanley, Jr. *Professional Public Relations and Political Power*. Baltimore: Johns Hopkins University Press, 1956.

Keogh, James. *President Nixon and the Press*. New York: Funk and Wagnalls, 1972.

Kernell, Samuel. "The Evolution of the White House Staff." In John E. Chubb and Paul E. Peterson, eds., *Can the Government Govern?* Washington, D.C.: Brookings, 1989.

——. *Going Public: New Strategies of Presidential Leadership*. Washington, D.C.: CQ Press, 1986.

King, Gary, and Lyn Ragsdale, eds. *The Elusive Executive*. Washington, D.C.: CQ Press, 1988.

Kirschten, Dick. "Buchanan Switches Strategy, Taking His Case to the Washington Press Corps." *National Journal*, 25 May 1985, 1218–21.

—. "Communications Reshuffling Intended to Help Reagan Do What He Does Best." *National Journal*, 28 January 1984, 153–57.

—. "The Communicator President." *National Journal*, 10 January 1981, 66.

—. "Damage Control Team." *National Journal*, 18 January 1986, 132–33.

—. "The Day After *The Day After*." *National Journal*, 26 November 1983, 2484.

—. "Deaver's Departure in May Paves the Way for Buchanan to Speak Loud and Clear." *National Journal*, 4 May 1985, 974–75.

—. "Decision Making in the White House: How Well Does It Serve the President?" *National Journal*, 3 April 1982, 584–89.

—. "For Reagan Communication Team It's Strictly One Week at a Time." *National Journal*, 8 March 1986, 594–95.

—. "Friday's at Blair House." *National Journal*, 6 February 1982, 251.

—. "In Reagan's White House, It's Gergen Who's Taken Charge of Communications." *National Journal*, 25 July 1981, 1329–31.

—. "Life in the White House Fish Bowl—Brady Takes Charge as Press Chief." *National Journal*, 31 January 1981, 180–83.

—. "The Pragmatism of the First Reagan Term May Be Giving Way to 'Toughing It Out.'" *National Journal*, 27 April 1985, 918–19.

—. "The President's Counselor." *National Journal*, 23 May 1987, 1332–37.

—. "Safety Net Semantics." *National Journal*, 1 May 1982, 776.

—. "Same Reagan, New Team." *National Journal*, 18 May 1985, 1078–87.

—. "Second-Term Legislative Strategy Shifts to Foreign Policy and Defense Issues." *National Journal*, 30 March 1985, 696–99.

—. "The White House Office: Where the Power Resides." *National Journal*, 25 April 1981, 678.

Klein, Herbert G. *Making It Perfectly Clear*. Garden City, N.Y.: Doubleday and Company, 1980.

Kumar, Martha Joynt. "Presidential Libraries: Gold Mine, Booby Trap, or Both?" In George C. Edwards III and Stephen J. Wayne, eds., *Studying the Presidency*. Knoxville: University of Tennessee Press, 1983.

Lang, John S. "Margita White: White House Voice." *New York Post*, 9 August 1975, Section 3, 1.

Lavine, Harold. *Smoke-Filled Rooms*. Englewood Cliffs, N.J.: Prentice-Hall, 1970.

Lowi, Theodore J. *The Personal President: Power Invested, Promise Unfulfilled*. Ithaca, N.Y.: Cornell University Press, 1985.

Lukas, J. Anthony. *Nightmare: The Underside of the Nixon Years*. New York: Viking Press, 1976.

Lydon, Christopher. "Rough Ex-Nixon Aide." *New York Times*, 4 June 1974, A24.

Maass, Arthur. "In Accord with the Program of the President." *Public Policy* 4 (1953): 77–93.

McCamy, James L. *Government Publicity*. Chicago: University of Chicago Press, 1939.

McGinniss, Joe. *The Selling of the President: 1968*. New York: Trident Press, 1969.

Magruder, Jeb Stuart. *An American Life: One Man's Road to Watergate*. New York: Atheneum, 1974.

Maltese, John Anthony. "The Selling of Clement Haynsworth: Politics and the Confirmation of Supreme Court Justices." *Judicature* 72 (April–May 1989): 338–47.

Mayer, Jane, and Doyle McManus. *Landslide: The Unmaking of the President, 1984–1988*. Boston: Houghton Mifflin Company, 1988.

Minow, Newton N., John Bartlow Martin, and Lee N. Mitchell. *Presidential Television*. New York: Basic Books, 1973.

Mock, James R., and Cedric Larson. *Words That Won the War: The Story of the Committee on Public Information (1917–1919)*. Princeton, N.J.: Princeton University Press, 1939.

Moe, Terry M. "The Politicized Presidency." In John E. Chubb and Paul E. Peterson, eds., *The New Direction in American Politics*. Washington, D.C.. Brookings, 1985.

Mollenhoff, Clark R. *Game Plan for Disaster*. New York: W. W. Norton and Company, 1976.

Nathan, Richard P. *The Plot That Failed: Nixon and the Administrative Presidency*. New York: John Wiley and Sons, 1975.

Nessen, Ron. *It Sure Looks Different from the Inside*. Chicago: Playboy Press, 1978.

Neustadt, Richard E. "Approaches to Staffing the Presidency." *American Political Science Review* 57 (December 1963): 855–64.

—. "Presidency and Legislation: Planning the President's Program." *American Political Science Review* 49 (December 1955): 980–1021.

—. *Presidential Power*. Rev. ed. New York: John Wiley and Sons, 1980.

"Newspapers on President's Source List." *Boston Herald American*, 27 June 1973, 4.

Nimmo, Dan. *Political Communication and Public Opinion in America*. Santa Monica, Calif.: Goodyear, 1978.

Nixon, Richard. *In the Arena*. New York: Simon and Schuster, 1990.

—. *The Memoirs of Richard Nixon*. New York: Grosset and Dunlap, 1978.

—. *Six Crises*. Garden City, N.Y.: Doubleday and Company, 1962.

"Nixon Hatchet Man: Call It What You Will, Chuck Colson Handles President Nixon's Dirty Work." *Wall Street Journal*, 15 October 1971, 1.

"Nixon Sees the News Media through 'Faulty Lens' of Aide, Says Friendly." *Variety*, 30 May 1973, 1.

Noonan, Peggy. *What I Saw at the Revolution: A Political Life in the Reagan Era*. New York: Random House, 1990.

"OGR Over News: Office of Government Reports Is Framework for Wartime Censorship-Propaganda System under White House Secretary." *Business Week*, 14 December 1940, 24.

Ornstein, Norman. *President and Congress: Assessing Reagan's First Year*. Washington, D.C.: American Enterprise Institute, 1982.

Osborne, John. *The Nixon Watch*. New York: Liveright, 1971.

Oudes, Bruce, ed. *From: The President—Richard Nixon's Secret Files*. New York: Harper and Row, 1989.

Paletz, David L., and Robert M. Entman. *Media Power Politics*. New York: Free Press, 1981.

Patterson, Bradley H., Jr. *The Ring of Power: The White House Staff and Its Expanding Role in Government*. New York: Basic Books, 1988.

Pichirallo, Joe. "Ex-Head of State Department Office Denies Illicit Propaganda Role." *Washington Post*, 11 October 1987, A16.

Pollard, James E. *The Presidents and the Press*. New York: Macmillan, 1947.

Porter, William E. *Assault on the Media: The Nixon Years*. Ann Arbor: University of Michigan Press, 1976.

Powell, Jody. *The Other Side of the Story*. New York: William Morrow and Company, 1984.

Press, Charles, and Kenneth Verburg. *American Politicians and Journalists*. Glenview, Ill.: Scott, Foresman and Company, 1988.

"The Press Covers Government: The Nixon Years from 1969 to Watergate." Study prepared by the Department of Communication, American University, Washington, D.C., 1973.

Public Papers of the Presidents: Lyndon B. Johnson (1963–64). Washington, D.C.: Government Printing Office, 1965.

Public Papers of the Presidents: Lyndon B. Johnson (1968–69). Washington, D.C.: Government Printing Office, 1970.

Public Papers of the Presidents: Richard Nixon (1973). Washington, D.C.: Government Printing Office, 1975.

Ranney, Austin. "The Carter Administration." In Austin Ranney, ed., *The American Elections of 1980*. Washington, D.C.: American Enterprise Institute, 1981.

Rather, Dan, and Gary Paul Gates. *The Palace Guard*. New York: Harper and Row, 1974.

Regan, Donald T. *For the Record*. New York: Harcourt Brace Jovanovich, 1988.

Riddlesperger, James W., Jr., and James D. King. "Jimmy Carter and the Administrative Presidency." Paper prepared for presentation at the Annual Meeting of the Southern Political Science Association, Memphis, Tennessee, 2 November 1989.

Roberts, Steven V. "Reagan's Rating Is Best since 1940's for a President." *New York Times*, 18 January 1989, A1.

Rose, Richard. *The Postmodern President: The White House Meets the World*. Chatham, N.J.: Chatham House, 1988.

Rozell, Mark J. *The Press and the Carter Presidency*. Boulder, Colo.: Westview Press, 1989.

Rubin, Bernard. *Public Relations and the Empire State*. New Brunswick, N.J.: Rutgers University Press, 1958.

Rubin, Richard L. *Press, Party, and Presidency*. New York: W. W. Norton and Company, 1981.

"Rx for Ailing White House Press Operation." *Broadcasting*, 7 July 1975, 39.

Safire, William. *Before the Fall: An Inside View of the Pre-Watergate White House.* New York: Doubleday, 1975.

Schieffer, Bob, and Gary Paul Gates. *The Acting President.* New York: E. P. Dutton, 1989.

Schram, Martin. *The Great American Video Game: Presidential Politics in the Video Age.* New York: William Morrow and Company, 1987.

—. *Running for President: A Journal of the Carter Campaign.* New York: Pocket Books, 1977.

Seidman, Harold. *Politics, Position, and Power.* 3d ed. New York: Oxford University Press, 1980.

Semple, Robert B., Jr. "Nixon Reported Wooing Democrat; Herbert Klein Is Named Communications Chief." *New York Times*, 26 November 1968, A1, A35.

—. "Nixon's Inner Circle Meets." *New York Times Magazine*, 3 August 1969, 6–9, 45, 50, 54, 58–59, 62–64.

—. "Vote for Brinkley a Welcome Script Change." *New York Times*, 24 August 1972, A46.

Seymour-Ure, Colin. *The American President: Power and Communication.* New York: St. Martin's Press, 1982.

Shabecoff, Philip. "Nixon Foes Held Source of Leaks." *New York Times*, 19 June 1974, A34.

Sheldon, Courtney R. "How Nixon Gets News." *Christian Science Monitor*, 16 December 1972.

Sidey, Hugh. "So Long to Old Herb Klein." *Time*, 18 June 1973, 24.

Sigal, Leon V. *Reporters and Officials.* Lexington, Mass.: D. C. Heath and Company, 1973.

Smith, Hedrick. *The Power Game: How Washington Works.* New York: Random House, 1988.

Smith, Terence. "Rafshoon Gathers List of Carter Advocates." *New York Times*, 3 May 1979, A20.

Speakes, Larry, with Robert Pack. *Speaking Out: The Reagan Presidency from Inside the White House.* New York: Charles Scribner's Sons, 1988.

Spear, Joseph C. *Presidents and the Press: The Nixon Legacy.* Cambridge, Mass.: MIT Press, 1984.

Stroud, Karen. *How Jimmy Won.* New York: William Morrow and Company, 1977.

"Superchief of Information." *Time*, 6 December 1968, 30.

"A Talk with Dave Gergen." *Washington Journalism Review*, April 1982, 41–45.

terHorst, Jerald F. "President Ford and the Media." In Kenneth W. Thompson, ed., *The Ford Presidency.* New York: University Press of America, 1988.

"They'll Take All the Help They Can Get." *National Journal*, 7 March 1981, 387.

Tulis, Jeffrey K. *The Rhetorical Presidency.* Princeton, N.J.: Princeton University Press, 1987.

—. "The Two Constitutional Presidencies." In Michael Nelson, ed., *The Presidency and the Political System*. Washington, D.C.: CQ Press, 1984.

Turner, Kathleen J. *Lyndon Johnson's Dual War: Vietnam and the Press*. Chicago: University of Chicago Press, 1985.

U.S. Congress. Senate. Select Committee on Presidential Campaign Activities. *Final Report*. 93d Cong., 2d sess., 1974. S. Rept. 93–981.

—. *Watergate and Related Activities, Phase I, Book 4*. 93d Cong., 1st sess., 1973.

Vaughn, Stephen. *Holding Fast the Inner Lines: Democracy, Nationalism, and the Committee on Public Information*. Chapel Hill: University of North Carolina Press, 1980.

von Damm, Helene. *At Reagan's Side*. New York: Doubleday, 1989.

Warner, Margaret Gerrard. "Ideologue-in-Residence: Will Patrick Buchanan Help or Hurt Ronald Reagan?" *Newsweek*, 27 May 1985, 26.

Wayne, Stephen J. "Congressional Liaison in the Reagan White House: A Preliminary Assessment of the First Year." In Norman J. Ornstein, ed., *President and Congress: Assessing Reagan's First Year*. Washington, D.C.: American Enterprise Institute, 1982.

Weaver, Warren, Jr. "G.O.P. Carefully Created Fresh Show for Viewers." *New York Times*, 24 August 1972, A46.

Weintraub, Bernard. "Buchanan Assumes a Powerful Position in the White House." *New York Times*, 11 April 1985, A1.

Weisman, Steven R. "The President and the Press: The Art of Controlled Access." *New York Times Magazine*, 14 October 1984, 34–37, 71–74, 80–83.

White, Theodore H. *Breach of Faith*. New York: Atheneum, 1975.

—. *The Making of the President: 1968*. New York: Atheneum, 1969.

—. *The Making of the President: 1972*. New York: Bantam, 1972.

"White House Media Services." *National Journal*, 3 October 1970, 2137.

"White House's Warren: Held Over in Confidence." *Broadcasting*, 3 March 1975, 73.

Wicker, Tom. *One of Us: Richard Nixon and the American Dream*. New York: Random House, 1991.

Wiedenkeller, Daniel. *Präsident und Medien: Eine Studie zur Machtausübung durch Kommunikation am Beispiel von Jimmy Carter*. Bern: Peter Lang, 1985.

Winkler, Allan M. *The Politics of Propaganda: The Office of War Information (1942–1945)*. New Haven: Yale University Press, 1978.

Wise, David. *The Politics of Lying*. New York: Vintage Books, 1973.

Witcover, Jules. *Marathon: The Pursuit of the Presidency*. New York: Viking, 1977.

—. "The Two Hats of Herbert Klein." *Columbia Journalism Review*, Spring 1970, 26–30.

Woodward, Bob, and Carl Bernstein. *The Final Days*. New York: Simon and Schuster, 1976.

INDEX

the White House Office of Communications, 26; announces Klein's appointment as White House director of communications, 27; compared with Klein, 28, 29, 30, 40, 75–76; use of advertising clichés, 29–30; media monitoring program and, 51; on Nixon's freeze-out directives, 51–52; on Agnew's antimedia speech, 54, 57; on Klein, 67; on Colson, 83; Nessen compares himself to, 119, 124

11/5/95

Philip — ? You
who knows? you
may need This some day.
Happy 30!
Ron